SUETONIUS: LIVES OF GALBA, OTHO & VITELLIUS

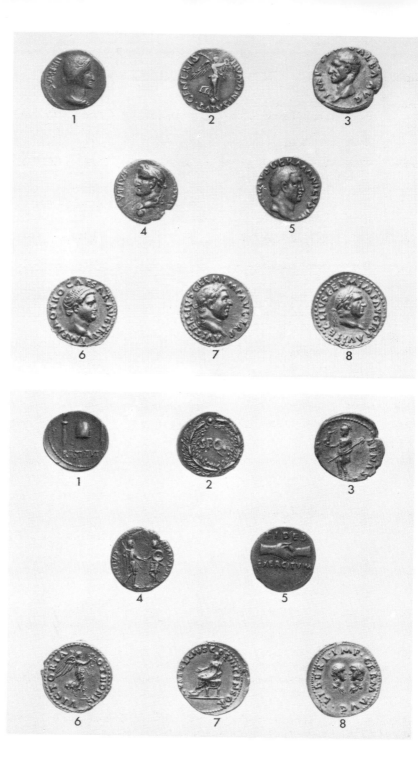

Frontispiece

1. Denarius	Obv.	Bust of *Libertas*	LIBERTAS
	Rev.	Cap of Freedom, between two daggers	P(opuli) R(omani) RESTITVTA
	(BMC, Civil Wars, 7)		
2. Denarius	Obv.	Victory, standing right on globe	SALVS GENERIS HVMANI
	Rev.	In oak-wreath	S(enatus) P(opulus) Q(ue) R(omanus)
	(BMC. Civil Wars, 33)		
3. Denarius	Obv.	Head of Galba, left	IMP(erator) SER(vius) GALBA AVG(ustus)
	Rev.	Roma, standing left	ROMA RENASC(ens)
	(BMC, Galba, 26)		
4. Denarius	Obv.	Head of Galba, left	GALBA IMP(erator)
	Rev.	Gallia and Hispania, clasping hands	GALLIA HISPANIA
	(BMC, Galba, 171)		
5. Denarius	Obv.	Head of Vitellius, right	A(ulus) VITELLIVS GERMANICVS IMP(erator)
	Rev.	Clasped hands	FIDES EXERCITVVM
	(BMC, Vitellius, 2)		
6. Aureus	Obv.	Head of Otho, right	IMP(erator) M(arcus) OTHO CAESAR AVG(ustus) TR(ibunicia) P(otestas)
	Rev.	Victory, flying right	VICTORIA OTHONIS
	(BMC, Otho, 21)		
7. Aureus	Obv.	Head of Vitellius, right	A(ulus) VITELLIUS GERM(anicus) IMP(erator) AVG(ustus) TR(ibunicia) P(otestas)
	Rev.	Lucius Vitellius, seated left on curule chair	L(ucius) VITELLIVS CO(n)S(ul) III CENSOR
	(BMC, Vitellius, 23)		
8. Aureus	Obv.	Head of Vitellius, right	A(ulus) VITELLIVS GERM(anicus) IMP(erator) AVG(ustus) TR(ibunica) P(otestas)
	Rev.	Busts of Vitellius' son and daughter, facing each other	LIBERI IMP(eratoris) GERM(anici) AVG(usti)
	(BMC, Vitellius, 27)		

Obv. = Obverses; Rev. = Reverses; *BMC = Coins of the Roman Empire in the British Museum* (Reproduced with the permission of the Trustees of the British Museum)

General Editor: Professor M.M. Willcock

SUETONIUS

Lives of
Galba, Otho & Vitellius

edited with translation and commentary by

David Shotter

Aris & Phillips – Warminster – England

ISBN cloth 0 85668 537 2
ISBN limp 0 85668 538 0

Classical Texts ISSN 0953 796 1

British Library Cataloguing-in-Publication Data
A catalogue record for this book is available from the
British Library

Printed and published in England by ARIS & PHILLIPS Ltd., Teddington House, Warminster, Wiltshire, BA12 8PQ, England.

Contents

Acknowledgements

It is a pleasure to acknowledge the help of Peter Lee (of Lancaster University Archaeological Unit) for drawing the maps which appear as figures 1–5; I am grateful also to Mrs Ghislaine O'Neill and Miss Susan Waddington (of the Department of History of Lancaster University) for their help in the preparation of the manuscript.

Finally, I am indebted to the Trustees of the British Museum for their permission to reproduce photographs of coins, which appear as the frontispiece.

Abbreviations

Abbreviations used in the Introduction and commentary

In the Introduction and Commentary, references to imperial biographies, unless otherwise specified, are to those of Suetonius

I Classical Authors and their Works

App.	*BC*	Appian	*The Civil War*
	Hisp.		*The Spanish Wars*
Apuleius	*Met.*	Apuleius	*Metamorphoses*
Augustus	*RGDA*	Augustus	*Res Gestae Divi Augusti*
Caes.	*Bell. Gall.*	Caesar	*The Gallic War*
Cic.	*Ad Att.*	Cicero	*Letters to Atticus*
	Ad Fam.		*Letters to His Friends*
	Phil.		*Philippic Orations*
	Verr.		*Orations against Gaius Verres*
Dion. Hal.		Dionysius of Halicarnassus	
Front.	*Strateg.*	Frontinus	*Strategemata*
Gellius	*NA*	Aulus Gellius	*Attic Nights*
Hor.	*Sat.*	Horace	*Satires*
Jos.	*Ant. J.*	Josephus	*Jewish Antiquities*
	Bell. Iud.		*The Jewish War*
Juv.	*Sat.*	Juvenal	*Satires*
Macrobius	*Sat.*	Macrobius	*Saturnalia*
Martial	*Epig.*	Martial	*Epigrams*
Ovid	*Ars Am.*	Ovid	*Ars Amatoria*
	Met.		*Metamorphoses*
Paul.	*Sent.*	Paulus	*Sententiae*
Persius	*Sat.*	Persius	*Satires*
Philo	*Leg.*	Philo	*Legation to Gaius*
Philostratus	*Vit. Apoll.*	Philostratus	*Life of Apollonius of Tyana*
Pliny	*Nat. Hist.*	Pliny (the Elder)	*Natural History*
Pliny	*Epp.*	Pliny (the Younger)	*Letters*
Plut.	*Rom.*	Plutarch	*Life of Romulus*
Quint.	*Inst. Or.*	Quintilian	*Institutiones Oratoriae*
Sall.	*Cat.*	Sallust	*Catilinarian Conspiracy*
Sen.	*Suas.*	Seneca (the Elder)	*Suasoriae*
Sen.	*Apocol.*	Seneca (the Younger)	*Apocolocyntosis*

	Ad Helv.		*Consolation to Helvia*
	De Ben.		*On Benefits*
	Ep. Mor.		*Epistulae Morales*
	Quaest. Nat.		*Quaestiones Naturales*
Stat.	*Silv.*	Statius	*Silvae*
Suet.	*Caes.*	Suetonius	*The Lives of the Caesars*
	Div. Iul.		*The Life of the Deified Julius*
	Div. Aug.		*The Life of the Deified Augustus*
	Tib.		*The Life of Tiberius*
	Cal.		*The Life of Caligula*
	Div. Claud.		*The Life of the Deified Claudius*
	Vitell.		*The Life of Vitellius*
	Div. Vesp.		*The Life of the Deified Vespasian*
	Div. Tit.		*The Life of the Deified Titus*
	Dom.		*The Life of Domitian*
	Gramm.		*On Grammatici*
SHA		Writers of the Augustan History	
Tac.	*Agr.*	Tacitus	*On the Life of Agricola*
	Ann.		*Annals*
	Dial.		*Dialogue on Orators*
	Germ.		*Germania*
	Hist.		*Histories*
Val. Max.		Valerius Maximus	
Varro	*Ling. Lat.*	Varro	*De Lingua Latina*
Veg.	*De Re Mil.*	Vegetius	*De Re Militari*
Vell.Pat.		Velleius Paterculus	
Victor	*Caes.*	Aurelius Victor	*On the Caesars*
	Epit.		*Epitome*
Virgil	*Aen.*	Virgil	*Aeneid*

II Concordances and Periodicals

AE	L'Année Epigraphique
AJP	American Journal of Philology
Anc Soc	Ancient Society
CAH	Cambridge Ancient History
CIG	Corpus Inscriptionum Graecarum
CIL	Corpus Inscriptionum Latinarum
CRAI	Comptes Rendus de l'Académie des Inscriptions et Belles-Lettres de Paris
Class Phil	Classical Philology

Class Quart	Classical Quarterly
G & R	Greece and Rome
IG	Inscriptiones Graecae
IGRR	Inscriptiones Graecae ad Res Romanas Pertinentes
ILS	Inscriptiones Latinae Selectae (H. Dessau)
JRS	Journal of Roman Studies
LCM	Liverpool Classical Monthly
Num Chron	Numismatic Chronicle
PBA	Proceedings of the British Academy
PBSR	Papers of the British School at Rome
PCPS	Papers of the Cambridge Philological Society
PIR	Prosopographia Imperii Romani
RIC	Roman Imperial Coinage
Riv di Fil	Rivista di Filologia

Bibliography

Ashby and Fell, 1921: Ashby T. and Fell R.A.L., The Via Flaminia, *JRS* XI, 125–190.

Balsdon, 1934: Balsdon J.P., *The Emperor Gaius (Caligula)*, Oxford.

Balsdon, 1969: Balsdon J.P., *Life and Leisure in Ancient Rome*, London.

Barbieri, 1954: Barbieri G., Mario Massimo, *Riv. di fil.* XXXII, 36–66.

Bardon, 1956: Bardon H., *La Littérature Latine Inconnue*, Paris.

Barrett, 1989: Barrett A.A., *Caligula: The Corruption of Power*, London.

Bauman, 1972: Bauman R.A., *Impietas In Principem*, Munich.

Birley A., 1967: Birley A.R., The Augustan History, pp. 113–138 in Dudley D.R. and Dorey T.A. (Edd), *Latin Biography*, London.

Birley E., 1953: Birley E.B., Senators in the Emperors' Service, *PBA* XXXIX, 197–214.

Blake, 1947: Blake M.E., *Ancient Roman Construction in Italy from the Prehistoric Period to Augustus*, Washington.

Blake, 1959: Blake M.E., *Roman Construction in Italy from Tiberius Through the Flavians*, Washington.

Boethius and Ward-Perkins, 1970: Boethius A. and Ward-Perkins J.B., *Etruscan and Roman Architecture*, London.

Bowman and Thomas, 1983: Bowman A.K. and Thomas J.D., *Vindolanda: The Latin Writing-Tablets*, London.

Broughton, 1952: Broughton T.R.S., *The Magistrates of the Roman Republic*, New York.

Brunt, 1959: Brunt P.A., The Revolt of Vindex and the Fall of Nero, *Latomus* XVIII, 531–559.

Cheeseman, 1914: Cheeseman G.L., *The Auxilia of the Roman Army*, Oxford.

Chilver, 1957: Chilver G.E.F., The Army in Politics, A.D. 68–70, *JRS* XLVII, 29–35.

Crawford, 1974: Crawford M.H., *Roman Republican Coinage*, Cambridge.

Crook, 1955: Crook J.A., *Consilium Principis*, Cambridge.

Crook, 1957: Crook J.A., Suetonius Ab Epistulis, *PCPS* IV, 18–22.

Dessau, 1889: Dessau H., Uber Zeit und Personlichkeit der Scriptores Historiae Augustae, *Hermes* XXIV, 337ff.

Duff, 1928: Duff A.M., *Freedmen in the Early Roman Empire*, Oxford.

Durry, 1938: Durry M., *Les Cohortes Prétoriennes*, Paris.

Earl, 1963: Earl D.C., *Tiberius Gracchus, a Study in Politics*, Brussels.

Ferguson, 1970: Ferguson J., *The Religions of the Roman Empire*, London.

Frere, 1987: Frere S.S., *Britannia*, London (3rd Edition).

Furneaux, 1896: Furneaux H., *The Annals of Tacitus*, Oxford.

Gelzer, 1969: Gelzer, M., *The Roman Nobility*, Oxford.

Gjerstad, 1962: Gjerstad E., *Legends and Facts of Early Rome*, Lund.

Griffin, 1984: Griffin M., *Nero: The End of a Dynasty*, London.

Hadas, 1930: Hadas M., *Sextus Pompey*, New York.

Hainsworth, 1962:   Hainsworth J.B., Verginius and Vindex, *Historia* XI, 86–96.
Jones, 1960:   Jones A.H.M., *Studies in Roman Government and Law*,
                         Oxford (Blackwell).
Jones, 1970:   Jones A.H.M., *Augustus*, London.
Kahane et al, 1968:   Kahane A., Threipland L.M., and Ward-Perkins J.B.: The
                         Ager Veientanus, North and East of Rome, *PBSR* XXXVI.
Kokkinos, 1992:   Kokkinos N., *Antonia Augusta*, London.
Kraay, 1949:   Kraay C.M., The Coinage of Vindex and Galba, A.D. 68, and
                         the Continuity of the Augustan Principate, *Num. Chron.*[6] IX,
                         129–149.
Lacey, 1917:   Lacey R.H., *Equestrian Officials of Trajan and Hadrian*,
                         Princeton.
Levick, 1976:   Levick B., *Tiberius The Politician*, London.
Lintott, 1993:   Lintott A.W., *Imperium Romanum*, London.
Loftstedt, 1948:   Loftstedt E., On the Style of Tacitus, *JRS* XXXVIII, 1–8.
Lugli, 1960:   Lugli G., *Mons Palatinus*, Rome.
Macé, 1900:   Macé A., *Essai sur Suétone*, Paris.
Marañon, 1956:   Marañon G., *Tiberius, A Study in Resentment*, London.
Marec and Pflaum, 1952: Marec E. and Pflaum H.G., Nouvelle Inscription sur la
                         carrière de Suétone, l'historien, *CRAI* (1952), 76–85.
Mattingly, 1954:   Mattingly H., Verginius at Lugdunum, *Num. Chron.*[6] XIV,
                         32–39.
Maxfield, 1981:   Maxfield V.A., *The Military Decorations of the Roman Army*,
                         London.
McCrum and   McCrum M. and Woodhead A.G., *Select Documents of the*
Woodhead, 1960:   *Principates of the Flavian Emperors, A.D. 68–96*,
                         Cambridge.
McKay, 1975:   McKay A.G., *Houses, Villas and Palaces in the Roman*
                         World, London.
Milne, 1971:   Milne J.G., *A Catalogue of Alexandrian Coins*, London.
Mooney, 1930:   Mooney G.W., *C. Suetoni Tranquilli De Vita Caesarum Libri*
                         VII - VIII, Dublin.
Nicolet, 1980:   Nicolet C., *The World of the Citizen in Republican Rome*,
                         London.
Ogilvie, 1969:   Ogilvie R.M., *The Romans and Their Gods*, London.
Pallotino, 1974:   Pallotino M., *The Etruscans*, London (Third Edition).
Parker, 1928:   Parker H.M.D., *The Roman Legions*, Oxford.
Pflaum, 1950:   Pflaum H.G., *Les Procurateurs Equestres*, Paris.
Platner and Ashby, 1929: Platner S.B. and Ashby T., *A Topographical Dictionary of*
                         Ancient Rome, Oxford.
Potter, 1987:   Potter T.W., *Roman Italy*, London.
Raoss, 1958:   Raoss M., La Rivolta di Vindice ed il Successo di Galba,
                         Epigraphica XX, 46–120.
Raoss, 1960:   Raoss M., La Rivolta di Vindice ed il Successo di Galba,
                         Epigraphica XXII, 37–151.
Reifferscheid, 1860:   Reifferscheid A., *Suetonii Reliquiae*, Leipzig.

Roth, 1893:   Roth C.L., *C. Suetoni Tranquilli quae supersunt omnia*,
                              Leipzig.
Sherwin-White, 1966:   Sherwin-White A.N., *The Letters of Pliny*, Oxford.
Sherwin-White, 1973:   Sherwin-White, A.N., *The Roman Citizenship*, Oxford (2nd
                              edition).
Shotter, 1966:   Shotter D.C.A., The Elections under Tiberius, *CQ* XVI, 321–
                              332.
Shotter, 1967:   Shotter D.C.A., Tacitus and Verginius Rufus, *CQ* XVII,
                              370–381.
Shotter, 1968:   Shotter D.C.A., Tacitus, Tiberius and Germanicus, *Historia*
                              XVII, 194–214.
Shotter, 1971:   Shotter D.C.A., Julians, Claudians and the accession of
                              Tiberius, *Latomus* XXX, 1117–1123.
Shotter, 1974a: Shotter D.C.A., The Fall of Sejanus: two problems, *Class.
                              Phil.* LXIX, 42–46.
Shotter, 1974b: Shotter D.C.A., Gnaeus Calpurnius Piso, Legate of Syria,
                              Historia XXIII, 229–245.
Shotter, 1975:   Shotter D.C.A., A Time-table for the 'Bellum Neronis',
                              Historia XXIV, 59–74.
Shotter, 1977:   Shotter D.C.A., Tacitus and Antonius Primus, *LCM* II, 23–
                              27.
Shotter, 1978a: Shotter D.C.A., Principatus ac Libertas, *Anc. Soc.* IX, 235–
                              255.
Shotter, 1978b: Shotter D.C.A., Tacitus and Marius Celsus, *LCM* III, 197–
                              200.
Shotter, 1979:   Shotter D.C.A., Gods, Emperors and Coins, *G & R* XXVI,
                              48–57.
Shotter, 1983:   Shotter D.C.A., The Principate of Nerva: some observations
                              on the Coin Evidence, *Historia* XXXII, 215–226.
Shotter, 1989:   Shotter D.C.A., *A Commentary on Tacitus Annals IV*,
                              Warminster.
Shotter, 1991a: Shotter D.C.A., Tacitus' View of Emperors and the
                              Principate, pp. 3263–3331 in Haase W. and Temporini H.
                              (Eds), *Aufstieg und Niedergang der Romischen Welt* II. 33.5,
                              Berlin.
Shotter, 1991b: Shotter D.C.A., *Augustus Caesar*, London.
Shotter, 1992:   Shotter D.C.A., *Tiberius Caesar*, London.
Smallwood, 1967:   Smallwood E.M., *Documents illustrating the Principates of
                              Gaius, Claudius and Nero*, Cambridge.
Stevenson, 1939:   Stevenson G.H., *Roman Provincial Administration*, Oxford
                              (Blackwell).
Sutherland, 1951:   Sutherland C.H.V., *Coinage in Roman Imperial Policy, 31
                              B.C.-A.D. 68*, London.
Sutherland, 1984:   Sutherland C.H.V., The Concepts *Adsertor* and *Salus* as used
                              by Vindex and Galba, *Num. Chron.* CXLIV, 29–32.

Syme, 1937:   Syme R., The Colony of Cornelius Fuscus: an incident in the
                    Bellum Neronis, *AJP* LVIII, 7–18.
Syme, 1939:   Syme R., *The Roman Revolution*, Oxford.
Syme, 1955:   Syme R., Marcus Lepidus *capax imperii*, *JRS* XLV, 22–33.
Syme, 1958:   Syme R., *Tacitus*, Oxford.
Syme, 1971:   Syme R., *Emperors and Biography*, Oxford.
Syme, 1980a: Syme R., Biographers of the Caesars, *Museum Helveticum*
                    XXXVII, 104–28.
Syme, 1980b: Syme R., *Some Arval Brethren*, Oxford.
Syme, 1981:   Syme R., The Travels of Suetonius Tranquillus, *Hermes* CIX,
                    105–117.
Taylor, 1912:   Taylor L.R., *The Cults of Ostia*, Bryn Mawr.
Taylor, 1931:   Taylor L.R., *The Divinity of the Roman Emperor*,
                    Middletown.
Townend, 1959:   Townend G.B., The Date of Composition of Suetonius'
                    Caesares, *CQ* IX, 285–293.
Townend, 1960:   Townend G.B., The Sources of the Greek in Suetonius,
                    Hermes LXXXVII, 98–120.
Townend, 1961:   Townend G.B., The Hippo-Inscription and the career of
                    Suetonius, *Historia* X, 99–109.
Townend, 1964:   Townend G.B., Cluvius Rufus in the "Histories" of Tacitus,
                    AJP LXXXV, 337–377.
Townend, 1967:   Townend G.B., Suetonius and his Influence, pp.79–111 in
                    Dudley D.R. and Dorey T.A. (Ed.) *Latin Biography*, London.
Veyne, 1992:   Veyne P., *Bread and Circuses*, London.
Wallace-Hadrill, 1983: Wallace-Hadrill A., *Suetonius: The Scholar and his Caesars*,
                    London.
Ward-Perkins, 1961: Ward-Perkins J.B., Veii: The Historical Topography of the
                    Ancient City, *PBSR* XXIX.
Warmington, 1969:   Warmington B.H., *Nero: Reality and Legend*, London.
Webster, 1985:   Webster G.B., *The Roman Imperial Army*, London (3rd
                    Edition).
Wellesley, 1954:   Wellesley K., Can you Trust Tacitus? *G & R* 1, 13–35.
Wellesley, 1975:   Wellesley K., *The Long Year, A.D. 69*, London.
Wiedemann, 1992:   Wiedemann T., *Emperors and Gladiators*, London.
Wirszubski, 1950:   Wirszubski Ch., *Libertas as a Political Idea at Rome*,
                    Cambridge.

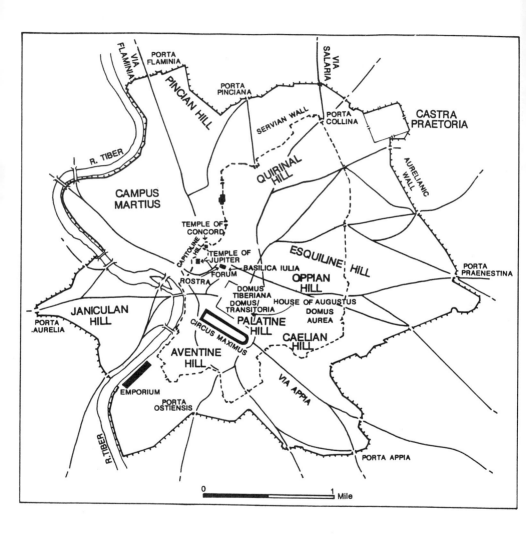

1. Plan of Ancient Rome.

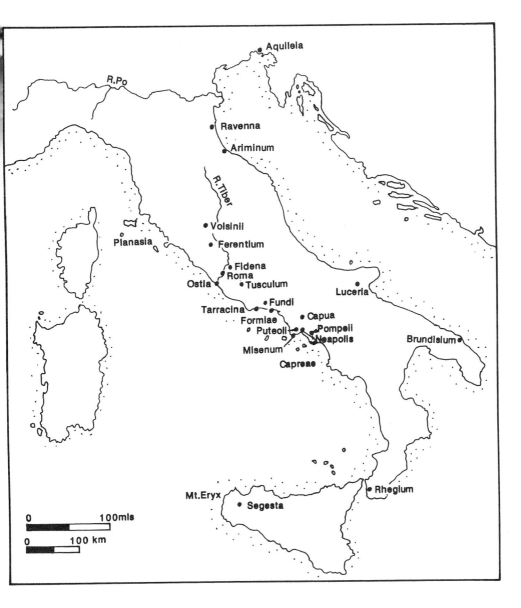

2. Map of Italy.

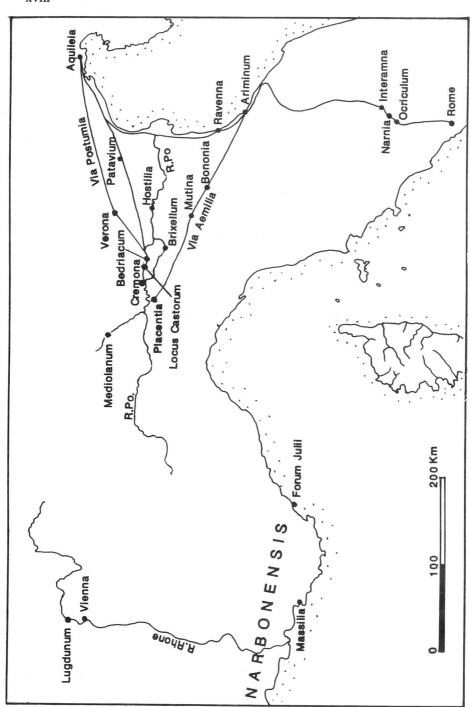

3. Northern Italy, to illustrate the campaigns of AD 69.

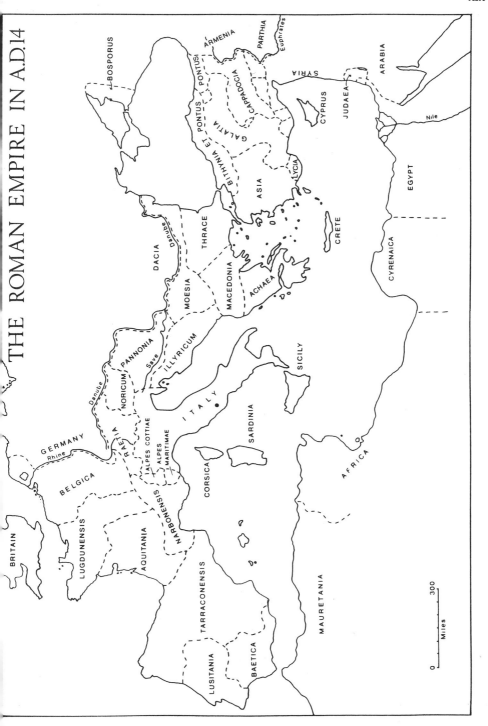

THE ROMAN EMPIRE IN A.D.14

BRITAIN

GERMANY
Rhine

BELGICA

LUGDUNENSIS

AQUITANIA

NARBONENSIS

RAETIA

NORICUM

ALPES COTTIAE
ALPES MARITIMAE

PANNONIA
Save

ILLYRICUM

Danube

DACIA

MOESIA

THRACE

MACEDONIA

ACHAEA

BOSPORUS

ARMENIA

PARTHIA
Euphrates

PONTUS
BITHYNIA ET PONTUS

GALATIA

CAPPADOCIA

ASIA

LYCIA

SYRIA

CYPRUS

JUDAEA

ARABIA

Nile

EGYPT

CYRENAICA

CRETE

ITALY

SICILY

SARDINIA

CORSICA

AFRICA

MAURETANIA

TARRACONENSIS

LUSITANIA

BAETICA

Danube

0   300
Miles

4. The Provinces of the Roman Empire.

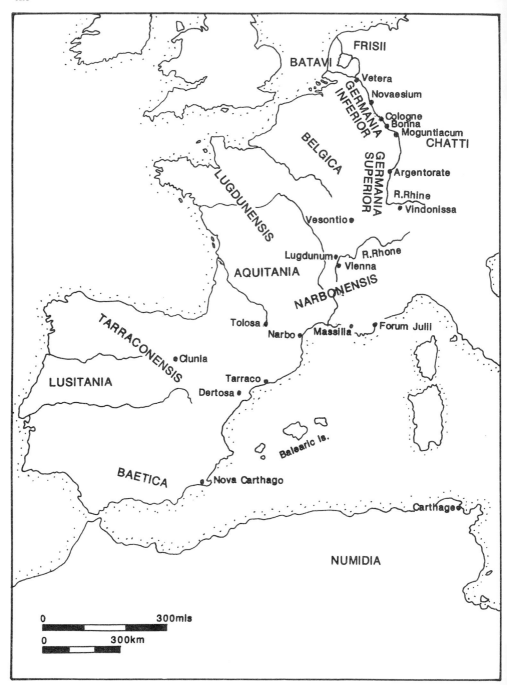

5. Spain, Gaul and the Germanies.

Introduction

1. The Life and Works of Suetonius

i) Life and career

A discussion and reconstruction of the life and career of Suetonius Tranquillus is beset with difficulties; comments and remarks made by Suetonius himself and by contemporary and later writers provide a part of the evidence, although a career-inscription of the biographer, found at Hippo (Bône in Algeria) in 1952[1], whilst not without its own problems, offers a framework for understanding Suetonius' public life.

We know little about Suetonius' family; a grandfather – whether maternal or paternal is not specified – is cited[2] as the source of a story concerning Caligula's building of the bridge of boats at Baiae. This grandfather was evidently placed close to intimate courtiers which might suggest that he was either a freedman or perhaps a soldier in the praetorian guard. Suetonius' father, Suetonius Laetus,[3] was an equestrian tribune in legion XIII at the time of the war between Otho and Vitellius, taking part in the battle of Bedriacum, and sufficiently close to Otho to know of that emperor's abhorrence of civil war. Suetonius' father had first-hand experience of the disgrace inflicted upon legion XIII by Vitellius, and of the terrible vengeance meted out by these ex-Othonian soldiers to the towns of Cremona and Bononia (Bologna).[4]

The year of Suetonius' birth cannot be fixed with precision, although a date in the early 70s seems most likely. Suetonius on a number of occasions[5] refers to himself as *adulescens*, a word meaning *young man* and normally applicable to the late teens. The most useful of these references is to the appearance of a "false Nero" around A.D. 88. Further, Pliny, who was born around A.D. 62, twice describes Suetonius as his "companion" (*contubernalis*), a term implying the kind of intimacy which would not normally bridge a significant age-gap.[6]

Similarly uncertain is Suetonius' place of birth; whilst arguments have been put forward for Rome, there are indications of other possibilities.[7] For example, the fact that the career-inscription was discovered at Hippo offers some support for that town as the biographer's birthplace, unless of course Hippo had some other reason for commemorating Suetonius.[8] Ostia has had some support because of the mention on the

---

1   The text and a discussion of the inscription can be found in Townend, 1961; See also Syme, 1958, ii. 778ff.
2   *Cal.* 19,3.
3   *Otho* 10,1.
4   See Tacitus *Hist.* II. 43ff and 67; III. 32.
5   *Nero* 57,2; *Dom.* 12; *On Grammarians* 4.
6   *Letters* I. 24; X. 94. It is worth noting that the elder Pliny (in the preface to *The Natural History*) refers to the *contubernium* in connection with himself and the emperor, Titus; Titus was at least sixteen years Pliny's junior.
7   Macé, 1900, 34.
8   Syme, 1958, ii. 780; Crook, 1957, 18ff.

Hippo-inscription of a priesthood of Vulcan; Ostia is known to have had such a priesthood.[9] Lanuvium is another possibility as Suetonius' relative, Caesennius Silvanus, came from there.[10] Pisaurum, a citizen-colony (*colonia*) in Italy, has also been suggested,[11] as the gentile name, Suetonius, appears to have had a centre there, and the biographer betrays some knowledge of the area.

Suetonius seems to have enjoyed a normal education in Rome,[12] and to have proceeded from that to a teaching-career; Pliny, in book I[13] (dated as a whole to A.D. 97), refers to Suetonius as a *scholasticus*, a term used to describe teachers of both secondary and tertiary levels (respectively *grammaticus* and *rhetor*). Suetonius' preoccupation with compilation might be thought to point to the former. The same letter of Pliny, which concerns a small farm which Suetonius wished to purchase, indicates the biographer to have been a man who was careful with money, staid and rather fussy.

Suetonius evidently attempted at some stage to embark upon a career at the bar although he does not appear to have progressed far in this; one of Pliny's letters[14] contains a reply to a request from Suetonius that Pliny should use his influence to secure the adjournment of a case in which Suetonius was due to speak. Evidently the superstitious Suetonius had had a dream which he regarded as a bad omen for his coming responsibility. It is not known whether Suetonius made any further attempts to speak in public.

A similarly indecisive attempt was made at a military career, for Suetonius persuaded Pliny to obtain for him one of the military tribunates available in the army commanded by Lucius Neratius Marcellus, who became governor of Britain in A.D. 101.[15] Having secured the commission, Suetonius changed his mind, requesting that it be transferred to Caesennius Silvanus. The next ten years appear to have been spent in teaching and writing; lightheartedly, Pliny attacked his friend for the length of time it took him to produce and polish his literature.[16]

The next record comes in the collection of letters (book X) which passed between Pliny and the emperor, Trajan, whilst the former was governor of Bithynia. In an exchange of letters,[17] Pliny requested the emperor to grant Suetonius the privileges attaching to fathers of three or more children (*ius trium liberorum*); Suetonius' marriage had proved childless, and the privilege requested would have allowed Suetonius amongst other things to benefit from the legacies of friends. A point of interest that arises from this letter surrounds the possible presence of Suetonius in Bithynia as a member of Pliny's staff (*cohors amicorum*); Pliny's governorship probably extended over the years A.D. 109–111,[18] but Suetonius' presence in the province depends to a large extent upon a disputed reading in Pliny's letter.

---

9   Taylor, 1912, 14ff; *ILS* 4176 and 4402.
10   Pliny, *Letters* III. 8,1; *ILS* 7212.
11   Syme, 1958, ii. 780.
12   For a detail, see *On Grammarians* 4.
13   *Letters* I. 24.
14   *Letters* I. 18.
15   *Letters* III. 8.
16   *Letters* V. 10.
17   *Letters* X. 94 and 95.
18   For a discussion of the chronological problems, see Sherwin-White, 1966, 80ff.

The death of Pliny, probably whilst still in Bithynia, will have left a considerable gap in Suetonius' life. It is evident, however, that before long this gap came to be filled by another close friend of Pliny's and a member of his literary circle, Gaius Septicius Clarus, who in A.D. 119 became one of the two prefects of the praetorian guard.[19] Septicius was the recipient of the dedications both of Pliny's *Letters* and Suetonius' *Lives of the Caesars*.

It may be assumed that it was Pliny's recommendation, together with Suetonius' association with Septicius Clarus, that led to Suetonius' advancement along the career for men of equestrian status. He received a co-optation (*adlectio*); although there is a number of bodies to which he might have been co-opted, most agree that it was to a group of senior judges, the *selecti iudices*. These were men of equestrian status and who under the principate were the highest-ranking amongst the judges.[20] It has been pointed out that the status was usually conferred upon equestrians who had not yet received administrative office, but who had fulfilled the normal *military* qualifications; that Suetonius had not emphasises the importance of Pliny's support.[21] It is possible that at this stage of his career Suetonius was awarded the priesthood of Vulcan to which the Hippo-inscription refers.

However, the chief difficulty in interpreting the Hippo-inscription, and thus in determining the shape of Suetonius' career, lies in the assessment of the chronology involved. The names of emperors are twice specified; the co-optation on to the panel of judges was due to Trajan, but no further imperial name is mentioned until that of Hadrian appears after the secretarial post (*ab epistulis*). Simply, the difficulty – which is hardly capable of certain resolution – is whether Trajan was responsible for the co-optation alone or whether Suetonius received all the cited offices from Trajan with the exception of the *ab epistulis*, for which Hadrian was responsible.[22] Although the two earlier secretarial posts (*a studiis, a bibliothecis*) could be held as a combined office, on balance it seems unlikely that Suetonius could have filled these offices (and others that have been lost in the inscription) between Hadrian's accession in A.D. 117 and his own dismissal from office, along with Septicius Clarus, probably in A.D. 122. The most likely solution is that Suetonius' career continued to develop in Trajan's later years and into Hadrian's reign, culminating in the promotion to *ab epistulis* in A.D. 119, the year that also saw the promotion of Septicius Clarus.

This discussion is hampered by problems surrounding the date of Suetonius' dismissal; the year A.D. 122 is usually accepted because the story concerning the over-familiarity of Suetonius and Septicius Clarus with Hadrian's wife, Sabina, is attached in Spartianus' biography to the account of Hadrian's visit to Britain in A.D. 122.[23] It has, however, been argued[24] that Suetonius was still in the emperor's entourage at the time of

19 Writers of the Augustan History (SHA), *Life of Hadrian* 9,4.
20 See Jones, 1960, 41ff.
21 See Townend, 1961, 100, who cites examples of similar privileged treatment – amongst them the second century writer, Aulus Gellius (*Attic Nights* 14.2,1).
22 The two points of view are argued by Crook, 1957, 18ff and Townend, 1961, 105.
23 *Life of Hadrian* 11,3. Syme (1958, ii. 779–780) accepts the connection.
24 Crook, 1957, 21; Hadrian's beneficence to African provincials is recorded in Spartianus' biography (13,4).

the visit to Africa in A.D. 128 and that the Hippo-inscription commemorates a man who had perhaps helped to secure imperial favours for the province. Against this, it might be asked whether the provincial leaders in Africa would have been wise to have commemorated one so recently disgraced. In any case, care has to be exercised in using Spartianus' biography; it has been shown that it depends upon two sources – a simple chronological account and a more anecdotal treatment of character – which may have been woven together in a rather indiscriminate fashion.

The reason for and circumstances of Suetonius' dismissal are similarly open to speculation. It is generally assumed that Sabina accompanied her husband on most of his imperial visits, and that the offending incident took place on one of them. The problem does not appear to have been one of immorality or intrigue, but perhaps centred on the observance of court-etiquette to which Hadrian was by nature opposed, but which was obviously of some importance in the provinces.[25] It may be suggested that in these circumstances Sabina reacted unfavourably to the behaviour of Suetonius and Septicius Clarus, thus forcing Hadrian for the sake of household-unity to take a step that he would have preferred to have avoided; as his biographer records,[26] "he used himself to say that had he been a private citizen he would have dismissed his miserable shrew of a wife".

Suetonius would have seen congenial employment in his secretarial posts.[27] The duty of *a studiis* was to act as a kind of literary adviser to the emperor, supervising his private libraries and bringing promising writers to his attention. The *a bibliothecis* had charge of the public libraries, whilst the highly influential *ab epistulis* handled all imperial mail, made the recommendations for promotion and had to have his finger on the empire's pulse. As we shall see, however, it is possible that the decisiveness which was required of the post's holder and the prominence which attached to it may have been foreign to Suetonius' nature.[28] On the other hand, the opportunities which all of these posts provided for the kind of research which Suetonius enjoyed are obvious, and it is clear from the early *Lives of the Caesars* that the biographer took full advantage of these opportunities whilst they were available – and suffered as a researcher when they were not. It is worth noting that although by Hadrian's reign such posts went almost exclusively to men of equestrian status, under earlier emperors, such as Claudius and Nero, they had been held by ex-slaves (*liberti*) – a fact which caused great resentment in senatorial circles.

It does not seem that Suetonius regained imperial favour; indeed, if it is true that he dedicated his *Lives of the Caesars* to Septicius Clarus, and if, as some suggest,[29] there are anti-Hadrianic references in the *Lives*, it does not appear that he set out to regain the emperor's confidence. Nor is it clear how long Suetonius lived; it has been suggested that his work, *On Public Offices*, may have been written to coincide with Hadrian's

---

25 Syme, 1958, ii.779; Dio Cassius LXIX. 10,1. It is worth here recalling Tiberius' displeasure at the over-informal behaviour of Germanicus in Egypt (Tacitus *Ann*. II. 59, 2–3; Shotter, 1968, 204ff).

26 *Life of Hadrian* 11,3.

27 For a discussion of the duties, see Duff, 1928, 156–9.

28 For the heaviness of responsibilities, see Statius' account of Abascantus who held the post under Domitian (*Silvae* V. 1, 83–100).

29 See Townend 1959, 290ff and 1967, 90. Continuing disfavour is at least implied in the *Life of Hadrian* 15.

reform of the civil service in the late 120s and 130s. It has further been argued that a reference to Domitia Longina (the wife of Domitian) implies that she was dead by the time of writing; her death has been placed in or a little before A.D.140.[30] In any case the long list of titles ascribed to Suetonius in Suidas' *Lexicon* suggest a long literary career after the biographer's dismissal from administrative office.[31]

ii) The character of Suetonius

Apart from what can be inferred from Suetonius' writings themselves, our chief evidence for his character comes from those letters in Pliny's collection which are either addressed to the biographer or concern him. As we have already seen, there is an apparent contrast between the character of the man and the kind of life he must have led in the senior levels of the emperor's service. Pliny's letters suggest that Suetonius was a man who, whilst diligent almost to the point of excess, especially with regard to his literary productions, was not interested in the publicity which came with high office and was perhaps ill-at-ease with its responsibilities. He preferred the quiet life of books and teaching to a more exciting (and risky) existence in the army; yet Suetonius' indecisiveness was such that he let Pliny go to the trouble of securing a military commission for him before he decided to reject it. A similar lack of decisiveness surrounded Suetonius' projected entry into the world of public speaking; so superstitious was he that a dream caused him to seek Pliny's good offices in securing an adjournment. It thus causes little surprise when we notice his preoccupation with dreams and omens in the *Lives of the Caesars*.

His personal and family-life appear to have been honourable and straightforward; in this, as in other things, we can imagine him to have been careful, perhaps to the point of fussiness, and very staid. Such a picture emerges clearly from the stipulations surrounding the nature of the small country-estate which he had asked Pliny to obtain for him; it had to be cheap, and it had to provide peace and quiet.[32]

The quality and character of Suetonius, however, are plainly shown by the excessive trouble to which Pliny was prepared to go on his behalf. No better testimonial exists than the opening of the letter in which Pliny recommends his friend to Trajan:[33] "Sir, I have for a long time now considered Suetonius Tranquillus amongst my closest friends; he is a man of absolute honour and integrity – and an outstanding scholar. It is this combination of character and erudition that has made us so close." Pliny was clearly delighted to have Suetonius in his circle and consulted him on literary matters.[34] In fact, true to his character, Suetonius appears to have been excessively careful both in researching and in publishing; indeed Pliny suggests that Suetonius was spending so much time polishing his work that he was in danger of rubbing it away altogether.

---

30   *Div. Tit.* 10. For reference to Domitia Longina, see *PIR*[2] D181; for her death, see *ILS* 272.
31   Macé, 1900, 235, placed Suetonius' death in or around A.D. 141. It is most unlikely that the Tranquillus mentioned in a letter of Fronto, which is dated to A.D. 161–2, should be identified with Suetonius.
32   *Letters* I. 24.
33   *Letters* X. 94, 1.
34   *Letters* IX. 34.

Attention to detail and diligence are qualities that come out clearly in *Lives of the Caesars* – care over particular facts (such as Caligula's birthplace), thoroughness in quotation from sources (such as Augustus' correspondence). The arrangement[35] of the *Lives* is generally careful, adopting the literary *divisio* ("division into topics") – even though this may confuse the modern reader who is not used to it. His predilection for scandal has often been noted; yet it is less likely to have been due to a natural *liking* for the salacious and the scurrilous than to his interest in the curious. For example, the fulsome details of Tiberius' supposed perversions on the island of Capreae[36] bear more the signs of diligent compilation than of anything else – the same kind of interest in the curious that will have persuaded him to compose his manual on terms of abuse.

However, whilst we need not see in Suetonius' writings signs of a malicious man, we can recognise a writer who found it congenial and easy to list, compile and categorise. At the same time perhaps we can appreciate the same indecisiveness that is apparent in his personal life. Amassing information was one thing; coming to critical decisions about it quite another.

iii) The writings of Suetonius

It is hardly surprising that one who devoted so much time to scholarly pursuits, both in private and in public, should have had a large output. It is evident in this that he must have overcome the diffidence in publishing noted by Pliny.[37]

Of a long list of titles, however, only *Lives of Famous Men* and *Lives of the Caesars* survive in any substance. The chronology of publication is not clear, although *Famous Men* is generally reckoned to have been published earlier than the *Caesars*, and may have been the work that prompted Pliny's remark about excessive polishing. That neither of these works appeared in published form during Pliny's lifetime is a reasonable deduction from the latter's failure to mention the fact. *Famous Men* was a collection of literary biographies; from it, *On Grammarians* survives more or less complete, and there are pieces from *On Rhetoricians*. It appears that there were sections also on poets, orators and historians. Of the poets, *Lives* of Terence, Horace, Lucan and Donatus' Virgil survive; possibly from this source also are the extant *Lives* of Tibullus and Persius. There are thought to have been thirty-three biographies of poets in all. Much less survives from the sections on orators and on historians. It is thus difficult to form an estimate of the work as a whole, though, as in the early *Caesars*, it appears that Suetonius was prepared to quote at length to establish his points.

The publication of *Lives of Caesars* is usually placed in the period A.D. 119–122, though the *Lives* are divided between separate books and because of the variable quality of the *Lives* there is room to doubt whether in fact they fall into a single publishing period. There are eight books:-

I	Julius Caesar
II	Augustus

---

35   Townend, 1967, 84ff.
36   *Tib*. 43–45.
37   For Suetonius' publications and surviving fragments of them, see Roth's edition in the Teubner series (Leipzig 1860), pp.275–320; also Bardon, 1956, 206.

The work was dedicated to Septicius Clarus, although the statement of dedication and the opening sections of *Julius Caesar* are now lost.

It has been noted that Suetonius has abundant quotations from Augustus' correspondence in the *Augustus* and in the subsequent *Lives* where that correspondence was relevant, but no quotations from the letters of later emperors. From this it might be suggested[38] that the *Julius Caesar* and the *Augustus* were thoroughly researched and published whilst Suetonius' imperial office gave him access to relevant raw material and before he and Septicius Clarus were dismissed in A.D. 122. The dedication to Septicius would thus be a natural preliminary to the publication of an initial section of respectable size: subsequent sections could thus be published at intervals. Suetonius could not be expected to know how dramatically his circumstances were to alter.

The *Lives* after that of Augustus bear other indications of difference beyond simply that of the use made of quotations from private correspondence. They are generally shorter and more sketchy, and there is an increasing tendency on the author's part towards uncritical generalisations.[39] Also observable is a greater hostility towards the principate and possibly criticism of Hadrian – features absent from the earlier *Lives*, despite opportunities.

Suetonius' other works are known by little more than their titles, but they betray the wide-ranging interests of a man for whom every subject presented an opportunity for factual compilation and the chance to research into the curious. The variety between such titles as *Roman Games and Festivals*, *Public Offices*, *Terms of Abuse*, *Courtesans* is ample evidence of the enquiring mind and thorough research of Suetonius Tranquillus.

2. Biography in antiquity and the Lives of the Caesars

i) Biography in antiquity

Although frequently united in modern usage by the description "biography", Suetonius' *Lives of the Caesars* and Tacitus' *Life of Agricola* are two very different types of work. Tacitus' is a eulogy, and professedly so; as such it follows a recognisable tradition in both Greece and Rome – Xenophon's *Life of Agesilaus*, Isocrates' *Life of Evagoras*, and Cornelius Nepos' biographies of Epaminondas, Agesilaus and Atticus. There is little

---

38   Townend, 1959, 285ff; 1967, 88.
39   From the *Tiberius* we may note 32,2 (where "governors" refers to Aemilius Rectus alone) and 61, where there are examples designed to demonstrate the supposed cruelty of the emperor. The most outrageous of these is the observation concerning the raping of virgins prior to execution which is almost certainly a generalisation based on the single case of Sejanus' daughter (61,5).

doubt that this kind of writing was related to the practice of commemorating famous deeds of famous men, and so could be said to have been linked with epic poetry and with the commemorative orations known to have been "sung" in Rome in a number of contexts.[40] Different contexts will have called for different approaches: for example, in his *Histories*, Tacitus was critical of the behaviour of Verginius Rufus in the events of A.D. 68–69; such an approach would clearly, however, have been out of place when, as consul in A.D. 97, Tacitus delivered Verginius' funeral oration.[41]

Another sort of biography was that which attempted to view the subject's character from a somewhat more ethical point of view; into this category fall some of Nepos' biographies and most of Plutarch's. Yet again, there were attempts at more critical and factual work; the origin of this type lay probably with the scholars of Alexandria in the third century B.C., who, in their editing of Greek texts, prefixed a work with a short account of the author's life which probably attempted some kind of chronological development and analysis of conflicting pieces of evidence – in other words, *critical biography*.

It is this latter type that best describes Suetonius' *Lives of the Caesars*; although Suetonius may not always be regarded as a successful critical writer, his work is nevertheless neither eulogistic nor ethical, but an effort to portray a subject's life in such a way as to illustrate both character and times. Care is taken to achieve chronological accuracy, and evidence is weighed.

The nature of Roman oratory under the principate may also have contributed, although of all the authors left to us from this period Suetonius must rate as one of the least rhetorical in style. Oratory had, however, for some become a vehicle for criticism and assessment – however rudimentary. Political pressures, however, had undermined open criticism; Tacitus notes in the introductions to both his *Histories* and his *Annals* that critical assessment had been made more difficult partly because of "governmental secrecy" and partly because of the developing tendency to flatter living emperors and to blackguard dead ones. Tacitus attempted a critical middle road; that Suetonius did also is to be deduced from those *Lives* in which he was most successful – the *Julius Caesar* and the *Augustus*. With his access to unique source-material Suetonius stood a better chance than many of achieving a reasonably objective account.

The biographer has, of course, been much criticised in modern times; some of the criticism directed towards the later *Lives* is merited. The fact remains, however, that Suetonius has been most frequently assailed by those who have hoped to use him as if he were an historian. The biographer's writings lack a clear chronological perspective, but he does share with Tacitus an attempt to apply an analytical method to the evaluation of the recent past.

ii) *The Lives of the Caesars*
As we have noticed, there is evidence to suggest that the *Lives of the Caesars* was published in at least two parts – the *Julius Caesar* and *Augustus* probably around A.D. 121–122, and the remainder perhaps as late as A.D. 135–140. The work is complete

---

40   Cicero *Tusculan Disputations* IV. 3.
41   Tacitus *Hist.* I. 8,2 and II. 68,4; for the oration, see Pliny *Letters* II. 1,6. In general, see
       Shotter, 1967, 379f.

apart from the beginning of the *Julius Caesar*, which will have contained, besides the dedication to Septicius Clarus, the family background, birth and its preceding omens, childhood and upbringing of Julius Caesar. It is evident that this lost portion was still in existence in the sixth century, but had perished before the ninth, which is the date ascribed to the earliest manuscript – the *Codex Memmianus*.

The general plan of the biographies is made clear early in the *Augustus*:[42] "After a brief outline of Augustus' life, I shall treat it in separate sections; I shall not use a chronological framework, but subject-headings in order to make the work more comprehensible to my readers."

Macé long ago[43] noted that this "cataloguing"-methodology was well-suited to an ex-schoolmaster and accords well with the apparent nature of many other of Suetonius' recorded titles.

It will be immediately apparent that with the sacrifice of chronology, we lose two things. First, the historical perspective which will sometimes be crucial for the understanding of the full significance of the point being made; and secondly, there is by this method no real development of character. In this respect, we are probably more aware of the sacrifice than Suetonius' ancient audience will have been, since they thought less of character-development than of relevation, where actions and situations simply revealed a character which already existed. Such a view is reasonably clear from Tacitus' summary of the life of Tiberius.[44]

The *Lives* follow a similar general pattern: starting with a survey of family, early life and career to the point of accession, the subjects' lives are then treated under such headings as wars, legislation, buildings, virtues, vices and so on, concluding with physical characteristics and death preceded by relevant omens; all of these sections are illustrated by a collection of facts and stories, though the amount of information varies.

Within these categories there is some variation: for example, the account of death precedes that of physical characteristics in *Nero* and *Domitian*, whilst in the *Titus* the physical characteristics are discussed in the context of the emperor's youth.[45] The opening sections also vary, particularly as the early lives of the subjects varied; *Julius* is, of course, here in a class of its own, as the subject came to power so late in life. *Augustus* contains a long section on the civil wars,[46] whilst *Tiberius* has one on Rhodes.[47] *Caligula* is different again in that there is a mini-biography of the subject's father, Germanicus.[48] Emperors' memorable sayings are generally scattered throughout each *Life*, although in two cases they were evidently thought to be of sufficient significance to be gathered together in a single section.[49]

Particular divisions can in some cases appear obfuscated – at least to the modern reader; this generally results from the author's composing of a section which is

---

42   *Div. Aug.* 9.
43   Macé, 1900, 54.
44   *Ann.* VI. 51, 5–6.
45   *Div. Tit.* 3.
46   *Div. Aug.* 9–18.
47   *Tib.* 10–13.
48   *Cal.* 1–10.
49   *Div. Vesp.* 22 and *Dom.* 20.

introduced by a sentence stating that illustrations of a number of qualities are to follow, but then failing to make the illustration of each individually clear. A straightforward example occurs in *Augustus* and a more confusing one in *Nero*.[50] It is only in the *Julius Caesar* and *Augustus* that Suetonius offers clear guidance to divisions.[51] In the later *Lives*, indications of major divisions are less frequent, though *Caligula* and *Nero* carry explicit distinctions between tolerable and bad actions.[52] It is probable that Suetonius considered repeated major expositions of his practice in each *Life* to be unnecessary, although it must remain an open question whether he intended all the variations in division that do occur.

The care with which Suetonius approached his task has often been discussed – and with varying conclusions. On a superficial level, it is noticed that the careers and characters of the first six Caesars are treated with more care and fullness than is the case with the six that follow; more specifically, a change in the nature of treatment appears to set in after *Augustus*. Suetonius' readiness to quote *verbatim* particularly from the imperial correspondence falls away after *Augustus*; indeed in the ensuing *Lives*, such *verbatim* quotations as there are come mainly from Augustus' correspondence and were probably noted when the *Augustus* was in preparation.[53] The only similar reference to an emperor later than Augustus is to Nero and the suggestion that his poems were not original.[54] There have been a number of suggestions to explain this, varying from loss of interest to hurried publication;[55] possibly Hadrian disapproved of the publication of Augustus' correspondence, though this did stop Suetonius using the source in later *Lives* where it was relevant. However, the simplest explanation is loss of access – that is, after his dismissal. The same may also explain the noted decline in tactfulness with regard to Hadrian himself.[56]

Thus, we may detect a change of attitude to complement the author's change of circumstance. There are other indications, too, of a changed attitude to his work; the tendency to omit names from examples, whilst they may be supplied by the reader of

---

50   *Div. Aug.* 51–52; in *Nero* 26–33 five major vices are introduced in 26,1 and then illustrated without further announcement by 26–27, 27–29, 30–31, 32 and 33. The latter then leads into an account of further cruelties. See also *Div. Claud.* 21,1 for another example which is presented very confusingly.

51   The plan for the second half of the *Julius Caesar* is made clear at 45,3 and may have complemented a statement now lost in the opening of the work.

52   *Cal.* 22,1:"so much for Caligula the emperor; the rest of this account must deal with Caligula the monster" (cf. *Nero* 19.3).

53   *Tib.* 21,2; *Cal.* 8; *Div. Claud.* 4. Such quotations may have been noted with the specific purpose of refuting statements he had read elsewhere (Townend, 1959, 285ff). It should be noted that Augustus' correspondence is used also in the *Lives* of Horace and Virgil.

54   *Nero* 52; cf. *Nero* 23,1 for a quotation from a Neronian rescript: it is possible that such later "quotations" were taken from a library-source used by Suetonius (Townend, 1959, 285).

55   Macé, 1900, 210-11.

56   Three instances have been highlighted (Townend, 1959, 290ff):
         1) The death of Claudius (*Div. Claud.* 44,2) which may have been intended to recall the death of Trajan (Dio LXIX. 1,3).
         2) The murder of ex-consuls at the beginning of a reign (*Tib.* 6,1).
         3) Uncomplimentary references to Nero's frontier policy (*Nero* 18).

Tacitus or Dio, nonetheless suggests a plurality of crimes, where only one of the type can in fact be instanced.[57] On other occasions names are withheld, where they were clearly known.[58] The same thing may be noted in a tendency to pluralise sources,[59] though this is not unusual in other writers.

Although Suetonius does not observe the dictates of chronology, following his scheme of division, there are passages in which apparently deliberate chronological distortions take place to blacken the subject: an example is the illustration of Tiberius' handing-out of posts to his drinking companions.[60] Besides this, chronological inaccuracies occur.[61] There are occasions, too, when Suetonius is inconsistent with himself over facts – as in his references to the death of Claudius[62] and the fire of Rome in A.D. 64.[63] He will give fragmentary accounts of events, leaving them in the state where they will apparently inflict most damage on the subject's reputation,[64] or even more confusingly give casual references to events that may well have had major significance.[65]

Suetonius' interests focussed entirely upon the individuals who were the subject of each biography; everything is excluded save that which illustrates that central person in some way. Whilst this is no criticism of the author of a biography, the modern reader, who is reading Suetonius as a historical source for the events of the first century A.D., will find it particularly tantalising that there is, for example, no mention of Agricola in the *Domitian*; another view of Tacitus' highly personalised account would have been especially welcome. Suetonius' reputation in antiquity was high; not only are there complimentary notices in Pliny's *Letters*, but a similar enthusiasm may be found in later authors. Flavius Vopiscus, one of the writers of the *Augustan History*, twice stresses Suetonius' impartiality and thoughtfulness.[66] Such praise reflects the fact that, true to his original profession, Suetonius was a cold and unemotional cataloguer of his subjects' characteristics. Even the most commonly-heard criticism – his fondness for a lewd or outrageous anecdote – can be ascribed to his conviction that he should not suppress anything that he had read or heard; a caveat of "it is said that ..." may have been sufficient for conscience. The fact remains, however, that whatever his overall intentions, Suetonius nearly always wrote down the worst version of an incident that he knew.[67]

Suetonius expected a lot of his reader, for he did not see himself primarily as the *assessor* of the information he set down – except in so far as he may have been selective.

---

57   For example, *Tib.* 61; *Nero* 11,1 (cf. Dio LXI. 19,2); *Tib.* 32,2 (cf. Dio LVII. 10,5); *Nero* 15,2 (cf. Tac. *Ann.* XV. 72); *Nero* 24,1 (cf. Dio LXIII. 8,5). See Townend, 1959, 290 and notes 1–3.
58   *Tib.* 32 and 35; *Nero* 26,2 and 31,4.
59   *Nero* 28,2 (Fabius Rusticus); *Otho* 7,1 (Cluvius Rufus).
60   *Tib.* 42,1.
61   *Galba* 23; *Otho* 11; *Vitellius* 18; *Tib.* 11.
62   *Div. Claud.* 44,2 (cf. *Nero* 33,1 and 39,3).
63   *Nero* 38,1 and 43,1 (cf. Tac. *Ann.* XV. 38,1).
64   For example, the trials narrated in *Tib.* 49,1; also *Nero* 37,1 (cf. Tacitus *Ann.* XVI. 1ff).
65   *Div. Claud.* 25,4; *Nero* 36,1.
66   *Life of Firmus* 1; *Life of Probus* 2.
67   For example *Div. Iul.* 49; *Div. Aug.* 68; *Galba* 22.

As a compiler, he clearly expected the reader to make the assessment: facts were often left to speak for themselves, and large collections of facts may be put together with no attempt made to discuss them.[68] An example of his zeal as a compiler is to be seen in the long lists of dreams and omens which he drew up;[69] not only was Suetonius, like his emperor, Hadrian, a superstitious man, but he was evidently well-read in the subject,[70] and eager therefore to display his scholarship.

Despite the fact that Suetonius sometimes showed his *critical* metal by refuting a statement in another author,[71] he generally did not see it as his task to draw conclusions. Nor did he worship uniformity of presentation: quotations from latin and Greek sources stand side-by-side with his own narrative, providing variety and thus enhancing readability. This latter quality Suetonius displays in abundance, as is eminently demonstrated by passages such as those describing the deaths of Julius Caesar and Nero;[72] it is typical, however, that in the latter of these passages a whole series of questions is prompted in the reader's mind which Suetonius clearly feels no need to answer.

Suetonius remained external to his subjects, making no general estimate of character, and omitting the philosophical or moral reflections which we might have expected from Plutarch. There is in fact what amounts to a refusal to enter into a character's thoughts: indeed it is probably this cold recital which lacks an attempt to comprehend that makes Suetonius often appear hostile, despite the fact that in essence there is little that he says, for example, about Tiberius or Nero that is not mentioned in other sources.[73]

When Suetonius and Tacitus have described the same event, the difference between them is immediately obvious. For example,[74] in their accounts of the death of Vitellius, whilst characteristically Suetonius provides more items of information, it is Tacitus who comes nearer to understanding Vitellius and appreciating the loneliness of the man-in-power, no matter how unscrupulous he may have been. Suetonius' account is external and inquisitive, whilst Tacitus' is aimed at revealing the mind of Vitellius, and at providing the reader with the means to understand. Tacitus' understanding of the event is encapsulated in Vitellius' pathetic, but pertinent, observation, "yet I was your emperor", whilst Suetonius' indifference is demonstrated by the fact that he appears more concerned to press on to the derivation of *Becco*, the childhood name of the Flavian general, Antonius Primus.

---

68 For example, *Div.Claud.* 39.
69 *Div. Iul.* 59; 77; *Div. Aug.* 90–96; *Tib.* 14; 69; 74; *Cal.* 42; 51; 57; *Div. Claud.* 22; 46; *Nero* 46; *Galba* 4; 18–19; *Otho* 7–9; *Vitell.* 11; 15; *Div. Vesp.* 5; 23; 25; *Div. Tit.* 5; 10; *Dom.* 15; 23.
70 See *Div. Aug.* 94,4, where he cites the obscure *Theologumena* of Asclepiades of Mende; for Suetonius' own superstitiousness, see Pliny *Letters* I. 18.
71 For example, with regard to the "rival" versions of Caligula's birthplace (*Cal.* 8).
72 *Div. Iul.* 81–2; *Nero* 47–49.
73 Compare, for example, Suetonius' account of Nero's death with Dio's version of the same event (LXVIII. 27–8).
74 *Vitell.* 16–17; Tac. *Hist.* III. 84. For a detailed discussion of the passages, see Loftstedt, 1948.

iii) The influence of Suetonius[75]

The especial influence of Suetonius amongst later writers lay in his method of arrangement of division into topics. His earliest follower appears to have been Marius Maximus (A.D. 165–230),[76] who continued the Suetonian *Lives* by producing biographies of the next twelve emperors (Nerva to Elagabalus). Marius Maximus was the son of an Italian *procurator*, who apparently entered the senate under the auspices of the emperor Commodus (A.D. 180–192); a supporter of Septimius Severus,[77] he governed Belgica, Lower Germany and Syria Coele under that emperor, was *proconsul* of Africa and Asia simultaneously under Caracalla, prefect of the city under Macrinus, and became consul for the second time in A.D. 223 under Severus Alexander.

Marius Maximus is generally supposed to have followed Suetonius, although there appear to have been differences; whilst the *Writers of the Augustan History* sometimes link the two biographers and claim to use Marius Maximus as a source, it is evident that clear differences of style and attitude were observed between the two authors.

Flavius Vopiscus, for example, whom we have already noted as an admirer of Suetonius, described Marius Maximus as the "most loquacious of writers".[78] It is in any case evident that his works were fuller, for the *Life of Marcus* occupied two books, and Marius probably achieved this by quoting from documents at sometimes excessive length.[79] Nonetheless, he was probably the only continuous source for the emperors of the second century A.D.

The *Writers of the Augustan History*[80] themselves provided an extremely variable collection of biographies from Hadrian to Carinus; six authors were involved, apparently writing in the period covered by the reigns of Diocletian and Constantine (c. A.D. 284–337) –Aelius Spartianus, Julius Capitolinus, Vulcadius Gallicanus, Trebellius Pollio, Aelius Lampridius and Flavius Vopiscus. Besides biographies of emperors, the work also includes accounts of heirs (*Caesars*) and usurpers (*Tyrants*). In some cases, the Suetonian pattern is followed by covering the subject's life in topics, though in the main the better biographies in the collection treat their subjects in chronological fashion. In two cases – *Maximinus/Balbus* (4) and *Probus* (2) – the authors, respectively Capitolinus and Vopiscus, explicitly claim to be following Suetonius' method, and topic-divisions can sometimes be made out.[81] Documents and speeches are frequently quoted, allegedly taken from public records, but in many cases are probably forgeries.

In the fourth century, Aurelius Victor and Eutropius again attempted to follow the Suetonian method. Aurelius Victor published his *On the Caesars* in A.D. 360; down to Domitian's reign this simply contains information taken from Suetonius, whilst the rest is modelled on him. The work goes down to Constantius II (A.D. 337–361). Similarly,

---

75   This topic is fully explored in Townend, 1967, 96ff.

76   On him, see Barbieri, 1954, 36ff.

77   Writers of the Augustan History, *Life of Severus* (5,3) probably refers to him amongst others; for his career, see *ILS* 2935–6.

78   *Life of Firmus* 1,1.

79   Writers of the Augustan History, *Life of Commodus* 18,1 and *Life of Pertinax* 15,8.

80   For a succinct account, see Birley A., 1967, 113 ff. A much fuller treatment is to be found in Syme, 1971.

81   For example, the *Life of Severus Alexander* 29,1.

Eutropius' *Breviarium* derives much in material and method from Suetonius, to the extent that the work has been employed in making emendations to the text of Suetonius.

Of later works, the most "Suetonian" is Einhard's *Life of Charlemagne*, composed shortly after the king's death in A.D. 814.[82] The work is most firmly based on the *Julius Caesar* and *Augustus*, and chronology is ignored. After an excursus on the family, Charlemagne's birth, boyhood and youth are mentioned, followed by a statement (4,2) which lays out the plan for the rest of the work. After a list of wars, Einhard proceeds to summarise conquests, treaties and buildings before passing on to character, introduced by a "topic-division" (18,1) which is itself ignored; in this section the author's partiality towards his subject is obvious in a way that would never have been found in Suetonius. After character, there are chapters on appearance and habits, religion, death (with epitaph) and omens thereof – a pattern which recalls the *Tiberius*. In fact, the chapter on personal appearance (22) forms a close parallel to *Tiberius* (68), and it has been noticed that features which are there described can be paralleled in Suetonius' description of various of the emperors.

Einhard's attempt to write Suetonian biography – or at least partly to desert panegyric – is the last obvious effort in this direction. Yet there is enough to show that the influence of Suetonius over quasi-historical productions was considerable for some 700 years after his death.

3. The Civil Wars of A.D. 68–69[83]

For nearly two years from the spring of 68, the Roman empire was convulsed in the chaos of civil war; Nero's principate, which ended in confusion and the emperor's suicide, was followed by the short and disturbed reigns of Galba, Otho and Vitellius, until eventually at the very end of 69 the forces supporting Vespasian triumphed bloodily over Vitellius' demoralised and dispirited partisans.

Two truths emerged from it – that emperors could be created elsewhere than at Rome,[84] and that the dynastic arrangements instituted by Augustus could not be relied upon to produce a ruler who merited the respect of his contemporaries.[85] It also became clear, as was to be the case after Domitian's death in 96,[86] that different sections of the population might entertain totally divergent ideas of what kind of emperor suited them.

In A.D. 68–69, the predominant factors were the ambitions and rivalries of the senatorial element within the military command-structure, and the readiness of the troops, both for profit and *esprit de corps*, to identify their interests with those of their commanders. In other words, the instability which had plagued the late republic, and

---

82   For a consideration of this, see Townend, 1967, 98ff.
83   For a general account of the events of A.D. 68–69, see Wellesley, 1975.
84   Tac. *Hist*. I. 4,2.
85   The idea, which probably formed the basis of Tacitus' optimism about contemporary politics (*Agr*. 3,1), is laid out clearly in the oration put by Tacitus into the mouth of Servius Galba on the occasion of the latter's adoption of Piso Licinianus (*Hist*. I. 15–16; for a discussion, see Shotter, 1978a).
86   Shotter, 1983.

which Augustus seemed to have resolved, still lay beneath the surface ready to re-appear. The reason for this lay in the development of Nero's reign and the contrast between the exaggerated promise with which it had commenced and the realities that became apparent as Nero shed himself of his advisers and tried more directly to control his own destiny.[87]

i) The Fall of Nero

Nero's reign had begun in A.D. 54 amidst elaborate senatorial sycophancy; many remained the emperor's fawning servants, but his political murders (especially that of his mother in 59), and his gradual development of a more absolutist "hellenistic" style of monarchy, progressively alienated elements within the senate – particularly the group around Thrasea Paetus who pursued a "political stoicism", which amounted to a campaign of civil disobedience.[88] The chief effect of this combination of sycophany and civil disobedience was to accelerate trends already apparent in Nero's rule;[89] he took more of the government to himself, relying on the help of people whom he did not find it necessary to fear, such as freedmen, equestrians and those senators whose social inferiority, he hoped, would make them less of a challenge to himself.[90] This almost inevitably produced a weakening of the command-structure in the legionary groups which guarded the empire's frontiers.

Opposition to Nero graduated from "civil disobedience" to active conspiracy in the none-too-salubrious cabal of Gaius Piso in A.D. 65.[91] The failure of this made Nero more suspicious and tyrannical, which led apparently to the abortive and ill-documented coup of 66,[92] the aim of which seems to have been to secure the throne for Nero's eastern commander, Domitius Corbulo. This time the tangible result was Nero's invitation – not refusable – to Corbulo and the two German commanders to commit suicide. Thus, army-commanders were now involved against Nero, and the emperor's popularity-seeking tour of Greece in A.D. 67–68 allowed the breathing-space in the west in which new moves were planned to unseat him.

The understanding of the events which led to Nero's fall is made particularly difficult by the chronological imprecision of our main sources;[93] it is clear, however, that the dismay that already existed in senatorial circles over the emperor's unsuitability was enhanced as a result of the antics of his tour of Greece. The growth of unrest prompted Helius, the emperor's freedman, to warn Nero repeatedly of the advisability of returning to Italy.[94] He eventually made the journey to Greece to see Nero in person, and Nero

---

87   Warmington, 1969; Griffin, 1984.
88   E.g. Tac. *Ann.* XIV. 12,2 and XVI. 21–35. For Tacitus' comment, see *Agr.* 42,4.
89   See, for example, Nero's later coinage – Sutherland, 1951, 148ff; Shotter, 1979, 50f.
90   Chilver, 1957, 29ff.
91   Tac. *Ann.* XV. 48–74; Shotter, 1975, 59.
92   Suet. *Nero* 36,1.
93   Dio LXIII. 22–29; Suet. *Nero* 40–49; *Galba* 9–11; Plutarch *Galba* 4–10. I have tried to clarify the chronology in Shotter, 1975, especially the table on pp.73f.
94   Dio LXII. 19,1.

finally returned to Rome early in 68, although he had left it again, this time for Naples, by the middle of March.[95]

Helius, however, had been right; for by the time Nero had returned to Italy, the moves which eventually unseated him were already underway. The instigator of these moves was a Romanised Gaul, Gaius Julius Vindex, who was the governor of Lugdunensis, and who had by letter approached provincial governors and dissidents in order to gauge the level of support that an anti-Nero crusade might attract.[96] It would appear that although Vindex received little open encouragement, privately some must have shown him sympathy. However, the fact that so few openly indicated their support has been the major contributor to the difficulties experienced in trying to analyse Vindex's aims and assess the level of his support.[97]

Although Vindex had the support of some Gallic groups, there was certainly no open commitment on the part of any provincial governors or army-commanders when the rebellion was actually declared in March – perhaps symbolically on the Ides. He had raised locally ten thousand recruits, but surely cannot have expected these to be able to do battle with either of the nearest army-commanders – Galba in Spain, or Verginius Rufus in Upper Germany. Indeed, in both cases evidence can be adduced which is suggestive of private collusion between each of these commanders and Vindex.[98] Further afield, Fonteius Capito in Lower Germany, to judge from his later execution by Galba,[99] was hostile to Vindex.

Vindex needed time for his approaches to bear fruit, and it may be that the siege of the pro-Neronian town of Lugdunum (Lyons) with which he began his campaign was intended to "buy time", as well as to eliminate a source of support for Nero. At any rate, it was soon after this – probably on April 2nd – that at Nova Karthago, Galba openly entered the fray, raising a new legion (VII Galbiana) in addition to the one already available to him (VI Victrix), and carefully styling himself "legate of the Roman senate and people". Galba's entry brought in other colleagues in the Iberian peninsula – notably T. Vinius Rufinus (legionary *legatus* in Tarraconensis), Caecina (quaestor in Baetica) and Otho (governor of Lusitania).

Nero had shown little inclination for planning when he heard of Vindex's declaration; nor is there any reason why he should have done since with no Roman supporters openly in the field on Vindex's behalf at that stage, the emperor would have had no reason to attach much significance to it. All changed, however, in mid-April when news reached him of Galba's declaration against him; this not only meant civil war, but also carried the

---

95 Suet. *Nero* 40,4; see Warmington, 1969, 157f. Although official prayers were offered for Nero's safe return from Greece (*CIL* VI.2044), there were some who prayed that he might be lost at sea (Dio LXII. 19,2).

96 Plutarch *Galba* 4,2. Vindex's approaches probably explain Nero's later threat, uttered during a tantrum, to kill all provincial governors and exiles (Suet. *Nero* 40,4).

97 The whole subject has encouraged a lengthy bibliography, to which the principal contributions have been Raoss, 1958; 1960; Brunt, 1959; Hainsworth, 1962; Shotter, 1967; 1975; in addition the important, though not always clear, numismatic evidence has been presented and assessed by Kraay, 1949 and Mattingly, 1954.

98 It is possible that Philostratus (*Life of Apollonius* V.10) refers to contacts between Vindex and Galba; for Verginius' position, see Shotter, 1967, 375, and Syme, 1937, 12.

99 Tac. *Hist*. I. 71.

threat that the "infection" might spread. At any rate, the emperor now made positive plans for the defence of Italy,[100] choosing top commanders – Rubrius Gallus and Petronius Turpilianus – and deploying troops (including the legions I Italica, XIV Gemina Martia Victrix and eight cohorts of Batavians attached to the latter) to prevent the insurgents from entering Italy. Although no details are known, it is reasonable to suppose that they were to utilise the line of the river Po, a strategy which would be repeated twice more before the end of 69. It was probably at this time also that approaches were made to Clodius Macer,[101] the commander of legion III Augusta in north Africa, to intervene on Nero's behalf – perhaps militarily in Spain – though in the event Macer preferred to raise his own standard of rebellion.

Verginius Rufus, who had probably been at Moguntiacum (Mainz) when he heard of the news of Vindex's rebellion, mobilised his legions as if for war, advanced to Vesontio (Besançon) and laid siege to the town – as a pretext, according to Dio.[102] The reason for the pretext must surely have been to allow the commander himself to come within reasonable distance of Vindex, presumably for further negotiations, but without alarming the German legions, whose loyalty was still intact at that stage; indeed they will have assumed that they had been mobilised to defeat Vindex in the name of Nero.

It is evident that the two commanders managed to continue their discussions in secret,[103] but that before a conclusion was reached their two armies, unaware of these discussions, clashed in battle. The result was a predictable victory for the Upper German legions, and Vindex's death (either by his own hand or by another's). Verginius retired in shock to his tent;[104] he refused his army's offer of the throne,[105] ignored Galba's invitation that they should now concert their efforts,[106] and is very unlikely to have done anything as positive as clearing up the remnants of revolt in Gaul.[107] Almost certainly, he retired to Mainz, determined to have nothing further to do with such traumatic matters, whilst his army, unable to persuade him to take power, resumed a rather uncomfortable allegiance to Nero. Verginius' own claims over his positive role in these events are countered (albeit unwittingly) by the younger Pliny, whose guardian Verginius was.[108] Ironically, however, the confusions within the Upper German army, when incorrectly relayed to Rome, were instrumental in pushing Nero into his final

---

100 Suet. *Nero* 43,2.
101 Tac. *Hist.* I. 73, where Tacitus describes the journey to Africa of Calvia Crispinilla, Nero's "magistra libidinum", though Tacitus leaves it unclear whether the journey was intended as a help to or a betrayal of Nero.
102 Dio LXIII. 24.1.
103 Dio LXIII. 24.2.
104 John of Antioch (frag. 91; v.22–25).
105 Dio LXIII. 25; Plut. *Galba* 6,3.
106 Suet. *Galba* 11; Plut. *Galba* 6,4.
107 Mattingly, 1954, 38.
108 Verginius' claim is quoted, together with contemporary criticism, in Pliny *Letters* IX. 19. Elsewhere (*Letters* II. 1,1), Pliny describes the retirement from which Verginius did not emerge: *Triginta annis gloriae suae supervixit* ("He outlived his glory by thirty years"). (See Shotter, 1967, 370ff).

panic.[109] Nor would it seem, to judge from Galba's harsh treatment of Fonteius Capito, that the Lower German army had deserted the *princeps*.

Following the battle of Vesontio, May of A.D.68 must have been an uneasy month; Vindex was dead, and Verginius had retired from active participation; Galba had withdrawn into the interior of Spain to await his fate,[110] whilst other provinces, probably nervously, watched events.[111] The chief spotlight, however, now shifted to the army Nero had organised in Italy: The Illyrian troops amongst them are said to have made approaches to Verginius Rufus;[112] the vigorous Cornelius Fuscus persuaded his *colonia* (probably Aquileia) to declare for Galba,[113] whilst the Batavian cohorts attached to legion XIV boasted later that they had put pressure on that legion and robbed Nero of Italy.[114]

It is possible that of the Italian commanders, the pliant Rubrius Gallus may have deserted; his subsequent favour with the Flavians does not suggest a prolonged allegiance to Nero.[115] Desertion of Nero is definitely alleged against his colleague, Petronius Turpilianus, and news of it is said to have completed Nero's despair;[116] Plutarch,[117] on the other hand, affirms Petronius' loyalty to Nero, and Galba's subsequent murder of him, which created a bad impression, seems to confirm this. Perhaps again, confusion was the victor and Nero was misled by news of his desertion by the Batavian cohorts into thinking that Petronius too had gone over to the other side.

Contrary to Nero's belief, he had not lost the allegiance of large bodies of his army; as Galba's chosen successor, Piso Licinianus, was to say on another occasion: "It was Nero who deserted you, not you Nero".[118] On the night of June 8th/9th, Nero escaped from Rome towards Phaon's villa, and on the 9th heard that the senate had withdrawn its support from him; so too the praetorian guard whose commander, Nymphidius Sabinus, had promised a donative in Galba's name – which was never paid.[119] At this, Nero with the aid of his secretary, Epaphroditus, killed himself; *qualis opifex pereo* ("so great an artist dies in me"[120]), was a fitting comment on a life distinguished more for its cultural than for its political contribution.

Galba heard a week later that he was the senate's – if not everyone's – choice: the senate, however, was less important than those army-units whose attitudes had caused Nero so much alarm. The German armies had not supported Galba, and did not want him now; it was the particular service of Fabius Valens, *legatus* of legion I Germanica,

---

109   Tac. *Hist.* I. 98,2, where it is indicated that rumour was more potent in Nero's removal than force of arms.
110   Suet. *Galba* 11; Plut. *Galba* 6,4.
111   For example, Greece (Mattingly, 1954, 35f.).
112   Tac. *Hist.* I.9 ,3. (cf. *ILS* 982 from Milan).
113   Tac. *Hist.* II. 86,3. (Syme, 1937, 7ff.).
114   Tac. *Hist.* II. 27,2.
115   Josephus *Jewish Wars* (VII. 91) and Juvenal *Sat.* IV. 104–6.
116   Dio LXIII. 27,1a.
117   Plut. *Galba* 15,2 and 17,3.
118   Tac. *Hist.* I. 30,2; cf. Suet. *Nero* 47,1.
119   Tac. *Hist.* I. 5,1; Plut. *Galba* 2, 1–2.
120   Suet. *Nero* 49,1.

to bring the German legions to Galba's side.[121] This act, however, contained two ominous warnings for the new *princeps*: first, the German legions clearly lacked enthusiasm for the new emperor; after all, they believed they had destroyed his cause at Vesontio. Secondly, Fabius Valens was just one of those who thought his services to Galba was deserving of substantial reward. The omens for the new reign were not good.

ii) The Principate of Galba

Galba's short reign lasted from June 9th, A.D. 68, until his murder by Otho's partisans on January 15th of the following year. From the start, its tone was discordant: not just the competing claims for the succession to Galba, but also the contrast between the martinet that was Galba's reputation and which frequently surfaced during his reign and the disastrously lax attitude he displayed towards the activities of his closest advisers, Titus Vinius, Cornelius Laco and the freedman Icelus.[122] In a masterly summary, Tacitus encompasses the interaction of the rivalries and inconsistencies in the prelude to the opening of his *Histories* on January 1st, A.D. 69, the beginning of the year that was the last for its consuls (Galba and Vinius) and almost the last for the state (*annum sibi ultimum, reipublicae prope supremum*).[123]

In June of 68, there was general relief at Nero's demise; only the ordinary people missed him for the entertainments which he had provided. As we have seen, however, that is not to say that all those who were glad at Nero's death held similar expectations of what would follow. Clearly, a hand was required that was both firm and respected, yet at the same time able to adapt to fluid situations. Galba certainly recognised the need for reconstruction and a return to basic principles; he recognised too that Nero's reign represented a crisis in the Augustan principate. An examination of the coinage issued during Vindex's rebellion and during Galba's principate emphasises the desire for the return of something traditional that Nero's reign had destroyed. Such coin-types as LIBERTAS RESTITVTA, SALVS HVMANI GENERIS, and the oak-wreath enclosing OB CIVES SERVATOS demonstrate the link between Vindex and Galba and the need to return to the principles of the principate's founding father, the Deified Augustus.[124] Indeed Galba's view of *libertas* is expressed in the oration given him by Tacitus, and which may have been linked in the historian's mind with the situation that greeted Nerva as he succeeded Domitian in 96.[125] There was a determination to replace a dynastic succession with the principle of choice based on merit. On a material level, Agricola, who was praetor in 68 was charged with the task of investigating treasures which Nero had misappropriated from temples and other sources.[126]

However, whilst the sentiments were fine, there were features in Galba's character and actions which militated against the harmony and integrity of government he was attempting to achieve; particularly he failed in practice to appreciate the need for harmony in the armies which the coinage rather emptily proclaimed (CONSENSVS

---

121 Plut. *Galba* 10,3.
122 Tac. *Hist*. I. 13,1.
123 Tac. *Hist*. I. 11,3, at the conclusion of the introduction to the *Histories*.
124 See *RIC* I² pp. 197ff.
125 Tac. *Hist*. I. 15–16; see also Shotter, 1978a; 1983; and Syme, 1958, i. 130 and 150; ii. 576.
126 Tac. *Agr*. 6,5.

EXERCITVVM). Galba perhaps did not fully understand that the armies' sensitivity over their own role in the events of 68 left the need for careful handling and a realisation that the aspirations of different groups needed to be taken into account. The string of murders[127] which marked the opening of the reign militated against such harmony and created a bad impression.

Galba was plainly unable to come to terms with all who had opposed him in the first half of 68; most were murdered, whilst Verginius Rufus was simply removed from his command.[128] The replacements for those murdered or removed were hardly inspiring; the aged and gout-ridden Hordeonius Flaccus replaced Verginius in Upper Germany, whilst the Lower army was first of all without a commander, and then received A. Vitellius; his qualification was nothing more than having had a highly-qualified father.[129] Effective control in those armies fell to two legionary commanders – Fabius Valens and Alienus Caecina;[130] both had supported Galba in 68, but neither felt he had been sufficiently appreciated. Thus, both began to work on the German legions to desert Galba in favour of Aulus Vitellius.

Galba's entry into Rome in the autumn of 68 was similarly inauspicious; murders of prominent citizens, which were seen as unjust,[131] were a prelude to large-scale and uncontrolled butchery of soldiers who, due to Nero's troop-movements, were present in the city. In addition, the praetorian guard had lost its commander, Nymphidius Sabinus, and the donative promised by him in Galba's name was not paid. The praetorian guard, therefore, soon came to regret the loss of Nero and looked for an alternative; its new commander, Cornelius Laco, is described by Tacitus as utterly idle and was no match for Otho's approach to his soldiers. Like Nerva in A.D. 96–97, Galba was faced with tides of dissension which he had little hope of controlling. Nerva, perhaps learning from Galba's experience, had the sense to come to terms with the most powerful of those putting pressure on him – Trajan and the legions of Germany; that composed the situation and allowed Nerva a relatively peaceful last few months.

On January 1st A.D. 69, Galba was faced with three separate sources of revolt – the legions of Upper Germany and their colleagues in Lower Germany, (though these soon made common cause under Vitellius), and the praetorian cohorts and assorted soldiery in Italy who accepted Otho as their champion. Galba rightly recognised that a crucial issue was the succession, though it was, as for Nerva, a matter of making a choice out of the existing rivals for power. Galba's sense of unreality was aggravated by the degree of unpopularity achieved both by him and his immediate associates. A symbol of his complete divorce from reality is to be seen in his clear assumption that his choice of successor was free and open, and also in the fact that in Tacitus'[132] eyes he not only made a poor choice, but also showed himself to have constitutional principles which,

---

127 Otho is recorded as having presented these murders as a major cause of complaint against Galba (*Hist.* I. 37,3).

128 Verginius Rufus was removed under the guise of being required by Galba to serve amongst his *amici* (Tac. *Hist.* I. 8,2).

129 Tac. *Hist.* I. 9,1.

130 Tac. *Hist.* I. 52–53.

131 Cingonius Varro and Petronius Turpilianus (Tac. *Hist.* I. 6).

132 Tac. *Hist.* I. 15–16.

however honourable, had little place in the confusion that dominated Rome. Galba's "lecture" on *libertas* and *dominatio* was seen to be just about as relevant as the *libertas* of Brutus and Cassius after Caesar's assassination.

Otho, who expected that the succession to Galba would be his just reward for services in A.D. 68, had the support of Titus Vinius, but, according to Tacitus, was viewed by Galba as a kind of "second Nero".[133] It was as a consequence of this viewpoint, and believing that all he needed for rehabilitation was a strong successor, that Galba chose Piso Licinianus, a young *nobilis* of little experience, though of apparently impeccable character.

For Otho and his friends, this choice was beyond sufferance. Otho set about cynically exploiting the grievances of Galba's friends and enemies alike, and particularly the soldiers of the praetorian guard, displaying an ability to relate to people that was in marked contrast to the puritanical aloofness of Galba. Otho first captivated and then armed the guard, whilst Galba, once he recognised the danger, found himself unable to form a strategy as he faltered amid a welter of conflicting and self-interested advice.[134] He was too old and too weak to produce a positive strategy and carry it through; yet in individual instances, such as in the case of the soldier who claimed to have killed Otho, he displayed his characteristic strict sense of discipline[135] ("he showed the same outstanding characteristic of checking undisciplined soldiers: he was fearless in the face of threats, and beyond corruption by false friends").

Leaving the protection of the palace proved fatal to Galba: in the confusion and chaos, first Piso and then Galba himself were cut down; thus on January 15th, Otho had become emperor by armed insurrection. According to Tacitus' view[136] this was an act which was totally to vitiate Otho's short principate; presumably Otho had undermined the principle of personal loyalty upon which the successful operation of the principate was taken to depend. No action of his could retrieve that situation – a political rather than a moral judgement on Tacitus' part.

Galba has earned as an epitaph one of the most famous of the Tacitean epigrams, which goes to the heart of his life and short reign – *Omnium consensu capax imperii nisi imperasset* ("Everyone would have thought him capable of ruling, had he not tried").[137] There was a perceived contrast between the disciplinary qualities that were Galba's reputation and the confusion and indecision that marked his reign. He showed as a subordinate that he could operate within the confines of a defined job: but his virtues were not great, and his lack of them was concealed behind his strong sense of discipline: old age and a demanding job in demanding circumstances did not make the man. Rather they highlighted his fatal inadequacies.

---

133   Tac. *Hist*. I. 13, 2–3.
134   Tac. *Hist*. I. 35, 1: *nemo scire et omnes adfirmare, donec inopia veri et consensu errantium victus sumpto thorace Galba inruenti turbae, neque aetate neque corpore insistens, sella levaretur* ("Nobody knew what was happening, yet they all swore by their versions of events; in the end Galba was worn out by his vain search for the truth and the agreement of people whose information was wrong: he put on his breastplate, and although he was too old and infirm to resist the surge of the crowd, he was carried outside").
135   Tac. *Hist*. I. 35,2.
136   Tac. *Hist*. II. 50,1.
137   Tac. *Hist*. I. 49,4.

iii) The Principate of Otho

Otho's reign was the shortest of this confused year, lasting only until his suicide on April 16th. Tacitus appears to have found Otho's a difficult character to fathom, marked as it was by the foul murder which initiated the reign and the apparently noble suicide which brought it to a close. In the historian's eyes, the new emperor should have forfeited all claims to loyalty by his murder of Galba: yet he acted in contrast to his reputation as a voluptuary,[138] and demonstrated a considerable ability to attract loyalty both from his troops and from sound subordinate officers such as Marius Celsus[139] and Suetonius Paulinus.

Although Otho's brief reign was dominated by the war with Vitellius, it appears that not only did the new emperor give the lie to his reputation as a "second Nero", but that he tried to use his undoubted gifts of personality to create a harmonious atmosphere; he was conciliatory to those who had not supported him and displayed care for his subjects which pointed to the possibility of reconstruction,[140] had not his reign inevitably been dominated by a conflict which he could not avert. For a variety of reasons, Vitellius and the German legions were unlikely to be mollified by the new *princeps*.

From Vitellius' own point of view, he and Otho had been rivals for Galba's position; thus Otho's success was bound to drive Vitellius harder to the fulfilment of ambition. The Rhine army, which had supported Vitellius because of its own reluctance to accept Galba, now saw itself not just as having been thwarted, but as having lost out principally to a section of the army which it envied and regarded as over-privileged – the praetorian cohorts whose support of Otho had proved crucial. Effectively, therefore, the civil war progressed from the "local conflict" of Galba and Otho to something which had a far more "global" significance, bringing into play the latent rivalries which existed between the various groups of the Roman army.

Nominally, the conflict between Otho and Vitellius became one between the eastern and western parts of the empire. The western provinces, through inclination or fear of the Rhine legions, supported Vitellius, though the real core of his support remained large sections of the Rhine legions themselves. However, although Otho could count on the adherence of the legions of the Danube and the east, neither of these groups could come quickly to his aid, and he was therefore forced to rely on a modest force of praetorians and those legionaires who were in Italy: the core of the latter was represented by legion I Adiutrix, which had been recruited by Nero from the fleet in A.D. 67, and decimated by Galba in 68 – hardly a force of which one could expect skill or high morale.

Vitellius' force was driven by two men – Fabius Valens and Alienus Caecina –who were strongly antagonistic towards each other, but were now brought under the same colours by their shared loathing of Galba. Two forces were assembled – one to march south across the Alps under Caecina, the other, under Valens, to take a less direct route through Gaul. Otho's dilemma was clear: success depended on preventing a junction between the forces of Caecina and Valens, and thus upon quick action; yet without

---

138   Tac. *Hist*. I. 22,1.
139   For a discussion of his role, see Shotter, 1978b, 197ff.
140   See, for example, *ILS* 5947 and *IGRR* III. 1164: also Tac. *Hist*. I. 77,2 over Otho's "rehabilitation" of Verginius Rufus.

reinforcements, whose arrival meant waiting, Otho could hardly hope to take on even the separated Rhine forces.

In the event, Caecina reached Cremona on the north bank of the Po, whilst Otho's forces took up position at Placentia (on the south bank) and in the region of Hostilia in order to keep open the road from Aquileia along which reinforcements from the Danube would have to come. Caecina failed to dislodge the Othonians from Placentia, whilst part of Otho's force, halted at Bedriacum, was able to embarrass Caecina by attacks across the river.

At this point, Othonian strategy was disturbed by lack of clarity; the caution shown by Suetonius Paulinus and Marius Celsus was interpreted as treachery; at any rate it might be seen as mistaken in view of the fact that Caecina's position around Cremona was none-too-easy, particularly since his failure to win Placentia. Otho himself who had marched all the way from Rome on foot at the head of his troops now decided to stay back at Brixellum, perhaps partly so that he could exercise a role of overall supervision, partly too to guard the road south from Cremona and Bedriacum. Thus, overall battle-field command was left in the hands of his brother, Titianus, with individual army-groups under Suetonius Paulinus, Marius Celsus, Annius Gallus and Vestricius Spurinna. The perception of confusion and the risk of conflicting strategies can only have been heightened by this.

The situation on the other side, however, was in some ways not much better. The arrival of Valens, far from imparting a positive boost to Vitellian morale, proved divisive, as Caecina's inability to dislodge the Othonians was blamed on the dilatory tactics of Valens. The result was that Valens' army, in considerable confusion, rushed off to join Caecina at Cremona. In the event, the Vitellians appear to have regained their composure rather faster than their opponents, whose battle-plan depended on running considerable risks to be able to take a position west of Cremona at the confluence of the Adda and the Po. In fact, battle was joined at a point between Cremona and Bedriacum, and the Othonians received the worst of the encounter – though not disastrously, particularly taking into account that for Otho's side further reinforcements from the Danube were by this time not far off, whereas the Vitellian forces had no reinforcements to which to look.

Besides this, the morale of most of the Othonians, lowered by the defeat, was inclining towards surrender on reasonable terms; Otho himself had no stomach for further civil war and advised this same course of action. His own despair and perhaps desire to ameliorate his soldiers' conditions motivated Otho's suicide on April 16th. The irony that those German legions which had taken the lead in revolting against Galba had ultimately proved to be his avengers can hardly be missed.

iv) The Principate of Vitellius

Aulus Vitellius was a man of contrast; the distinguished records of many members of his family had seemed qualification enough to justify his appointment to the Rhine by Galba;[141] yet his own life had been dominated by indolence and gluttony, which may have given him a superficial attractiveness to some, but which indicated a man who could hardly stand up to the demands born of the pressing ambitions of the likes of

---

141   Tac. *Hist.* I. 9,1.

Caecina and Valens. Nor in the event could he resist the tides that issued from the prejudices and jealousies of the Rhine legions. Vitellius clearly appreciated the virtues of a conciliatory policy; his treatment of Otho's senior commanders, his rehabilitation of Galba's memory, and his attitude to the trappings of imperial power suggest it. What was lacking was an ability to act decisively in a fluid and dangerous situation.

Vitellius had taken a rather slower course to Italy than either Caecina or Valens, with the result that he was only about to enter Italy at the moment his armies were victorious. Partly, this was due to his self-indulgence, partly too to the need to recruit men to replace the depleted Rhine garrisons, where the presence of an army composed of veterans and raw recruits was to have disastrous consequences later in the year. The senate accepted Vitellius, as did the city of Rome through the offices of the city prefect, Flavius Sabinus, the brother of Vespasian. The eastern legions, too, initially took their oath of allegiance to the new emperor, though it is doubtful whether this, even if all other things had been equal, would have lasted. In the view of many, ancient and modern, the process of legionary muscle-flexing had to run its *full* course, and the eastern legions were bound to view with disquiet the ability of their western colleagues to dominate politics as they had done since early in 68.

However, the immediate catalyst to renewed disturbance was the manner of military settlement in Italy in the wake of Vitellius' victory. The attitude of the Vitellian armies was to treat Italy rather as if it were conquered foreign soil; looting and pillage were inspired from the top through the attitudes of Valens and Caecina. Thus, rapidly new sources of resentment were being created.

Otho's praetorians, admittedly his most loyal supporters, were disbanded, and replaced by sixteen new cohorts drawn from Vitellius' Rhine legions; we may infer that this had less to do with the perceived unreliability of Otho's praetorians in the new situation (which would have been reasonable enough) than to the envy of the German legions over the service-conditions of the praetorians. The Danubian legions, some of which had reached the Po, whilst others were still on their way, were sent back whence they had come, though legion XIII was first given the humiliating task of building amphitheatres at Cremona and Bononia – which was later to have terrible repercussions. The Batavian auxiliary cohorts were sent back to the Rhine, though not before they had been involved in a fracas with soldiers of legion XIV Gemina Martia Victrix which had resulted in the near-destruction of Turin. The catalogue of broken discipline and sordid rivalries ill-accorded with the coins of Vitellius proclaiming such virtues as CONCORDIA PRAETORIANORVM and FIDES EXERCITVVM; nor will Italy have been much impressed with the re-issue of the Galban type LIBERTAS RESTITVTA.[142]

Trouble was inevitable; it is not surprising that the focus of it shifted towards eastern Europe and the east, particularly since the eastern wars of Nero's reign had involved much interchange of legions between the east and the Danube. The Danube provinces, however, did not have amongst their commanders a suitable candidate for power; one (Aponius Saturninus in Moesia) was inclined towards Vitellius[143], whilst the others (Tampius Flavianus in Pannonia and Pomponius Silvanus in Dalmatia) are described as

---

142   *RIC* I^2 (Vitellius), 9 etc.
143   Tac. *Hist.* II. 96,1.

"old and rich",[144] – not that vigour was lacking at a lower level, particularly in the persons of Antonius Primus (*legatus* of legion VII Galbiana)[145] and Cornelius Fuscus (*procurator* in Pannonia).[146]

The east, however, had two senior and tried commanders – Licinius Mucianus (in Syria with four legions) and Flavius Vespasianus (in Judaea with a further three). Although the relationship between them was normally not good – as their diverse characters might explain – they had been persuaded by Vespasian's elder son, Titus, to settle their differences and work together.[147] They and their legions had taken little active part in the first twelve months of the civil war, recognising in turn Galba, Otho and initially Vitellius. It is not clear from where the impetus to nominate Vespasian first came; indeed the opening stages appear to have been subsequently obfuscated by Flavian propaganda which apparently amongst other things specifically suggested that Vespasian had been designated heir by Otho.[148] However it occurred, all of the eastern legions, including those of Egypt under Ti. Julius Alexander, had sworn allegiance to Vespasian by mid-July.

The battle-plan had three elements: approaches were made in order to undermine the sometimes rather flimsy allegiance to Vitellius amongst western legions. Two armies were put together – one under Mucianus, which would march to Italy through the Danube – provinces and thus obviously provide the main spearhead, whilst Vespasian led the other through the provinces on the southern side of the Mediterranean, amassing resources and presumably effecting control over Rome's corn-supply. On the Danube, Antonius Primus and Cornelius Fuscus, whose vigour and commitment far outshone those of seniors and contemporaries in the region,[149] had little difficulty in persuading the disgruntled legions to make common cause with Vespasian. It was clearly intended that Antonius and Mucianus would join forces for the attack on Italy, though in the event the Flavian campaign was dominated by the rivalry between them and Antonius Primus' desire for a quick finish.

The line of the Po was again inevitably the critical one, though on this occasion the precise location of significance was Hostilia which guarded the crossing of the river by which the Flavian forces would head for Rome. Vitellius personally behaved with considerable indolence when he heard the news of Vespasian's proclamation, and military preparations were left in the hands of Valens and Caecina. Four main problems can be highlighted; first, although still loyal, Vitellius' victorious army was now far from battle-ready after three months of looting. Secondly, the chances of reinforcements for the Vitellians were remote: Vettius Bolanus (in Britain) and the gout-ridden Hordeonius Flaccus (in Germany) were hardly in sympathy with Vitellius any longer, but in any case Antonius Primus[150] had persuaded the Batavians under Julius Civilis to create a diversion to occupy the Rhine legions – a plan which was, because of Civilis' outwitting

---

144   Tac. *Hist.* II. 86,3.
145   For an assessment of him, see Shotter, 1977.
146   For Cornelius Fuscus, see Syme, 1937, 7ff and 1958, ii. 683f.
147   Tac. *Hist.* I. 10 and II. 5.
148   Suet. *Div. Vesp.* 6,4.
149   Tac. *Hist.* II. 86.
150   Tac. *Hist.* IV. 13,2.

of Antonius, to have disastrous consequences, as the "diversion" rapidly took on the shape of a real nationalist rebellion against Rome. The third problem was Valens' suspect health, and fourth Caecina's equally suspect loyalty to Vitellius.[151]

The Vitellian troops held the Po from Hostilia and Cremona, and had loyally resisted Caecina's attempts to persuade them to change sides. Antonius Primus, although ordered to await Mucianus at Aquileia, decided that in view of the lateness of the season and because he felt no need of further reinforcements, pushed towards the Po, for the moment at least insisting on the highest standards of discipline amongst his troops. He made for Cremona, which, particularly for those on his side who had recently suffered a humiliation there, was a major prize; however, the sacking of Cremona was delayed by the fact that the Vitellian troops made a hurried march from Hostilia and insisted on immediate battle – wisely in view of their condition after the march and of their lack of real leadership. A dramatic night-battle was fought near Bedriacum[152], which ended in the Flavians' favour as the salute of the soldiers of legion III to the rising sun was interpreted by the Vitellians as an indication of the arrival of reinforcements. The unsavoury sequel to the battle was a four-day orgy of destruction in Cremona, which effectively rased the *colonia* to the ground.[153] This was the Danube-army's revenge for its earlier humiliation.

The Vitellians, particularly Valens, failed to attempt any regrouping: thus the road to Rome lay open to Antonius Primus. Although he encountered occasional resistance from Vitellian supporters, it is likely that the majority of the difficulties with which he met emanated from the hierarchy of his own side, fearful of the consequences of his having failed to wait for Mucianus and thus reaching Rome alone. The final skirmishes in and around Rome in December saw the remaining Vitellians fighting as vigorously as before, although Vitellius himself was probably more inclined by that stage to try to negotiate his way out of trouble. Antonius took Rome on December 20th, too late to save Vespasian's brother; Vitellius was dragged from the palace and put to death, whilst the seal was put on the victory and the new dynasty by the soldiers hailing Vespasian's younger son, Domitian, as "Caesar". Mucianus reached Rome right at the end of December, and the new year saw Vespasian and Titus initiating the new dynasty with a joint consulship, though both were still absent from Rome.

Thus the civil war had run its course, and had concluded with the establishment of a new dynasty which owed nothing, beyond patronage, to the Julio-Claudians. The self-assumed rights of the republican *nobiles* had thus finally ended, though the inception of a new dynasty showed that Galba's observations on the relationship between *libertas* and dynastic succession had not been heeded. On the other hand, it had to be noted that the army still readily identified itself with a dynastic type of loyalty; nor could anybody after the events of A.D. 68–69 underestimate the importance of what the army thought.

The wars had been costly in men and money; they had made and broken reputations; men, like Antonius Primus, had emerged who might never have made an impact in peacetime. In particular, the significance of military loyalty had been demonstrated; it might be bought or won by the men of charisma; it could not, however, be taken for

---

151   Tac. *Hist.* II. 101.
152   Tac. *Hist.* III. 22.
153   Tac. *Hist.* III. 34,1.

granted. The wars had demonstrated the effects of the ambitions of army-commanders, of the hatreds and enthusiasms of the ordinary soldiers; they had shown, too, that the Roman army was only the sum of its parts. Rivalries existed, which could be utilised – between different army-groups, between legions and auxiliaries, and between legions and praetorians. Auxiliaries, who normally served under their own commanders alongside the legions, could still breathe a dangerous and destructive nationalism.

That such dangers had been put aside under the umbrella of the Augustan Peace was now shown up as an illusion; in many respects the stability of the empire now had to be returned to the drawing-board, as a new Augustus and a new dynasty set out to produce a new *Pax Augusta*.

4. The Careers of Galba, Otho and Vitellius

The bulk of our information about these three short-lived emperors derives from four chief sources – Suetonius' *Lives*, Tacitus' *Histories*, Plutarch's *Lives* (of Galba and Otho), and *The Roman History* of Dio Cassius. These will of course have been dependent on a variety of contemporary sources no longer extant (see section 5). For the parts which they played in events prior to their principates, however, we are reliant largely on the information provided by Suetonius in his introductory sections in each case (*Galba* 2–9; *Otho* 1–4; *Vitellius* 1–7).

i) Galba
Of the three, Galba's family was unquestionably the most noble, stretching back into the republic. Members of Galba's family had been involved in notable events during the republic, including a Servius Galba, who, feeling himself insufficiently rewarded by Julius Caesar, joined the conspiracy against the dictator. The event provides an ironical foreshadowing of Galba's own fate at the hands of Otho in 69. It is possible that, like Labienus, this Galba was a partisan of Pompey's who served with Caesar in Gaul, and reverted to his true allegiance at the outbreak of the civil war.[154]

Galba's grandfather was best known as a historian who did not carry his public career beyond the praetorship. His father reached a suffect consulship[155] in 5 B.C., though possibly due more to his ability to intrigue with high-born women than from any real talent. Despite his lack of physical attractivenss he married two well-placed ladies; the first was Mummia Achaica, a descendant of the Mummius who sacked Corinth in 146 B.C., and who was the grand-daughter of the late republican optimate-leader, Quintus Catulus, whom the emperor Galba evidently regarded as the most impressive of his forbears. Mummia bore Gaius Galba two sons – Gaius and Servius (the later emperor).

The father subsequently contracted a second marriage – to Livia Ocellina, who was distantly related to the wife of Augustus. She took on responsibility for Gaius' sons, and was evidently so respected by Servius Galba that for a time he actually called himself Lucius Livius Ocella.[156] Galba's father is not known for anything beyond the consulate.

---

154 Syme, 1939, 67; *ILS* 8888.
155 Syme, 1939, 511 and Suet. *Galba* 3, 3–4.
156 Galba appears to have been using the *praenomen*, Lucius, at the time of his consulship.

The date of Galba's birth poses problems;[157] according to Suetonius (*Galba* 4,1), he was born in the year in which Marcus Valerius Messala shared the consulship with Gnaeus (*sic*) Lentulus[158] – presumably 3 B.C., though the Lentulus in question was actually Lucius. However, the various accounts of his death which indicate an age of around 73 in A.D. 69 suggest that a year of birth of 5 B.C., or even 6 B.C. might be more appropriate. That during his youth the patrician Galba was well connected is clear from the story (Suet. *Galba* 4,1) of his meeting with Augustus.

The elder brother, Gaius, was consul in A.D. 22;[159] in A.D. 36[160], he committed suicide, having been barred by Tiberius from participation in the drawing of lots for the proconsular provinces of Asia and Africa. Suetonius indicates that the reason for this must have been the self-induced poverty which had already caused Gaius Galba to retire from Rome, and which will have indicated him to Tiberius as a potentially unsafe provincial appointment.

Servius Galba too does not appear to have had an outstanding career; as Tacitus says[161], he was "free of vice rather than a possessor of great virtues", though even so he had a better time during other emperors' reigns than during his own. Like his father, he appears to have had an appeal to women; he was married to an Aemilia Lepida who was probably the daughter of Manius Lepidus (consul in A.D. 11)[162], and thus great-granddaughter of Lepidus, the *triumvir*. Suetonius (*Galba* 5,1) records that even before Lepida's death, the younger Agrippina had tried to seduce Galba – so openly that she provoked a sharp confrontation with Galba's mother-in-law. His attractiveness may in part have stemmed from his close relationship with Livia, though the incident involving Agrippina is said to have occurred when she was a widow – that is, after A.D. 40.

Plutarch (*Galba* 3) argues that Galba owed his consulship in A.D. 33 to Livia's influence, though since she had been dead for four years this does not seem likely. In any case, Suetonius says that Livia made Galba the principal beneficiary of her will, though he was subsequently cheated of his legacy by Tiberius on a technicality.

Galba's public career began earlier than the legal norm – perhaps because of Livia's influence, though Lepida bore him two sons who died young, albeit at an unspecified time; Galba may have won the normal advantage from his fatherhood. His consulship (A.D. 33) was held at the age of 38, indicating a favoured career; we may assume therefore that he was quaestor a little before A.D. 20, and praetor perhaps five years later when he is recorded as having introduced rope-walking elephants during his presidency of the *ludi Florales*. One propraetorian appointment – the governorship of Gallia Aquitania – is mentioned before the consulship.

---

157 Suetonius (*Galba* 23,1) says that he was in his seventy-third year; so too Tacitus (*Hist*. I. 49,2). Dio (LXIII. 6) puts him at seventy-two, Zonaras adding "and twenty-three days", indicating the *princeps*' birthday as December 24th. Plutarch (*Galba* 8) says that Galba was in his seventy-third year when he became emperor.

158 See Syme, 1939, 435. Lentuli with the *praenomen*, Gnaeus, had been consuls in 18 B.C. and 14 B.C. (Shotter, 1989, 174).

159 Tac. *Ann*. III. 52,1.

160 Tac. *Ann*. VI. 40,3 (cf. Suet. *Galba* 3,4).

161 Tac. *Hist*. I. 49,2, where he is described as of moderate capability (*medium ingenium*).

162 See Syme, 1955.

After Galba's consulship we hear of no further appointment in Tiberius' reign; indeed he next emerges in A.D. 39 as the successor of the rebellious Gn. Cornelius Lentulus Gaetulicus who had been *legatus* in Upper Germany since A.D. 29.[163] The arrogant Gaetulicus had evidently presided over an army whose discipline grew progressively more lax; Galba was therefore introduced both for his loyalty to Caligula and for his sense of discipline, which clearly singled him out as something of a martinet (Suet. *Galba* 6,2). It may well also be that he lacked the unpopular connection with Sejanus that had coloured Gaetulicus' career and which will not have been welcome to Caligula.

His work both against the enemy and in restoring discipline amongst the German legions earned him Caligula's approval and a reputation sufficiently high for many to expect him to put himself forward for the principate on Caligula's assassination in A.D. 41. Claudius clearly valued both his loyalty and his services, and in A.D. 45–46 secured for him the proconsulate of Africa; in view of tribal disturbances, which had last been resolved under Tiberius in A.D. 24, the appointment of Galba was not subject to the normal drawing of lots. Further, Suetonius' account (*Galba* 7,2) indicates that he had a military responsibility, which was strictly irregular since Caligula had confined the proconsul's duties in Africa to those of a civilian nature only.

The sum of Galba's achievement won him notable honours from Claudius – the triumphal insignia and membership of three priestly colleges (*the quindecemviri sacris faciundis*, the *sodales titii* and the *sodales augustales*).

After a period of retirement, his final appointment was made by Nero in A.D. 60 – to be *legatus* of Hispania Tarraconensis, a post which he still held with an apparently low profile, when news of Vindex's rebellion reached him in the spring of A.D. 68. Overall, his may be regarded as an efficient rather than a brilliant career: Galba was evidently effective where the parameters of action were well-defined; but ultimately he lacked the flair to exercise the surpreme authority. Indeed, the career of Galba could not be better summarised than it was by Tacitus: "by general agreement he would have been taken as a man capable of exercising supreme power, had he not tried it".[164]

ii) Otho

The family of M. Salvius Otho was of much more recent ennoblement than that of Galba; although traditionally the Salvii were descended from Etruscan war-lords, it was only in the generation of Otho's grandfather that the family achieved senatorial status. According to Suetonius (*Otho* 1,1), the grandfather was an equestrian client of Livia, through whose influence he was translated to the senate and progressed along the *cursus honorum* as far as the praetorship. He also, according to Suetonius, made a good marriage – possibly to a lady of the *gens Titia*.

Otho's father, Lucius, presumably because of his father's favour with Livia, prospered during the reign of Tiberius; he rose to achieve a suffect consulship in A.D. 33, thus not only achieving a consulship in the same year as Galba, but, like him, by this honour, suggesting that he had not been involved in any recognisable way with Sejanus. No detail is known of other steps in his career, apart from unspecified extraordinary

---

163 Barrett, 1989, 101ff.
164 Tac. *Hist.* I. 49,2.

imperia and the proconsulate of Africa which he may have held from A.D. 46 as Galba's successor.

His reputation for severity was displayed in his punishing of soldiers who out of loyalty to Claudius had put to death some of their officers. Although Suetonius (*Otho* 1,2) says that Lucius Otho lost favour with Claudius for this, he soon regained it by exposing a plot to assassinate the emperor. This won for him a statue on the Palatine hill, and elevation by Claudius, presumably during his censorship in A.D. 47–48, into the patricians[165]; Lucius Otho's wife, Albia Terentia, was probably of an equestrian family and they had three children – Marcus Otho, Lucius Titianus (the elder brother) and a daughter who in infancy was engaged to the uncongenial Drusus, son of Germanicus, who was starved to death in A.D. 33.[166]

Marcus Otho was born in A.D. 32, and his youth is described as wild, causing frequent interventions by his strict father. Suetonius gives no details of Otho's career beyond the "escapades"; but he became particularly close to Nero (*omnium ... consiliorum secretorumque particeps* – *Otho* 3,1), and was privy to the plot to murder Agrippina in A.D. 59. Subsequently, Nero involved Otho in his "courtship" of Poppaea Sabina, though (unfortunately) Otho fell in love with her; the marriage which Otho had contracted with her at Nero's insistence was annulled, and, Otho, possibly at Seneca's instigation, was removed from Rome under the guise of being made *legatus* of Lusitania.[167] Although this was normally a praetorian post Otho held it with only the rank of quaestor (Suet. *Otho* 3,2), but his tenure was distinguished by a spirit of moderation and good sense. In other words, his early career demonstrated the same paradoxes of character that Tacitus noticed in Otho's brief principate.

Otho's fear and jealousy of Nero made him one of the first to join Galba in A.D. 68 – a loyalty which he clearly hoped would bring him to the fore in Galba's quest for a successor. He was already busy insinuating himself into the favour of the praetorian guard when Galba's choice of Piso Licinianus as successor forced Otho's hand into making his successful bid for power.[168]

Otho's brother, Titianus, reached the consulship in A.D. 52, and was proconsul of Asia in A.D. 63–64, where he had the young Agricola as his quaestor.[169] Titianus played a prominent part in Otho's campaign against Vitellius in A.D. 69, when he enjoyed a second consulate. He was pardoned by Vitellius[170] after Bedriacum and appears to have taken no further part in politics. Titianus may have married a sister of the future emperor Nerva, as their son bore the name, Cocceianus[171]; he was later put to death by Domitian for celebrating his uncle's – (that is, Otho's) – birthday.[172]

iii) Vitellius

---

165   See Tac. *Ann.* XI. 25,3 for Claudius' creation of patricians at this time.
166   On Drusus and his fate, see Shotter, 1974a, 42–46.
167   Plutarch *Galba* 20,1; Tac. *Ann.* XIII. 46.
168   For Otho's cultivation of the army (and others) from the earliest days of his assocation with Galba, see Tac. *Hist.* I. 23,1, Plut. *Galba* 20, 2–4, Suet. *Galba* 14,2.
169   Tac. *Agr.* 6,2.
170   Tac. *Hist.* II. 60,2 (*pietate et ignavia excusatus*).
171   Syme, 1958, ii.628; Tac. *Hist.* II. 48,2.
172   Suet. *Dom.* 10,3.

The origins of Vitellius' family were shrouded in mystery, and Suetonius – undoubtedly wisely – regards the different stories as reflecting differing attitudes taken to the emperor (Suet. *Vitell.* 1,1). Immediately, the family came from Nuceria, and the emperor's grandfather, P. Vitellius, was an equestrian *procurator* under Augustus.

His four sons – Aulus, Quintus, Publius and Lucius – all, however, reached senatorial status; Aulus became suffect consul in A.D. 32, and was noted for his extravagance. Quintus entered the *cursus honorum* under Augustus' patronage as a *quaestor Augusti*, but in A.D. 17 was removed from the senate as having fallen beneath the required property-level (*census*) owing to his extravagances.[173] Publius Vitellius was a member of Germanicus' entourage both in Germany[174] and in the east, as proconsul of Bithynia; he was prominent amongst the accusers of Gn. Piso for Germanicus' murder.[175] Later, like a number of those who had been involved with Germanicus and Agrippina, he was accused of association with Sejanus[176], and committed to the custody of his brother (probably Aulus, as consul in A.D. 32); Tacitus says that he committed suicide whilst in his brother's custody, though Suetonius affirms that he *attempted* suicide, but died later. In the context of his prosecution of Piso, Tacitus asserts that Publius Vitellius was a man of great eloquence; further, it is clear from his time in Germany that he was not lacking in military ability.

Lucius was the most successful of the brothers: following his consulship in A.D. 34, he was put in charge of Syria – a difficult appointment owing to the current disturbed state of Parthian/Armenian/Roman relations[177] which Vitellius succeeded in settling. The efficiency and energy, however, displayed in this command stands in marked contrast to the obsequiousness also ascribed to him; Suetonius (*Vitell.* 2,5) says that Lucius was the first to introduce into Rome the worship of Caligula as a god (apparently to avert execution by a jealous emperor), and cited incidents (in which Tacitus generally concurs) of a similar nature under Claudius. At any rate, it is clear that Claudius valued the services of Lucius Vitellius, awarding him a second consulship in A.D. 43 in which he acted for the emperor in Rome during the latter's absence on the British expedition, and a third in A.D. 47, when he also shared the censorship with the emperor. He died shortly after this.

Lucius Vitellius married Sextilia, a lady of high reputation,[178] and she bore him two sons, Aulus and Lucius, who achieved the unusual distinction of enjoying a consulship in the same year – A.D. 48 when their father was censor, and Aulus was *ordinarius* and Lucius *suffectus*.

Aulus Vitellius was born on September 7th (or 24th) in A.D. 15; his early years were spent close to Tiberius' household, and he was apparently with the emperor on Capreae (Suet. *Vitell.* 3,2.). Like his father and uncles he had a penchant for obsequious behaviour and the enjoyment of leisure; Suetonius (*Vitell.* 4) cites his chariot-driving and dicing and shows how he abetted Nero's desire to perform in public.

---

173   Tac. *Ann.* II. 48,3.
174   Tac. *Ann.* I. 70.6.
175   Tac. *Ann.* II. 74,2 and III.10ff. See Shotter, 1974b, 238ff.
176   Shotter, 1989, 21. Tac. *Ann.* V. 8.
177   Tac. *Ann.* VI. 31–37 and 41–44.
178   For Sextilia's reputation, see Tac. *Hist.* II. 64,2; III. 67,1; Plut. *Otho* 5,2 and 16,2.

In addition to his consulship in A.D. 48, he enjoyed a number of priesthoods;[179] he was proconsul of Africa in A.D. 60 or 61, a post which he is said by Suetonius to have carried out well, and stayed there as a *legatus* when his brother succeeded him. He was also at some point a *curator operum publicorum*, a post with material temptations which Suetonius says (*Vitell.* 5) that Vitellius was unable to resist. It was to general surprise that Galba appointed him to Lower Germany to succeed the murdered Fonteius Capito; the appointment may have been due to Galba's hope that a member of a distinguished family would bring the right kind of authority to the job; alternatively, it may have been due to the influence of Galba's friend, Titus Vinius. It is certainly true that Vitellius' inattention to discipline in his new post provided the opportunity for the anti-Galba movement to gather momentum, a movement on which he himself of course was shortly to capitalise.

Vitellius had two marriages – the first to the daughter of P. Petronius (consul in A.D. 19), who appears to have had close contacts with Vitellius' father; they had a son whom Vitellius was accused of murdering. His second marriage was to Galeria Fundana, who was highly praised by Tacitus for her modesty[180]; they had a son, Germanicus, who was put to death along with his uncle in A.D. 70 on Mucianus' orders[181], and a daughter whom Vitellius tried to offer in marriage as a bribe to Antonius Primus, but who was eventually given a good marriage at the instigation of Vespasian.[182]

As political forces, therefore, none of these three imperial families survived to make any further impact upon Roman politics; nor, of course, did the Julii or the Claudii, whom they had displaced. All three could claim senatorial status in their families before their own generation; Vespasian, as a first-generation senator, represented a further break with past tradition – ironically probably one of those senators promoted by Nero in the expectation that his social inferiority would not dispose him to thoughts that were over-ambitious.[183]

5. Suetonius' sources of Information[184]

We have seen that the chief uniqueness of Suetonius as a biographer of emperors was his access to privileged material so long as he held official posts in the emperors' service. There is no doubt that he made extensive use of such material until his dismissal. As a result, the *Julius Caesar* and *Augustus* (and other *Lives* in which Caesarian or Augustan material was relevant) made full use of a type of source which evidently Suetonius did not have available for subsequent *Lives*. He was thus thrown back on to the same kinds

179 He was certainly a *frater Arvalis* under Nero, and at some stage a *quindecemvir sacris faciundis.*
180 Tac. *Hist.* II. 64,2.
181 Tac. *Hist.* IV. 80,1; Suetonius (*Vitell.* 18) says that Vitellius, his son and his brother perished together in December 69.
182 Tac. *Hist.* III. 78, 1; Suet. *Div. Vesp.* 14,1.
183 See Fabius Valens' assessment of Verginius Rufus (Tac. *Hist.* I. 52,4); also Chilver, 1957, 29ff.
184 In general, see Mooney, 1930, 27–39; Wallace-Hadrill, 1983, 50–66.

of material that were available to other writers – the *acts of the senate*, histories, biographies, monographs and memoirs of a wide collection of public and literary figures.

What he used and how he used his sources is a matter of some interest, and probably does not admit of a uniform response with regard to all of the *Lives*. In the *Julius Caesar* and *Augustus* sources are frequently cited and, contrary to the practice adopted by Tacitus, named. But in the main they are not those writers whom we take to be the standard sources for a history of the first century A.D.; they are, as Wallace-Hadrill has observed[185], "obscure, ephemeral or distinctly 'literary'", and consist of poets, orators and the writers of anonymous lampoons.[186] These were more profitable sources of the anecdotal material which the biographer preferred to use. Similarly, we may be certain that where such material was available, Suetonius made use of the memoirs and other writings of his subjects; he himself states that he used the memoirs of Julius Caesar, Augustus, Tiberius and Claudius, and he certainly employed Nero's poems and a more ephemeral essay on the care of hair which Domitian had composed.

This is not, of course, to say that he did not consult the writings of Roman historians; the similarities of accounts in Suetonius, Tacitus, Dio and Plutarch[187] indicate this – even to the point occasionally of close verbal correspondence. A comparison between Suetonius' and Tacitus' accounts of the capture and death of Vitellius[188] shows elements of correspondence, but it also shows that Suetonius had access to a more anecdotal source which Tacitus either did not use, or chose to ignore as inquisitive and irrelevant to his purpose.

Reputable historical sources are named at various points in the *Lives* – Asinius Pollio, Cremutius Cordus, the elder Pliny, and an anonymous consular historian sometimes (though almost certainly wrongly) assumed to have been Tacitus.[189] Although Suetonius will have used one or more of the relevant historical sources, it is not clear how much effort he will have been ready to put into the essential historiographical art of weighing and comparing previous accounts. This was not laziness on his part so much as an antipathy to sources which were not as anecdotal as he wished, and themselves not given to naming their own sources, thus making the assessment of them more onerous. Such sources, in short, did not lend themselves so obviously to compilation.

In the cases of *Galba*, *Otho* and *Vitellius* considerable ingenuity has been expended by modern scholars in attempting to place the relationship between Suetonius, Tacitus and Plutarch.[190] It emerges that there are sufficient significant differences for us to be reasonably certain that Suetonius did not make a great deal of use of Tacitus. It is generally agreed that Tacitus and Plutarch utilised a writer of the Flavian period and that this writer was used by Suetonius also, though supplemented by his own preferred types

---

185 Wallace-Hadrill, 1983, 64.
186 For example, in *Otho* 3,2.
187 On Suetonius' use of Greek sources, see Townend, 1960, 98ff.
188 See above on p.12.
189 It is much more likely to have been Servilius Nonianus, who was consul in A.D. 35.
190 This is summarised by Mooney, 1930, 35f.

of source – such as Sulpician family records over the ancestry of Galba[191] and "Quintus Elogius" and Cassius Severus (a noted lampoon-writer of the Augustan and Tiberian periods) over the ancestry of Vitellius.[192]

The identity of this source has been the subject of much discussion,[193] which it is inappropriate to reproduce in detail. It is generally agreed that there was a major source used by all of the writers on the events following the fall of Nero. It is likely that this source was the elder Pliny, who died in the eruption of Vesuvius in A.D. 79. His many works included an account of Rome's wars against the German tribes and a general history in thirty-one books, continuing the work of Aufidius Bassus, and carrying his account into the early years of Vespasian's reign. His work is cited at various points by Tacitus and Suetonius, and he was apparently in Rome during A.D. 68–69. Further, his interest in the curious, which is so apparent in his *Natural History*, may have proved an added attraction for Suetonius.

It seems clear, however, that even if Pliny was the *chief* source, one or more other writers were consulted. It is likely, for example, that the work of Cluvius Rufus was used, although we know very little about that work, nor even how far it extended beyond Nero's death. Cluvius had been consul under Caligula and had served as an obsequious, but in no way malicious, courtier under Nero. He transferred his support to Galba, and was made governor of Spain (Tarraconensis) by that emperor. Cluvius was thus away from Rome for much of the period of civil war. Subsequently, he transferred loyalty to Otho, and then to Vitellius, and finally to Vespasian, thus providing a striking illustration of the principle of offering service whoever the emperor happened to be.[194] One detail of Cluvius' writing that survives is the matter of his attitude to Verginius Rufus in A.D. 68;[195] this attitude was defended by Cluvius in a face-to-face encounter with Verginius himself. We may assume that, if Cluvius Rufus carried his account into A.D. 69, his writing will have reflected sympathy with the ultimate victor.

Two other writers have been canvassed as possible sources – Fabius Rusticus and Vipstanus Messalla. About the former we know very little, though he was mentioned twice by Tacitus as a source for events in Nero's reign; Vipstanus Messalla[196] was clearly valued by Tacitus who used him as one of the characters in the *Dialogue on Orators*. A participant in the war between Vitellius and Vespasian, Messalla is cited by Tacitus in connection with two incidents in that campaign.[197]

There will, of course, have been some men still living whilst Suetonius was undertaking his research for the *Lives* who had themselves participated in the events; the collecting and weighing of the material available from such sources was, according to the Athenian Thucydides, a major part of the historian's task. It would be very difficult to deny that such sources provided Suetonius with some of his anecdotal material, but

---

191 *Galba* 3.
192 *Vitell.* 1,2 and 2,1 (see notes there); for Cassius Severus, see particularly Tac. *Ann.* I. 72,4 and IV.21,5.
193 See particularly Syme, 1958, i. 178–9, 289–94, ii. 674–6; Townend, 1960 and 1964.
194 A favourite Tacitean theme; see Shotter, 1991a.
195 Pliny *Letters* IX.19,5; Shotter, 1967.
196 *Hist.* III. 9,3.
197 *Hist.* III. 25,2 and 28,1.

such evidence as exists in the *Lives* themselves suggests that he may not have strayed beyond books and reminiscences of his own and of members of his family and immediate circle.[198] In any case, the "privateness" which is so integral a part of Suetonius' character as portrayed in Pliny's *Letters* would probably have made such research a difficult matter for the biographer.

Like others engaged in research into the history and politics of the first century A.D., Suetonius would have had available to him a range of public documents. It is clear from Tacitus' observations, however, that the value of these in the early principate may not have been beyond dispute.[199] Indeed, Suetonius, as an imperial functionary, may have known better than most how far such documents were to be trusted. Nonetheless, he does on occasion cite both the senatorial record (*acta senatus*) and the public record (*acta publica*).[200] Emperors' own semi-official records of their reigns (*commentarii principales*) might be made available, but could be totally or partially suppressed.[201] Again, we may assume that, whilst in office, Suetonius had a better chance than most of seeing these, and in any case had probably formed a shrewd idea of their value.

In conclusion, it must be re-emphasised that Suetonius should not be seen as using sources as if he were an historian. He had his own interests, and his selection of sources ultimately was made to service these.

6. The style of Suetonius[202]

It has been suggested that one reason for the influence of Suetonius over later writers was to be found in his language and style, which were a great deal closer to late and mediaeval latin than was the case with Cicero or Tacitus.

To some extent, Suetonius' attitude to certain aspects of diction and style may be gathered from comments he makes about others in the course of his work. In general, it is clear that he preferred a "middle" style: that is, one that was free from various pretensions and conceits, not over-florid or over-brief. Like Quintilian and Pliny, he clearly did not approve of the "pointed" style as it was to be found in Seneca and Tacitus: his natural inclinations would have turned him rather to Cicero. Indeed, one can detect the tone of the admirer in the passage in which he rather sneeringly describes the lengths to which P. Clodius was prepared to go in his feud with Cicero.[203]

It is in his discussion of Augustus' style[204] that we get the clearest indication of what Suetonius admired: and it is obvious that he spent considerable effort in analysing that

---

198   For example, from his grandfather (*Cal.* 19,3), from his father (*Otho* 10,1) and from his own memory (*Nero* 57,2).
199   *Ann.* I.1, 4–6; *Hist.* I. 1,1.
200   For example in *Div.Aug.* 5 and *Tib.* 73 (*acta senatus*); in *Tib.* 5 and *Cal.* 8 (*acta publica*).
201   For example, *Cal.* 15 and Tac. *Hist.* IV. 40,3; the former refers to Caligula's suppressing of Tiberius' *commentarii*, the latter to Vespasian's refusal to make Nero's available to the senate to facilitate an attack on that emperor's helpers.
202   A detailed consideration is to be found in Mooney 1930, 611ff.
203   *Tib.* 2,4.
204   *Div. Aug.* 86.

emperor's habits of speaking and writing.[205] Augustus' principle is set out early in the chapter, and it was a principle that will have commended itself to a conscientious teacher: "he cultivated a simple and easy oratorical style, avoiding 'purple passages', artfully-contrived prose-rhythms, and the 'stink of far-fetched phrases', as he called it; his main object was to say what he meant as plainly as possible". Augustus was therefore prepared to sacrifice grace to clarity.[206]

Neither Augustus (nor Suetonius, for that matter) had any time for linguistic pedantry: "he expressed contempt for both innovators and archaisers, as equally mischievous". Three objects of Augustus' criticism are singled out – the "myrrh-distilling ringlets" of his friend, Maecenas, the "obsolete and difficult phrases" of Tiberius, whom Suetonius himself belaboured in schoolmasterly fashion,[207] and the madness of Marcus Antonius who wrote "as though he wanted to be wondered at, rather than understood". It is clear that Augustus' special point of criticism was that Antonius was both an archaiser, using words "which Sallust picked from the *Origines* of Cato", and adopted the "nonsenses of garrulous orators", who practised the "Asiatic" (or florid) style of oratory. Word-coinings and archaisms, the two faults which had aroused Augustus' criticism, were major stylistic affectations of Suetonius' own day; both were apparently espoused by Hadrian[208], who is said to have preferred Ennius to Virgil, Cato to Cicero, and Caelius Rufus to Sallust; if Hadrian found Sallust too modern, Suetonius found in him too much of an archaiser.[209]

Suetonius' own reputation in antiquity was for a faultless, clear and brief style;[210] yet his very brevity can produce a disjointed and unclear effect.[211] The fact that the cataloguer and compiler frequently show through his work is bound to produce the effect of lack of grace and polish, but his rejection of the rhetorical flourish in this sense can take him too far in the opposite direction, and he sometimes confuses brevity and simplicity.[212]

Again, however, we must remember Suetonius' profession: as a *grammaticus* he will have studied a wide variety of styles and a large number of methods of achieving effect. We should not imagine that he deliberately eschewed all of these. Some features noticed by the reader of Tacitus also find a place in Suetonius,[213] and it has been observed that

---

205 *Div. Aug.* 87–88.
206 Singled out for mention is the use of prepositions with the names of towns – a practice in which Suetonius also indulged (*Div. Iul.* 35,2).
207 *Tib.* 70,1. For a discussion of Tiberius' style, see Syme, 1958, i. 283–5, 319–20.
208 Writers of the Augustan History, *Life of Hadrian* 16,6. The biography (25) also provides an example of Hadrian's own writing, which was full of affected diminutives, one of the characteristics of the period, which can also be found in Suetonius (Mooney, 1930, 612).
209 *On Grammarians* 10.
210 Writers of the Augustan History, *Life of Firmus* 1.
211 For example, in *Div. Claud.* 39, where a disjointed list of instances of the emperor's foolishness is given.
212 For example, in *Tib.* 49, where examples are so truncated as to be misleading, even unintelligible.
213 An example is *quamquam* ("although") followed by the subjunctive.

his prose is not as flat and "unplanned" as may appear, for a large number of metrical devices has been detected in it, as is also the case with his friend, Pliny.[214]

In fact, an analysis of Suetonius' style produces evidence of many of the "silver-age" techniques which are familiar occurrences in Seneca and Tacitus – brevity, *variatio* (imbalance within or between sentences), and the use of a wide range of figures.[215] In syntax, too, most usages, then current, can be detected. Whilst Suetonius in general lacks the rhetorical climaxes and "purple passages"[216] familiar in writers of the "silver-age", and for this reason has been regarded as "cold"[217], we should do well to remember the excitement that he engenders in passages such as that describing the death of Nero.[218]

In other respects, too, his lack of polish may be subject to legitimate criticism. Like Cicero and Augustus,[219] Suetonius was ready to include Greek words; nor do these appear simply in quotations, but also in circumstances in which Suetonius, with his ready facility in Greek, plainly found a Greek word which more faithfully reflected his meaning than any latin word that he knew.[220] Although the use of Greek was an indication of learning, and "allowed" in correspondence, most Romans would not have used it in more "public" circumstances; thus Tiberius preferred a latin periphrasis to a single Greek word,[221] and Tacitus on one occasion translated into latin a comment which Tiberius in exasperation had muttered in Greek.[222]

The intrusion of Greek into latin texts would to Tacitus' mind not only have encumbered the stylistic flow, but it also hindered the reader's own grasp of a passage by diverting him unnecessarily. Transitions were important: for example, it would be equally diverting for a reader to be expected to pass abruptly from Tacitean style to, for example, that of the emperor Claudius. Thus historians, rather than quoting speeches, adapted them to some extent to their own style; Tacitus on one occasion[223] implies that he regularly adapted speeches. That he did not do so on the occasion in question was due to the fact that the particular speech was well-known.

Just how freely Tacitus interpreted his role as an adapter is to be seen in his treatment of the famous speech of Claudius.[224] Clearly by such a treatment not only was strict accuracy lost, but also a speech could be made to do more than the original intended; it could be fitted into its context in such a way as to convey the sense of other arguments

---

214 See Macé, 1900, 279 ff.
215 For example, see Mooney, 1930, 634ff.
216 A good example of the rhetorical embellishment that is typical of the period is to be found in Tacitus' description of a storm at sea (*Ann.* II. 23), which may be compared with that of Germanicus' officer, the poet Albinovanus Pedo, who was present (see Seneca *Suasoriae* I.14).
217 See Macé, 1900, 399.
218 *Nero* 47–9.
219 There are many examples in the correspondence of Augustus as cited by Suetonius (e.g. *Tib.* 21, 4–6; 57, 1 and 71).
220 For example, see *Cal.* 29,1, and particularly *Div. Claud.* 39.
221 *Tib.* 71.
222 *Ann.* III. 65,3.
223 *Ann.* XV. 67,3.
224 *Ann.* XI. 24; the original speech is preserved as *ILS* 212.

as well. Thus, the Tacitean version of Claudius' speech almost certainly tells us more about arguments used on the occasion by others than did Claudius' original.[225]

Suetonius demanded accuracy in the use of original material, even where this had the effect of producing a disjointed passage in his latin. There is no transition in his usage; speeches are abruptly introduced and cited. Indeed on one occasion, Suetonius seems to come into direct conflict with Tacitus over the practice; for Tacitus put a long speech into the mouth of Otho at a point where Otho did not have the time for such an oration[226] – a point which Suetonius explicitly makes.[227]

In short, Suetonius did not consider himself an artist in a primary sense; his aim was to produce information, and style was only a vehicle for this. He disapproved of certain current practices, though he did not carry this to the extent of pedantry, for whilst he avoided trends of his own age which he disliked, he settled for the "middle" style evident in Quintilian, Pliny, and to some extent in Tacitus' earlier works. Yet, as we have seen, his own work carried a fair measure of the features commonly-noted in the prose of his age; clarity and brevity were his requirements, and, like Augustus, he was prepared to sacrifice niceties to achieve these ends.

7. A Note on the manuscripts

A full discussion of the manuscript tradition would be out of place in the present work, but a brief note may be helpful.[228]

Research indicates that all the extant manuscripts derive from a single archetype, designated Ω, which was in the monastery at Fulda in the ninth century. A copy of this was made in the ninth century at the request of Servatus Lupus, Abbot of Ferrières. Both the Fulda manuscript and the copy of it have perished, but it is thought that all subsequent manuscripts derive ultimately from the copy of Ω; all lack the dedication and the opening chapters of *Julius Caesar*; it may therefore be assumed that Ω lacked them also, and that these portions disappeared between the sixth century, when they were known, and the ninth.

The oldest of the surviving manuscripts is the *Codex Memmianus* (M), written late in the ninth century: it is also the best, since, although it has gaps and errors, it has no interpolations, which are characteristic of the later manuscripts. It is fairly certain that it was made from Lupus' copy of Ω, and contains corrections which are no later than the twelfth century (M^2). No other surviving manuscript depends upon it. The next manuscript in point of age is the *Codex Gudianus* (G), dating to the eleventh century; it is inferior to M, but apparently derives from a similar original. It has many corrections, some made by the scribe(G^2), and some added in the fifteenth century (G^3).

Also of the eleventh century is the *Codex Vaticanus* (V), which is more reliable than G, and is frequently in agreement with M despite the fact that it contains careless errors and gaps; it is in any case deficient after *Cal.* 3,3. It has glosses which are similar in

---

225   See Wellesley, 1954, 13ff and Syme, 1958, i. 283–5 and 319–20.
226   *Hist.* I. 27–28.
227   *Otho* 7; Macé, 1900, 206–7.
228   For a full treatment, see Mooney, 1930, 44ff, where a stemma is constructed.

character to those of M^2. It has been suggested that another manuscript, now lost, derived from the same source as V and, designated X, was itself the source of a number of other manuscripts – L (with corrections L^2 and L^3), P, O and S, all of the twelfth century, and T which is of the fourteenth century. Of these, P, O, S and T have been corrected from another lost manuscript, designated Y, which was approximately contemporary with, but inferior in quality to, X. Three twelfth century manuscripts derive from Y – M, Q and R. The source of two fifteenth century manuscripts – S and δ – has been disputed.

Synopses of Suetonius' Lives of Galba, Otho and Vitellius

SUETONIUS

Lives of Galba, Otho and Vitellius

GALBA

1]   Progenies Caesarum in Nerone defecit: quod futurum compluribus quidem signis, sed vel evidentissimis duobus apparuit. Liviae olim post Augusti statim nuptias Veientanum suum revisenti praetervolans aquila gallinam albam ramulum lauri rostro tenentem, ita ut rapuerat, demisit in gremium; cumque nutriri alitem, pangi ramulum placuisset, tanta pullorum suboles provenit, ut hodieque ea villa "ad Gallinas" vocetur, tale vero lauretum, ut triumphaturi Caesares inde laureas decerperent; fuitque mos triumphantibus, alias confestim eodem loco pangere; et observatum est sub cuiusque obitum arborem ab ipso institutam elanguisse. Ergo novissimo Neronis anno et silva omnis exaruit radicitus, et quidquid ibi gallinarum erat interiit. Ac subinde tacta de caelo Caesarum aede capita omnibus simul statuis deciderunt, Augusti etiam sceptrum e manibus excussum est.

2]   Neroni Galba successit nullo gradu contingens Caesarum domum, sed haud dubie nobilissimus magnaque et vetere prosapia, ut qui statuarum titulis pronepotem se Quinti Catuli Capitolini semper ascripserit, imperator vero etiam stemma in atrio proposuerit, quo paternam originem ad Iovem, maternam ad Pasiphaam Minonis uxorem referret.

3]   Imagines et elogia universi generis exsequi longum est, familiae breviter 1 attingam. Qui primus Sulpiciorum cognomen Galbae tulit cur aut unde traxerit, ambigitur. Quidam putant, quod oppidum Hispaniae frustra diu oppugnatum inlitis demum galbano facibus succenderit; alii, quod in diuturna valitudine galbeo, id est remediis lana involutis, assidue uteretur; nonnulli, quod praepinguis fuerit visus, quem galbam Galli vocent; vel contra, quod tam exilis, quam sunt

GALBA

1] Nero's death brought the family of the Caesars to its end; there were several portents of this, but two in particular pointed to it most clearly. Once, when Livia, following her marriage to Augustus, was returning to her estate at Veii, an eagle flew over and dropped into her lap a white chicken which held in its beak a sprig of laurel; this was how the eagle had caught it. Livia decided to look after the bird, and to plant the laurel-sprig; so great was the flock that ensued that even to-day the villa is called "The Chicken Run". Furthermore, so vigorous was the resulting laurel-grove that whenever the Caesars were about to set out on a triumphal celebration they would pick their laurels there. It became the custom that those who triumphed would immediately afterwards plant their laurels in the grove; and it was noticed that whenever a Caesar died the laurel-tree he had planted withered away. Thus it was, in Nero's last year of power, that the whole grove withered totally, and all the hens that were there died. Not only that, but shortly after the temple of the Caesars had been struck by lightning, simultaneously the heads fell from all the statues, and even Augustus' sceptre was knocked from his hand.

2] Nero was succeeded by Galba, although the latter had no connection at all with the Caesarian family. This, of course, is not to say that he was not himself of a most noble origin; indeed, he hailed from such an old and great family that on the inscriptions on his statues he always added that he was the great-grandson of Quintus Catulus Capitolinus. Furthermore, when he was emperor he fixed up a family-tree in the hall of his palace, in which he traced his paternal roots back to Jupiter, and his mother's to Minos' wife, Pasiphae.

3] It would take far too long to list the whole family's distinctions and famous 1 forebears; instead I shall briefly outline those that relate to Galba's own branch of it. It is a matter of dispute which of the Sulpicii first took the surname of Galba; so too the reason for it and the source of the name. Some think that it derived from an occasion when a member of the family who had besieged a Spanish settlement for a long time and to no effect, finally set fire to it with torches which had been smeared with a type of resin called *galbanum*. Another story is that one of them during a long illness regularly applied a compress (*galbeum*) – a remedy that was wrapped in wool. Others say that it derived from a member of the family who was exceptionally fat – a condition which the Gauls call *galba*; or alternatively one of the ancestors was so thin that he got the name

animalia quae in aesculis nascuntur appellanturque galbae.

Familiam illustravit Servius Galba consularis, temporum suorum vel 2 eloquentissimus, quem tradunt Hispaniam ex praetura optinentem, triginta Lusitanorum milibus perfidia trucidatis, Viriatini belli causam exstitisse. Eius nepos ob repulsam consulatus infensus Iulio Caesari, cuius legatus in Gallia fuerat, conspiravit cum Cassio et Bruto, propter quod Pedia lege damnatus est. Ab hoc sunt imperatoris Galbae avus ac pater: avus clarior studiis quam 3 dignitate – non enim egressus praeturae gradum – multiplicem nec incuriosam historiam edidit; pater consulatu functus, quanquam brevi corpore atque etiam gibber modicaeque in dicendo facultatis, causas industrie actitavit. Uxores 4 habuit Mummiam Achaicam, neptem Catuli proneptemque L. Mummi, qui Corinthum excidit; item Liviam Ocellinam ditem admodum et pulchram, a qua tamen nobilitatis causa appetitus ultro existimatur et aliquanto enixius, postquam subinde instanti vitium corporis secreto posita veste detexit, ne quasi ignaram fallere videretur. Ex Achaica liberos Gaium et Servium procreavit, quorum maior Gaius attritis facultatibus urbe cessit prohibitusque a Tiberio sortiri anno suo proconsulatum voluntaria morte obiit.

4]   Ser. Galba imperator M. Valerio Messala Cn. Lentulo cons. natus est VIIII. 1 Kal. Ian. in villa colli superposita prope Tarracinam sinistrorsus Fundos petentibus, adoptatusque a noverca sua Livia nomen et Ocellare cognomen assumpsit mutato praenomine; nam Lucium mox pro Servio usque ad tempus imperii usurpavit. Constat Augustum puero adhuc, salutanti se inter aequales, apprehensa buccula dixisse: καὶ σὺ τέκνον τῆς ἀρχῆς ἡμῶν παρατρώξῃ. Sed et Tiberius, cum comperisset imperaturum eum verum in senecta: "Vivat sane," ait, "quando id ad nos nihil pertinet." Avo quoque eius fulgur procuranti, 2 cum exta de manibus aquila rapuisset et in frugiferam quercum contulisset,

from a type of insect which lives in oak-trees and is called *galba*.

The earliest member of the family on record as winning fame was the ex- 2 consul, Servius Galba, the greatest orator of his day, who is said to have won Spain as his province after his praetorship; he treacherously slaughtered thirty thousand Lusitanians and caused the war with Viriathus. His grandson at one time served as an aide to Julius Caesar in Gaul, but became Caesar's bitter enemy following his defeat in the consular elections; he joined the conspiracy of Brutus and Cassius, and for this was condemned under the law of Quintus Pedius. The father and grandfather of the emperor Galba were descended from 3 this man. His grandfather made a name for scholarship rather than political achievements, for although he did not move beyond the praetorship, he wrote a copious and well-researched history. Galba's father rose to the consulship, and although he was short – even hunchbacked – and only a moderate speaker, he worked hard on cases in which he was involved.

Galba's father married twice; his first wife was Mummia Achaica, grand- 4 daughter of Catulus and great-granddaughter of the Lucius Mummius who razed Corinth to the ground. His second wife was Livia Ocellina, a woman who was both rich and beautiful. It is thought that it was his aristocratic status that appealed to her; indeed, she redoubled her effort when at her insistence he took off his clothes in private to display his deformity to her, so that she should not think that he was trying to hide the truth from her.

Achaica bore him two sons – Gaius, the elder, and Servius; when Gaius went through his fortune and quit Rome, Tiberius prevented him from participating in the ballot when he was due for a proconsulship. As a result, he committed suicide.

4] Servius Galba, the emperor, was born on December 24th in the year when 1 Marcus Valerius Messala and Gnaeus Lentulus were consuls (3 B.C.); his birthplace was a hillside-villa near Tarracina, on the left as one travels towards Fundi. He was adopted by his step-mother, and took Livius as his gentile name with Ocella as his surname. He also changed his forename from Servius to Lucius, using the latter until he became emperor. There is a well-known story that once, when as a boy Galba came with others of his own age to greet Augustus, the emperor pinched him on the cheek and said in Greek, "you too, my child, will one day have a taste of this power of mine". When Tiberi learned that Galba would become emperor, but not till old age, he remarked, "Then he can live, since that has no relevance to me".

On another occasion, when his grandfather was sacrificing to avert the evil 2 portended by a lightning-flash, an eagle snatched the entrails from his hands and

responsum est summum sed serum imperium portendi familiae; et ille irridens: "Sane," inquit, "cum mula pepererit." Nihil aeque postea Galbam temptantem res novas confirmavit quam mulae partus, ceterisque ut obscaenum ostentum abhorrentibus, solus pro laetissimo accepit memor sacrificii dictique avi.

Sumpta virili toga somniavit Fortunam dicentem, stare se ante fores 3 defessam et nisi ocius reciperetur, cuicumque obvio praedae futuram. Utque evigilavit, aperto atrio simulacrum aeneum deae cubitali maius iuxta limen invenit idque gremio suo Tusculum, ubi aestivare consueverat, avexit et in parte aedium consecratum menstruis deinceps supplicationibus et pervigilio anniversario coluit.

Quanquam autem nondum aetate constanti veterem civitatis exoletumque 4 morem ac tantum in domo sua haerentem obstinatissime retinuit, ut liberti servique bis die frequentes adessent ac mane salvere, vesperi valere sibi singuli dicerent.

5] Inter liberales disciplinas attendit et iuri. Dedit et matrimonio operam; 1 verum amissa uxore Lepida duobusque ex ea filiis remansit in caelibatu neque sollicitari ulla condicione amplius potuit, ne Agrippinae quidem, quae viduata morte Domiti maritum quoque adhuc necdum caelibem Galbam adeo omnibus sollicitaverat modis, ut in conventu matronarum correpta iurgio atque etiam manu pulsata sit a matre Lepidae.

Observavit ante omnis Liviam Augustam, cuius et vivae gratia plurimum 2 valuit et mortuae testamento paene ditatus est; sestertium namque quingenties praecipuum inter legatarios habuit, sed quia notata, non perscripta erat summa, herede Tiberio legatum ad quingenta revocante, ne haec quidem accepit.

6] Honoribus ante legitimum tempus initis praetor commissione ludorum 1 Floralium novum spectaculi genus elephantos funambulos edidit; exim provinciae Aquitaniae anno fere praefuit; mox consulatum per sex menses ordinarium gessit, evenitque ut in eo ipse L. Domitio patri Neronis, ipsi Salvius Otho pater

flew off with them to an oak-tree that was laiden with acorns; this was interpreted as indicating that supreme power would come to the family, but not until late. Galba laughed and said, "yes, when mules have foals". Later, when Servius Galba was contemplating the overthrow of Nero, nothing encouraged him more than a mule happening to give birth to a foal. Whilst others shuddered at this, as a terrible omen, Galba alone took it as a particularly favourable sign, remembering the sacrifice and what his grandfather had said.

Years before, when he came of age, he dreamed that the goddess Fortuna 3 spoke to him, saying that she was tired of standing outside his door, and that unless he quickly let her in, she would pass her favours to the first person she met. When he woke up, he opened his hall-door, and found by the step a bronze statue of the goddess more than a cubit high. This he carried with great care to Tusculum where he usually spent the summer; he consecrated it in a room of the house, and thereafter worshipped it with prayers each month and an all-night vigil once a year.

Even when he was still a young man, with great persistence he kept up an 4 old and obsolete national custom which was observed only in his household, whereby twice each day the freedmen and slaves presented themselves to him, and individually wished him 'good morning' or 'good night', as appropriate to the time of day.

5]   Galba was keenly interested in the liberal arts, and particularly in the law. 1 He also put effort into his marriage; but, after the death of his wife, Lepida, and their two sons, he remained a widower for the rest of his life; he could not be tempted by any match, not even with Agrippina after the death of her husband, Domitius. Agrippina in fact had tried every trick to seduce Galba whilst his wife was still alive; this led to an incident at a meeting of married women when Lepida's mother had words with Agrippina and ended up slapping her.

He was always especially respectful towards Livia Augusta; during her 2 lifetime he enjoyed great favour, and came close to becoming a rich man under the terms of her will. She named him principal of her legatees, and left him half a million aurei; but because the sum was indicated in figures, not in words, Tiberius, as his mother's heir, reduced the sum to one thousand *aurei*, and Galba did not receive even that.

6]   He began his public career before the legal age, and, as praetor in charge 1 of the Floral games, exhibited a novel type of spectacle – elephants walking on tight-ropes; he was then governor of Aquitania for almost a year. He held the consulate for a six-month period, and in this office succeeded Lucius Domitius, the father of Nero, and was himself followed by the father of the future emperor,

Othonis succederet, velut praesagium insequentis casus, quo medius inter utriusque filios exstitit imperator.

A Gaio Caesare legatus Germaniae superioris in locum Gaetulici substitutus, 2 postridie quam ad legiones venit, sollemni forte spectaculo plaudentes inhibuit data tessera, ut manus paenula continerent; statimque per castra iactatum est: "Disce miles militare; Galba est, non Gaetulicus."

Pari severitate interdixit commeatus peti. Veteranum ac tironem militem 3 opere assiduo corroboravit matureque barbaris, qui iam in Galliam usque proruperant, coercitis, praesenti quoque Gaio talem et se et exercitum approbavit, ut inter innumeras contractasque ex omnibus provinciis copias neque testimonium neque praemia ampliora ulli perciperent; ipse maxime insignis, quod campestrem decursionem scuto moderatus, etiam ad essedum imperatoris per viginti passuum milia cucurrit.

7] Caede Gai nuntiata multis ad occasionem stimulantibus quietem praetulit. 1 Per hoc gratissimus Claudio receptusque in cohortem amicorum tantae dignationis est habitus, ut cum subita ei valitudo nec adeo gravis incidisset, dilatus sit expeditionis Britannicae dies. Africam pro consule biennio optinuit extra sortem electus ad ordinandam provinciam et intestina dissensione et barbarorum tumultu inquietam; ordinavitque magna severitatis ac iustitiae cura etiam in parvulis rebus. Militi, qui per expeditionem artissima annona residuum 2 cibariorum tritici modium centum denariis vendidisse arguebatur, vetuit, simul atque indigere cibo coepisset, a quoquam opem ferri; et is fame extabuit. At in iure dicendo cum de proprietate iumenti quaereretur, levibus utrimque argumentis et testibus ideoque difficili coniectura veritatis, ita decrevit ut ad lacum, ubi adaquari solebat, duceretur capite involuto atque ibidem revelato eius esset, ad quem sponte se a potu recepisset.

8] Ob res et tunc in Africa et olim in Germania gestas ornamenta triumphalia 1

Otho. This was like a portent of future events when he became emperor between the sons of these two men.

He was appointed by Gaius Caesar (Caligula) to replace Gaetulicus, and, 2 on the day after he reached the legions, when he happened to see them applauding during a solemn religious festival, he issued an order that they should in future keep their hands inside their cloaks. Immediately the word went around the camp, "Learn, you soldiers, how to fight; Gaetulicus has gone, and Galba's here".

He was just as hard over requests for leave; veterans and new recruits were 3 toughened up by a continuous schedule of work; the enemy, who had broken through almost to the frontier of Gaul, was sharply pushed back whence he had come. During all of this Gaius was himself present in Germany, and had such high praise for Galba and the German army that of all the countless troops brought together from every province none received warmer approval or higher rewards. Galba himself won particular distinction for directing field-manoeuvres – with his shield on his shoulder and at the same time running alongside the emperor's chariot for twenty miles.

7]   When Gaius was assassinated, there were many who encouraged Galba to 1 proclaim himself emperor; instead he preferred to remain in the background. Claudius was extremely grateful to him for this and included him in his circle of close friends. Indeed, he held him in such esteem that when Galba suffered a sudden, but not serious, illness, the sailing of the expedition to Britain was put off until he was better. Later he was selected without ballot for the proconsulship of Africa and held the post for two years; he was given the job so that he could reorganise the province which was at the time plagued by internal feuds and threatened by a native uprising.   He carried out his commission with great strictness yet with due observance of justice that extended to the smallest detail. Whilst on campaign, when corn supplies were extremely short, a soldier was 2 accused of selling for one hundred *denarii* what was left over from his grain-ration: Galba gave orders that when this solder himself ran short of food nobody should help him out, and the soldier starved to death.   Again, when he was presiding over a court-case concerning the ownership of a package-animal, he found the evidence and the witnesses unconvincing; because he could see no other way of arriving at the truth, he gave instructions that the animal should be blindfolded and led to its normal watering-place. Ownership should be awarded to the person to whom the animal went after drinking and when the blindfold had been removed.

8]   For his achievements in Africa and earlier in Germany he was awarded the 1

accepit et sacerdotium triplex, inter quindecimviros sodalesque Titios item Augustales cooptatus; atque ex eo tempore prope ad medium Neronis principatum in secessu plurimum vixit, ne ad gestandum quidem umquam iter ingressus quam ut secum vehiculo proximo decies sestertium in auro efferret, donec in oppido Fundis moranti Hispania Tarraconensis oblata est. Acciditque, ut cum 2 provinciam ingressus sacrificaret, intra aedem publicam puero e ministris acerram tenenti capillus repente toto capite canesceret, nec defuerunt qui interpretarentur significari rerum mutationem successurumque iuveni senem, hoc est ipsum Neroni. Non multo post in Cantabriae lacum fulmen decidit repertaeque sunt duodecim secures, haud ambiguum summae imperii signum.

9] Per octo annos varie et inaequabiliter provinciam rexit, primo acer et 1 vehemens et in coercendis quidem delictis vel immodicus. Nam et nummulario non ex fide versanti pecunias manus amputavit mensaeque eius adfixit, et tutorem, quod pupillum, cui substitutus heres erat, veneno necasset, cruce adfecit; implorantique leges et civem Romanum se testificanti, quasi solacio et honore aliquo poenam levaturus, mutari multoque praeter ceteras altiorem et dealbatam statui crucem iussit. Paulatim in desidiam segnitiamque conversus est, ne quid materiae praeberet Neroni et, ut dicere solebat, quod nemo rationem otii sui reddere cogeretur.

Carthagine nova conventum agens tumultuari Gallias comperit legato 2 Aquitaniae auxilia implorante; supervenerunt et Vindicis litterae hortantis, ut humano generi assertorem ducemque se accommodaret. Nec diu cunctatus condicionem partim metu partim spe recepit; nam et mandata Neronis de nece sua ad procuratores clam missa deprenderat et confirmabatur cum secundissimis auspiciis et ominibus virginis honestae vaticinatione, tanto magis quod eadem illa carmina sacerdos Iovis Cluniae ex penetrali somnio monitus eruerat ante ducentos annos similiter a fatidica puella pronuntiata. Quorum carminum sententia erat oriturum quandoque ex Hispania principem dominumque rerum.

triumphal insignia, and three priesthoods, being enrolled as a member of the board of fifteen, of the brotherhood of Titius and of the priests of Augustus. From then until Nero's middle years he lived most of his time in retirement; he never went out even for a drive unless a second carriage drove with him carrying ten thousand *aurei*. At length, however, when he was staying at the town of Fundi, the province of Hispania Tarraconensis was offered to him. Once it 2 happened, soon after his arrival in the province, that he was conducting sacrifice in a temple: during it the hair of one of the boy-servants who was carrying the incense turned completely white. Some who were there interpreted this as indicating a change in fortune – that an old man would succeed a young man: in other words, he would succeed Nero. Shortly afterwards, a thunderbolt struck a lake in Cantabria; twelve axes were found in this lake, an unmistakeable symbol of supreme power.

9] Galba administered the province for eight years in an uneven fashion; at 1 first he was sharp and vigorous, and rather excessive in the punishment of crimes. For example, a money-changer whose activities were fraudulent had his hands chopped off and nailed to the counter. Galba crucified a man who had poisoned his ward in order that he might inherit the property. When the man begged for justice and protested that he was a Roman citizen, Galba pretended that he was going to lighten the punishment and compensate the man with some distinction, and he gave orders that the cross should be changed for one that was painted white and which stood much higher than the rest. Gradually, however, Galba became idle and lazy, so as to avoid giving Nero any excuse for attacking him, and, as he himself used to say, because nobody can be required to account for his leisure-time.

Galba was conducting assizes at New Carthage when he received news that 2 the Gallic provinces were in revolt through a plea for help from the governor of Aquitania. This was followed immediately by a letter from Vindex urging him to put himself forward as the leader of the rising and the liberator of mankind. With little hesitation he accepted, partly out of fear but partly through hope; for Galba had intercepted confidential letters which Nero had sent to his agents containing instructions for his death. His confidence, on the other hand, was enhanced by favourable signs and omens, and also by a prophecy uttered by a girl of noble birth; this was the more convincing because the priest of Jupiter at Clunia, following a warning in a dream, had discovered those self-same lines in the temple-shrine: they had been uttered in this same manner two hundred years before by a girl in a trance. The sense of these lines was that one day the emperor and master of the world would arise in Spain.

10] Igitur cum quasi manumissioni vacaturus conscendisset tribunal, propositis 1
ante se damnatorum occisorumque a Nerone quam plurimis imaginibus et
astante nobili puero, quem exsulantem e proxima Baliari insula ob id ipsum
acciverat, deploravit temporum statum consalutatusque imperator legatum se
senatus ac populi R. professus est.   Dein iustitio indicto, e plebe quidem 2
provinciae legiones et auxilia conscripsit super exercitum veterem legionis
unius duarumque alarum et cohortium trium; at e primoribus prudentia atque
aetate praestantibus vel instar senatus, ad quos de maiore re quotiens opus esset
referretur, instituit. Delegit et equestris ordinis iuvenes, qui manente anulorum 3
aureorum usu evocati appellarentur excubiasque circa cubiculum suum vice
militum agerent. Etiam per provincias edicta dimisit, auctor singulis universisque
conspirandi simul et ut qua posset quisque opera communem causam iuvarent.

Per idem fere tempus in munitione oppidi, quod sedem bello delegerat, 4
repertus est anulus opere antiquo, scalptura gemmae Victoriam cum tropaeo
exprimente; ac subinde Alexandrina navis Dertosam appulit armis onusta, sine
gubernatore, sine nauta aut vectore ullo, ut nemini dubium esset iustum piumque
et faventibus diis bellum suscipi: cum repente ex inopinato prope cuncta turbata
sunt.   Alarum altera castris appropinquantem paenitentia mutati sacramenti 5
destituere conata est aegreque retenta in officio, et servi, quos a liberto Neronis
ad fraudem praeparatos muneri acceperat, per angiportum in balneas transeuntem
paene interemerunt, nisi cohortantibus in vicem ne occasionem omitterent,
interrogatisque de qua occasione loquerentur, expressa cruciatu confessio esset.

11] Accessit ad tanta discrimina mors Vindicis, qua maxime consternatus
destitutoque similis non multum afuit quin vitae renuntiaret. Sed supervenientibus
ab urbe nuntiis ut occisum Neronem cunctosque in verba sua iurasse cognovit,
deposita legati suscepit Caesaris appellationem iterque ingressus est paludatus
ac dependente a cervicibus pugione ante pectus; nec prius usum togae reciperavit

10] So, on the pretext that he was putting time aside for manumission cases, he 1
mounted the steps of the tribunal; facing him on it were as many busts as could
be found of those condemned to death by Nero. By his side stood a young lad
of noble birth whom he had had brought from exile on the nearest of the Balearic
Islands precisely for this purpose. He complained about contemporary conditions,
and when he was hailed as emperor, he said that he was merely the representative
of the Roman senate and people. He then declared a cessation of public business, 2
and enrolled legions and auxiliaries from the ordinary people of the province to
reinforce his original army which consisted of one legion, two units of auxiliary
cavalry and three of infantry. From those of the province's aristocracy who had
the wisdom of a lifetime's experience he formed a body similar to the senate; he
could refer to them on important matters when he felt it necessary.

He hand-picked some young equestrians who kept the gold ring which was 3
their status-symbol, but to whom he referred as volunteers and used as guards
outside his private quarters in place of regular soldiers. He then sent edicts
through the provinces, calling upon people individually and collectively to join
the common cause and asking for as much help as each could give.

At about this same time, whilst he was fortifying the town which he had 4
chosen as his base, an antique ring was found; its setting carried an engraving
of Victory with a trophy. Suddenly a ship from Alexandria put in at Dertosa; it
was laiden with arms, but had no pilot, no sailors and no passengers, and left no
doubt in anyone's mind that the coming war was just and holy and had the gods'
blessing. Even so, suddenly and unexpectedly the whole plan nearly fell
through.

Galba was approaching the camp when one of the two cavalry-regiments 5
regretted its change of allegiance, tried to desert and was kept on Galba's side
only with great difficulty. Some slaves, whom he had been given by one of
Nero's freedmen who had primed them for treachery, came close to killing
Galba as he was making his way along an alley to the baths; they were
encouraging each other not to let the opportunity slip, and when asked what
opportunity they meant, they confessed under torture.

11] As if these were not dangers enough, he had to cope in addition with the
death of Vindex; he was panic-stricken by this, and so near to despair that he
came close to committing suicide. Soon after, however, messengers came from
Rome with the news that Nero was dead and everyone had sworn allegiance to
him; he then laid aside the title of 'representative' and assumed that of
'emperor', setting out on his march to Rome wearing his general's cloak and
with a dagger hanging from his neck and covering his chest. He did not resume

quam oppressis qui novas res moliebantur, praefecto praetori Nymphidio Sabino Romae, in Germania Fonteio Capitone, in Africa Clodio Macro legatis.

12] Praecesserat de eo fama saevitiae simul atque avaritiae, quod civitates 1 Hispaniarum Galliarumque, quae cunctantius sibi accesserant, gravioribus tributis, quasdam etiam murorum destructione punisset et praepositos procuratoresque supplicio capitis adfecisset cum coniugibus ac liberis; quodque oblatam a Tarraconensibus e vetere templo Iovis coronam auream librarum quindecim conflasset ac tres uncias, quae ponderi deerant, iussisset exigi. Ea 2 fama et confirmata et aucta est, ut primum urbem introiit. Nam cum classiarios, quos Nero ex remigibus iustos milites fecerat, redire ad pristinum statum cogeret, recusantis atque insuper aquilam et signa pertinacius flagitantis non modo inmisso equite disiecit, sed decimavit etiam. Item Germanorum cohortem a Caesaribus olim ad custodiam corporis institutam multisque experimentis fidelissimam dissolvit ac sine commodo ullo remisit in patriam, quasi Cn. Dolabellae, iuxta cuius hortos tendebat, proniorem. Illa quoque verene an falso 3 per ludibrium iactabantur, adposita lautiore cena ingemuisse eum, et ordinario quidem dispensatori breviarium rationum offerenti paropsidem leguminis pro sedulitate ac diligentia porrexisse, Cano autem choraulae mire placenti denarios quinque donasse prolatos manu sua e peculiaribus loculis suis.

13] Quare adventus eius non perinde gratus fuit, idque proximo spectaculo apparuit, siquidem Atellanis notissimum canticum exorsis:

"Venit Onesimus a villa"

cuncti simul spectatores consentiente voce reliquam partem rettulerunt ac saepius versu repetito egerunt.

14] Maiore adeo et favore et auctoritate adeptus est quam gessit imperium, 1 quanquam multa documenta egregii principis daret; sed nequaquam tam grata erant, quam invisa quae secus fierent.

wearing a toga until he had removed those who had plotted against him – Nymphidius Sabinus, the prefect of the praetorian guard in Rome, and the governors, Fonteius Capito in Germany and Clodius Macer in Africa.

12] A reputation for cruelty and stinginess went before him; it was reported that 1 he had punished some of the communities in the Spanish and Gallic provinces which had been slow to come out in support of him; he had levied heavier taxes, in some cases he had razed their walls, and he had even put to death some army-officers and imperial officials together with their wives and children. What is more, it was even said that he had melted down the golden crown from an ancient temple of Jupiter which had been presented to him by the people of Tarraco, and, finding it three ounces underweight, had ordered the shortfall to be exacted from them.

From the moment he entered Rome, this reputation was confirmed and 2 enhanced; the oarsmen from the navy, whom Nero had promoted from oarsmen to regular soldiers, he ordered to return to their original status. They objected and made persistent demands for a legionary eagle and standards; at this he not only had their meeting broken up with a cavalry-charge, but literally decimated them as well. There was also a cohort of German soldiers which had been formed years before by the Caesars to act as a personal bodyguard. It had proved its great loyalty on many occasions when put to the test, but Galba now disbanded it, and sent it back to Germany with no gratuity, on the grounds that it was too favourably disposed to Gnaeus Dolabella, near whose estate it had its camp.

Although it is not certain whether they were true or false, stories were 3 circulated to ridicule him; for example, when a rather lavish banquet was served before him, he groaned, or again when his steward presented him with a summary of the accounts, he rewarded the poor man's unstinting efforts with a plate of beans; or finally when Canus the flute-player had given him especial pleasure, he presented him with five *denarii* out of his own private purse.

13] For these reasons his arrival in Rome was not an occasion for particular pleasure, and this was clearly demonstrated at the first theatrical show. The actors in the Atellan farce struck up the song, "Onesimus is back, back from the farm"; instantly the whole audience with one voice completed the rest of it, repeating that line over and over again.

14] He gained more favour and respect in his winning of power than he did in 1 the exercise of it, although he provided many examples of what an excellent emperor he was. These excited a level of approval far lower than the disapproval excited by acts of a different nature.

Regebatur trium arbitrio, quos una et intra Palatium habitantis nec umquam 2 non adhaerentis paedagogos vulgo vocabant. Ii erant T. Vinius legatus eius in Hispania, cupiditatis immensae; Cornelius Laco ex assessore praefectus praetorii, arrogantia socordiaque intolerabilis; libertus Icelus, paulo ante anulis aureis et Marciani cognomine ornatus ac iam summae equestris gradus candidatus. His diverso vitiorum genere grassantibus adeo se abutendum permisit et tradidit, ut vix sibi ipse constaret, modo acerbior parciorque, modo remissior ac neglegentior quam conveniret principi electo atque illud aetatis.

Quosdam claros ex utroque ordine viros suspicione minima inauditos 3 condemnavit. Civitates R. raro dedit, iura trium liberorum vix uni atque alteri ac ne iis quidem nisi ad certum praefinitumque tempus. Iudicibus sextam decuriam adici precantibus non modo negavit, sed et concessum a Claudio beneficium, ne hieme initioque anni ad iudicandum evocarentur, eripuit.

15] Existimabatur etiam senatoria et equestria officia bienni spatio 1 determinaturus nec daturus nisi invitis ac recusantibus. Liberalitates Neronis non plus decimis concessis per quinquaginta equites R. ea condicione revocandas curavit exigendasque, ut et si quid scaenici ac xystici donatum olim vendidissent, auferretur emptoribus, quando illi pretio absumpto solvere nequirent. At contra 2 nihil non per comites atque libertos pretio addici aut donari gratia passus est, vectigalia immunitates, poenas innocentium impunitates noxiorum. Quin etiam populo R. deposcente supplicium Haloti et Tigillini solos ex omnibus Neronis emissariis vel maleficentissimos incolumes praestitit atque insuper Halotum procuratione amplissima ornavit, pro Tigillino etiam saevitiae populum edicto increpuit.

16] Per haec prope universis ordinibus offensis vel praecipua flagrabat invidia 1 apud milites. Nam cum in verba eius absentis iurantibus donativum grandius

He was under the control of three men; because they lived in the palace with 2 him and never left his side, they were called his "childminders". These men were Titus Vinius, his aide in Spain who was a man of limitless greed; Cornelius Laco who had been promoted from the job of judge's assistant to become prefect of the praetorian guard, and he was a man of unbearable arrogance and idleness; and finally there was his ex-slave, Icelus; this man had shortly before been awarded the gold rings and the surname Marcianus, and was now a candidate for the highest post on the equestrian career-ladder. Each of these men occupied himself in a different kind of criminality, and Galba surrendered himself so completely to and was so used by them that his behaviour appeared inconsistent. At one moment he was rather harsh and mean; at the next he was too slack and careless for a man of his age, let alone one who had been chosen to be emperor. He condemned a number of well-known senators and equestrians on very slight 3 evidence and giving them no opportunity to defend themselves. He rarely made awards of Roman citizenship, whilst the privileges normally given to those with three children were awarded to a mere one or two men, and then only for a limited period which was fixed in advance. When the jurymen petitioned for the addition of a sixth panel, he not only refused, but also cancelled the concession given to them by Claudius, that they were not summoned to give judgements during the winter and at the beginning of the year.

15] It is thought, too, that he wished to limit to a two-year period the tenure of 1 senatorial and equestrian posts, and to give them only to those who did not want them or who refused them. He set up a commission of fifty Roman knights to cancel and recover the gifts handed out by Nero, allowing the beneficiaries to retain no more than ten percent of them. He also made a particular provision that if actors and athletes had sold anything that had been given to them, it should be recovered from the purchasers in those cases where the original recipients had spent the purchase-money and could not refund it.

In contrast, there was nothing which he did not allow his retinue and ex- 2 slaves to sell at a price or give as a favour; this included tax-collections, exemptions from taxes, punishing the innocent and letting off the guilty. Indeed, when the people demanded the executions of Halotus and Tigellinus, who were easily the worst of Nero's agents, Galba singled them out for his protection; what is more, he gave Halotus a choice-procuratorship, and in an edict castigated the people for their cruelty to Tigellinus.

16] Through such actions he angered almost all sections of the community, 1 though resentment burnt most strongly in the army. For the commanders had promised an abnormally large donative to those soldiers who swore allegiance

solito praepositi pronuntiassent, neque ratam rem habuit et subinde iactavit legere se militem, non emere consuesse; atque eo quidem nomine omnis, qui ubique erant, exacerbavit. Ceterum praetorianos etiam metu et indignitate commovit, removens subinde plerosque ut suspectos et Nymphidi socios. Sed 2 maxime fremebat superioris Germaniae exercitus fraudari se praemiis navatae adversus Gallos et Vindicem operae. Ergo primi obsequium rumpere ausi Kal. Ian. adigi sacramento nisi in nomen senatus recusarunt statimque legationem ad praetorianos cum mandatis destinaverunt: displicere imperatorem in Hispania factum; eligerent ipsi quem cuncti exercitus comprobarent.

17] Quod ut nuntiatum est, despectui esse non tam senectam suam quam orbitatem ratus, Pisonem Frugi Licinianum nobilem egregiumque iuvenem ac sibi olim probatissimum testamentoque semper in bona et nomen adscitum repente e media salutantium turba adprehendit filiumque appellans perduxit in castra ac pro contione adoptavit, ne tunc quidem donativi ulla mentione facta. Quo faciliorem occasionem M. Salvio Othoni praebuit perficiendi conata intra sextum adoptionis diem.

18] Magna et assidua monstra iam inde a principio exitum ei, qualis evenit, 1 portenderant. Cum per omne iter dextra sinistraque oppidatim victimae caederentur, taurus securis ictu consternatus rupto vinculo essedum eius invasit elatisque pedibus totum cruore perfudit; ac descendentem speculator impulsu turbae lancea prope vulneravit. Urbem quoque et deinde Palatium ingressum excepit terrae tremor et assimilis quidam mugitui sonus. Secuta sunt aliquanto 2 manifestiora. Monile margaritis gemmisque consertum ad ornandam Fortunam suam Tusculanam ex omni gaza secreverat; id repente quasi augustiore dignius loco Capitolinae Veneri dedicavit, ac proxima nocte somniavit speciem Fortunae querentis fraudatam se dono destinato, minantisque erepturam et ipsam quae dedisset. Cumque exterritus luce prima ad expiandum somnium, praemissis qui rem divinam apparent, Tusculum excucurrisset, nihil invenit praeter tepidam

to Galba in his absence, but the emperor refused to confirm it and frequently boasted that it was his practice to levy soldiers, not buy them. This aggravated the troops in all parts of the empire; but he caused the praetorians particular fear and anger, for he would often remove some of their number on the grounds that he suspected them of being allies of Nymphidius Sabinus.

However, the Upper German army was particularly indignant that it had 2 been robbed of its just rewards for having defeated Vindex and his Gallic mercenaries. So they were the first to venture as far as breaking their allegiance, refusing on new year's day to take an oath to anyone except the senate. Straightaway, they sent representatives to the praetorians with the message that they had no time for an emperor who was created in Spain, and that the praetorians should choose one who would suit all the armies.

17] When Galba heard of this, he reckoned that it was not so much his advanced age that made people look down on him, as the fact that he had no son and heir. So, from the midst of his morning-callers he picked out Piso Frugi Licinianus, a young aristocrat with a blameless reputation, whom he liked very much, and had long ago made heir to his property and name. He referred to him as his son, took him to the praetorian guard's camp and publicly adopted him; once again no mention was made of a donative. This gave Marcus Salvius Otho a better chance to bring his plans to fruition within six days of the adoption.

18] From the outset of his reign a steady stream of significant omens portended 1 an end like that which he actually suffered. For the whole length of his route from Spain to Italy, in town after town, sacrificial victims were slaughtered on the right hand and on the left; at one, a bull, crazed by a blow from the axe, broke away and charged at Galba's chariot; raising its feet, it saturated him with its blood. What is more, as Galba alighted from the chariot, one of his bodyguards, pushed forward by the crowd, almost speared him. Later, as he reached the city and entered the palace, there was an earth-tremor, accompanied by a bellowing-sound.

After this, there were signs whose significance was clearer still. There was 2 a necklace, encrusted with pearls and other jewels, which he had kept back from all the treasure he had amassed and with which he intended to adorn his private statue of Fortuna at Tusculum; at the last minute, on the ground that it deserved a more hallowed place, he dedicated it to Venus on the Capitolium. Next night, he dreamt that Fortuna came to him complaining that she had been robbed of a gift intended for her and threatening that she, too, would take back her gift to him. Galba was terrified, and at dawn, in order to avert the threatened calamity, sent on men to prepare a sacrifice, and himself then hurried to Tusculum. When

in ara favillam atratumque iuxta senem in catino vitreo tus tenentem et in calice
fictili merum. Observatum etiam est Kal. Ian. sacrificanti coronam de capite 3
excidisse, auspicanti pullos avolasse; adoptionis die neque milites adlocuturo
castrensem sellam de more positam pro tribunali oblitis ministris et in senatu
curulem perverse collocatam.

19] Prius vero quam occideretur sacrificantem mane haruspex identidem 1
monuit, caveret periculum, non longe percussores abesse.

Haud multo post cognoscit teneri castra ab Othone, ac plerisque ut eodem
quam primum pergeret suadentibus – posse enim auctoritate et praesentia
praevalere – nihil amplius quam continere se statuit et legionariorum firmare
praesidiis, qui multifariam diverseque tendebant. Loricam tamen induit linteam,
quanquam haud dissimulans parum adversus tot mucrones profuturam. Sed 2
extractus rumoribus falsis, quos conspirati, ut eum in publicum elicerent, de
industria dissiparant, paucis temere affirmantibus transactum negotium,
oppressos, qui tumultuarentur, advenire frequentis ceteros gratulabundos et in
omne obsequium paratos, iis ut occurreret prodiit tanta fiducia, ut militi cuidam
occisum a se Othonem glorianti: "Quo auctore?" responderit, atque in Forum
usque processit. Ibi equites, quibus mandata caedes erat, cum per publicum
dimota paganorum turba equos adegissent, viso procul eo parumper restiterunt;
dein rursum incitati desertum a suis contrucidarunt.

20] Sunt qui tradant, ad primum tumultum proclamasse eum: "Quid agitis 1
commilitones? Ego vester sum et vos mei," donativum etiam pollicitum. Plures
autem prodiderunt optulisse ultro iugulum et ut hoc agerent ac ferirent, quando
ita videretur, hortatum. Illud mirum admodum fuerit, neque praesentium
quemquam opem imperatori ferre conatum et omnes qui arcesserentur sprevisse
nuntium excepta Germanicianorum vexillatione. Ii ob recens meritum, quod se
aegros et invalidos magno opere fovisset, in auxilium advolaverunt, sed serius
itinere devio per ignorantiam locorum retardati.

he got there he found nothing except a pile of warm ashes on the altar, and beside it an old man dressed in black holding the incense in a glass dish and the wine in an earthenware cup. It was also noticed that on January 1st, when he was 3 conducting sacrifice, the garland fell from his head, and when he was taking the auspices the sacred chickens flew off; further, on the day of Piso's adoption, when he was about to address the soldiers, the servants forgot to put in place the camp-stool, usually set at the front of the dais; and in the senate-house his state-chair was knocked aside.

19] On the morning of his murder he was sacrificing, when a soothsayer gave 1 him repeated warnings to be on the look-out for danger, as assassins were close at hand. Not long after this he heard that the praetorian camp was in Otho's hands; many of his associates advised him that he too should go there as soon as possible, on the ground that his status and presence would ensure his success. But he decided that he would simply stay in the palace and protect himself with a bodyguard formed from legionary soldiers who were billeted in various parts of the city. He put on a linen tunic, although he made no secret of the fact that it would offer him little protection against so many swords.

But he was enticed out of his safe retreat by false stories which the conspirators had deliberately put about for this purpose: a few even rashly asserted that the affair was over, the conspiracy suppressed, and that everyone else was converging on the palace to offer him congratulations and total loyalty. Thus, he left the palace to meet them, so full of confidence, that to a soldier who boasted that he had killed Otho, Galba replied, "on whose authority?" He got as far as the forum; there, some horsemen who had been given the job of 2 assassinating him, drove their horses through the streets, scattering the crowds in their path. When they saw Galba in the distance they halted for a moment; then they picked up speed again and slaughtered him, now deserted by all his associates.

20] Some report that at the first sign of disturbance, he shouted out, "My fellow-soldiers, what are you doing? I am yours and you are mine"; he even promised a donative. The more usual story, however, is that he bared his throat and encouraged them to do their work and strike him down, since that is what they thought right. The most surprising feature was that none of those present tried to help their emperor and that all who had been summoned to Galba's aid ignored the message, except for a detachment from the German army. Because 1 of recent kindnesses he had shown them when they were sick and weak, they flew to his aid, but came too late: they were delayed by the roundabout-route which they took out of their ignorance of the city's landmarks.

Iugulatus est ad lacum Curti ac relictus ita uti erat, donec gregarius miles 2 a frumentatione rediens abiecto onere caput ei amputavit; et quoniam capillo arripere non poterat, in gremium abdidit, mox inserto per os pollice ad Othonem detulit. Ille lixis calonibusque donavit, qui hasta suffixum non sine ludibrio circum castra portarunt adclamantes identidem: "Galba Cupido, fruaris aetate tua," maxime irritati ad talem iocorum petulantiam, quod ante paucos dies exierat in vulgus, laudanti cuidam formam suam ut adhuc floridam et vegetam respondisse eum:

ʺΕτι μοι μένος ἔμπεδόν ἐστιν.

Ab iis Patrobii Neroniani libertus centum aureis redemptum eo loco, ubi iussu Galbae animadversum in patronum suum fuerat, abiecit. Sero tandem dispensator Argivus et hoc et ceterum truncum in privatis eius hortis Aurelia via sepulturae dedit.

21] Statura fuit iusta, capite praecalvo, oculis caeruleis, adunco naso, manibus pedibusque articulari morbo distortissimis, ut neque calceum perpeti nec libellos evolvere aut tenere omnino valeret. Excreverat etiam in dexteriore latere eius caro praependebatque adeo ut aegre fascia substringeretur.

22] Cibi plurimi traditur, quem tempore hiberno etiam ante lucem capere consuerat, inter cenam vero usque eo abundantis, ut congestas super manus reliquias circumferri iuberet spargique ad pedes stantibus. Libidinis in mares pronior et eos non nisi praeduros exoletosque; ferebant in Hispania Icelum e veteribus concubinis de Neronis exitu nuntiantem non modo artissimis osculis palam exceptum ab eo, sed ut sine mora velleretur oratum atque seductum.

23] Periit tertio et septuagesimo aetatis anno, imperii mense septimo. Senatus, ut primum licitum est, statuam ei decreverat rostratae columnae superstantem in parte Fori, qua trucidatus est; sed decretum Vespasianus abolevit, percussores sibi ex Hispania in Iudaeam submisisse opinatus.

He was murdered by the Lacus Curtius, and was left as he had fallen, until 2 an ordinary soldier returning from a foraging-expedition, put down his load and cut the head from Galba's body. Since he could not catch hold of it by the hair, he hid it in his tunic, and later put his thumb in the mouth and took the head to Otho. Otho gave it to the camp-servants, who fixed it on a spear-point and laughingly carried it round the camp, repeatedly shouting, "Galba, my desire, enjoy the fruits of your youth"; they were provoked into this contempt because a few days before a story had gone the rounds that when someone had praised the still youthful vigour of his appearance, he had quoted the line, "My vigour is undiminished still".

An ex-slave of Patrobius Neronianus bought the head from them for one hundred *aurei*, and threw it into the place where by Galba's own order his patron had been executed. Later, Galba's steward, Argivus, collected the head and the rest of the body and gave them burial on Galba's estate by the side of the Aurelian Way.

21] He was of medium height, completely bald, with blue eyes and a hooked nose; his hands and feet were disfigured by gout, so that he could not bear to wear shoes or unroll a scroll or even hold it. On his right side, his flesh was so badly ruptured that it hung down so far that it could scarcely be supported by a truss.

22] He is said to have had a colossal appetite for food, and in winter would have his breakfast even before daybreak; at dinner there was so much food that he ordered the left-overs to be gathered up in huge handfuls and distributed to the table-servants. He had homosexual tendencies, and preferred those who were mature in years and very strong. The story is told of him in Spain that when his long-standing lover, Icelus, told him of Nero's death, Galba not only smothered him with passionate kisses, but begged him to be shaved smooth and seduced him on the spot.

23] Galba was in his seventy-third year when he died, and had been emperor for nearly seven months. As soon as it was able, the senate had decreed that a statue to him should be erected on a beaked column already standing in that part of the forum where he had been murdered. Vespasian, however, reversed the decree, because he thought that Galba had secretly sent assassins from Spain to Judaea to kill him.

OTHO

1] Maiores Othonis orti sunt oppido Ferentio, familia vetere et honorata atque 1
ex principibus Etruriae. Avus M. Salvius Otho, patre equite R., matre humili
incertum an ingenua, per gratiam Liviae Augustae, in cuius domo creverat,
senator est factus nec praeturae gradum excessit.

Pater L. Otho, materno genere praeclaro multarumque et magnarum 2
propinquitatium, tam carus tamque non absimilis facie Tiberio principi fuit, ut
plerique procreatum ex eo crederent. Urbanos honores, proconsulatum Africae
et extraordinaria imperia severissime administravit. Ausus etiam est in Illyrico
milites quosdam, quod motu Camilli ex paenitentia praepositos suos quasi
defectionis adversus Claudium auctores occiderant, capite punire et quidem
ante principia se coram, quamvis ob id ipsum promotos in ampliorem gradum
a Claudio sciret. Quo facto sicut gloriam auxit, ita gratiam minuit; quam tamen 3
mature reciperavit detecta equitis R. fraude, quem prodentibus servis necem
Claudio parare compererat. Namque et senatus honore rarissimo, statua in
Palatio posita, prosecutus est eum et Claudius adlectum inter patricios conlaudans
amplissimis verbis hoc quoque adiecit: "Vir, quo meliores liberos habere ne
opto quidem." Ex Albia Terentia splendida femina duos filios tulit, L. Titianum
et minorem M. cognominem sibi; tulit et filiam, quam vixdum nubilem Druso
Germanici filio despondit.

2] Otho imperator IIII. Kal. Mai. natus est Camillo Arruntio Domitio 1
Ahenobarbo cons. A prima adulescentia prodigus ac procax, adeo ut saepe
flagris obiurgaretur a patre, ferebatur et vagari noctibus solitus atque invalidum
quemque obviorum vel potulentum corripere ac distento sago impositum in
sublime iactare. Post patris deinde mortem libertinam aulicam gratiosam, quo 2
efficacius coleret, etiam diligere simulavit quamvis anum ac paene decrepitam;
per hanc insinuatus Neroni facile summum inter amicos locum tenuit

OTHO

1] Otho's family came from the town of Ferentium; it was old and respected, 1 and derived ultimately from Etruscan kings. His grandfather was Marcus Salvius Otho, whose father was of the equestrian order, but whose mother was of low birth – perhaps even a slave's daughter. The grandfather was made a senator by the influence of Livia Augusta, in whose house he had been brought up: but he did not progress beyond the rank of praetor.

His father was Lucius Otho, whose mother's family was aristocratic, and 2 who had many influential connections. He was a favourite of the emperor Tiberius, and so like him in appearance, that it was widely believed that he was, in fact, Tiberius' son. He was very strict in his conduct of a number of posts in Rome, the proconsulship of Africa and some extraordinary commands. He even had the courage to execute some soldiers in Illyricum who, during Camillus' rebellion, had regretted their complicity and murdered their officers for having stirred up the rebellion against Claudius; what is more, he had this sentence carried out in his presence in front of his headquarters, although he was well aware that they had been promoted by the emperor for their action.

He enhanced his reputation by this, though he lost favour at court. But he 3 quickly regained this too when he uncovered the treachery of a member of the equestrian order, who was betrayed by his slaves and found to be plotting the emperor's death. For this he received an unusual distinction from the senate – a statue on the Palatine hill; Claudius made him a patrician, and added the highly flattering comment that Otho was a man whom he would not wish even his own children to excel. His marriage to the well-born Albia Terentia produced two sons, Lucius Titianus, and a younger one, Marcus, who bore his father's surname. They also had a daughter who, whilst still a child, was engaged to Drusus, the son of Germanicus.

2] The future emperor, Otho, was born on April 28th when Camillus Arruntius 1 and Domitius Ahenobarbus were consuls. From his earliest youth he was such a spender and so wild that he was often beaten by his father; he was said to have been in the habit of wandering the city at night, and grabbing any weak or drunken person he encountered; Otho would put him in a stretched-out cloak and toss him in the air.

Later, after his father's death, he wanted to cultivate an influential freed- 2 woman at court; to do this he pretended to be devoted to her even though she was elderly and almost on her last legs. By her influence he wormed his way into

congruentmorum, ut vero quidam tradunt, et consuetudine mutui stupri. Ac
tantum potentia valuit, ut damnatum repetundis consularem virum, ingens
praemium pactus, prius quam plane restitutionem ei impetrasset, non dubitaret
in senatum ad agendas gratias introducere.

3] Omnium autem consiliorum secretorumque particeps die, quem necandae 1
matri Nero destinarat, ad avertendas suspiciones cenam utrique exquisitissimae
comitatis dedit; item Poppaeam Sabinam tunc adhuc amicam eius, abductam
marito demandatamque interim sibi, nuptiarum specie recepit nec corrupisse
contentus adeo dilexit, ut ne rivalem quidem Neronem aequo tulerit animo.
Creditur certe non modo missos ad arcessendam non recepisse, sed ipsum etiam 2
exclusisse quondam pro foribus astantem miscentemque frustra minas et preces
ac depositum reposcentem. Quare diducto matrimonio sepositus est per causam
legationis in Lusitaniam. Et satis visum, ne poena acrior mimum omnem
divulgaret, qui tamen sic quoque hoc disticho enotuit:

"Cur Otho mentito sit, quaeritis, exsul honore?

Uxoris moechus coeperat esse suae."

Provinciam administravit quaestorius per decem annos, moderatione atque
abstinentia singulari.

4] Ut tandem occasio ultionis data est, conatibus Galbae primus accessit; 1
eodemque momento et ipse spem imperii cepit magnam quidem et ex condicione
temporum, sed aliquanto maiorem ex affirmatione Seleuci mathematici. Qui
cum eum olim superstitem Neroni fore spopondisset, tunc ultro inopinatus
advenerat imperaturum quoque brevi repromittens.

Nullo igitur officii aut ambitionis in quemquam genere omisso, quotiens 2
cena principem acciperet, aureos excubanti cohorti viritim dividebat, nec minus
alium alia via militum demerebatur; cuidam etiam de parte finium cum vicino

Nero's favour, and because of the similarity in their characters found no difficulty in holding the premier place amongst the emperor's entourage. Some even suggest that this was due to the fact that Otho and Nero seduced each other. So potent was his influence that he had no qualms about bringing into the senate-house an ex-consul who had been condemned for extortion; Otho agreed on a huge sum as a consideration, even though he had not yet succeeded in gaining the man a full restoration.

3] He became the confidant of all of the emperor's plans and secret ideas: thus, 1 on the day which Nero had marked down to murder his mother, to avert suspicion the emperor invited both Agrippina and Otho to a dinner which was unsurpassed for its jovial atmosphere. At the same time, Otho went through a kind of marriage with Poppaea Sabina. She was the mistress of Nero who had taken her from her husband and entrusted her to Otho for the time-being, as it were. Seducing her, however, was not enough, and Otho became so infatuated with her that he could not bear even Nero as a rival.

There is at any rate a story that he locked his doors against Nero's men who 2 had been sent to fetch Poppaea: not only that, but on one occasion even kept Nero himself outside his front door vainly mingling threats and pleading for the return of the property he had put into Otho's safe-keeping. So Otho and Poppaea were divorced and Otho was sent to Lusitania under the guise of the governorship of that province. Nero contented himself with this, worried that a more severe punishment might have brought the whole farce into the light of day. None-theless, the story was celebrated in the following verse:

"Why, you may ask, is Otho an exile under pretence of promotion?
Why? He had begun to seduce his own wife."

He governed his province as an ex-quaestor for ten years, and won a reputation of outstanding moderation and restraint.

4] At length the chance of revenge presented itself, and Otho was the first to 1 join Galba's conspiracy. At the very same time he conceived a hope of winning power for himself; this hope sprang partly from the state of the times, but even more from an assurance he had received from Seleucus, the astrologer. Years before, this man had guaranteed to Otho that he would outlive Nero, but then had come to him of his own free will and further promised that Otho would become emperor – and quite soon.

As a result, Otho used every opportunity to show attention to and seek 2 popularity with everyone; whenever he entertained the emperor to dinner, he gave an *aureus* to each man on guard-duty; he was no less assiduous in putting the soldiers under obligation to him in a variety of ways. On one occasion, Otho

litiganti adhibitus arbiter totum agrum redemit emancipavitque, ut iam vix ullus esset, qui non et sentiret et praedicaret solum successione imperii dignum.

5]   Speraverat autem fore ut adoptaretur a Galba, idque in dies exspectabat. 1 Sed postquam Pisone praelato spe decidit, ad vim conversus est instigante super animi dolorem etiam magnitudine aeris alieni. Neque enim dissimulabat, nisi principem se stare non posse, nihilque referre ab hoste in acie an in Foro sub creditoribus caderet. Ante paucos dies servo Caesaris pro impetrata dispensatione 2 decies sestertium expresserat; hoc subsidium tanti coepti fuit.   Ac primo quinque speculatoribus commissa res est, deinde decem aliis, quos singuli binos produxerant; omnibus dena sestertia repraesentata et quinquagena promissa. Per hos sollicitati reliqui, nec adeo multi, haud dubia fiducia in ipso negotio pluris adfuturos.

6]   Tulerat animus post adoptionem statim castra occupare cenantemque in 1 Palatio Galbam adgredi, sed obstitit respectus cohortis, quae tunc excubabat, ne oneraretur invidia, quod eiusdem statione et Gaius fuerat occisus et desertus Nero. Medium quoque tempus religio et Seleucus exemit.

Ergo destinata die praemonitis consciis, ut se in Foro sub aede Saturni ad 2 miliarium aureum opperirentur, mane Galbam salutavit, utque consueverat osculo exceptus, etiam sacrificanti interfuit audivitque praedicta haruspicis. Deinde liberto adesse architectos nuntiante, quod signum convenerat, quasi venalem domum inspecturus abscessit proripuitque se postica parte Palati ad constitutum.   Alii febrem simulasse aiunt eamque excusationem proximis mandasse, si quaereretur.   Tunc abditus propere muliebri sella in castra 3 contendit ac deficientibus lecticariis cum descendisset cursumque cepisset, laxato calceo restitit, donec omissa mora succollatus et a praesente comitatu

was called upon to arbitrate in the case of a man who had gone to law with his neighbour in a boundary-dispute; Otho bought the whole plot, and gave it to the man. As a result, there was hardly anyone who did not believe that Otho was the only man deserving to succeed Galba; and they were prepared to say as much openly.

5]   His hope had been that Galba would adopt him as successor, and every day 1 he expected it to happen. Galba's preference for Piso, however, dispelled that hope, and Otho turned to violence, spurred on partly by resentment, but also by his massive debts. He made no pretence of the fact that (as he said himself) he would not be able to stay on his feet unless he became emperor, and that it made no difference to him whether he fell in battle at the hands of his enemies, or in the forum at the hands of his creditors.

A few days earlier he had extracted one million *sestertii* from one of the 2 emperor's slaves in return for gaining a stewardship for him; this sum was a great help in financing an undertaking of such a size. To begin with, the project was confided to five guardsmen, then to a further ten, as each of the original five introduced two more. To each of them he gave ten thousand *sestertii* and promised fifty thousand more. These men were responsible for drawing in others – though not many; they were confident, however, that more would join when the call to action came.

6]   His intention had been to seize the camp of the praetorian guard immedi- 1 ately after Piso's adoption, and to kill Galba whilst he was dining in the palace. But he changed his mind because he did not want to burden with guilt the unit of the guard which was then on duty: for the same unit had been on guard when Caligula was murdered and when Nero was deserted. A further delay was then caused by the warnings which Seleucus gave him about the omens.

So he fixed a day; and when it came, he first warned his accomplices to wait 2 for him in the forum, near the temple of Saturn at the golden mile-stone. Then in the morning he went to pay his respects to Galba, and was as usual received with a kiss; he stayed whilst Galba was at sacrifice to listen to what the soothsayer predicted. Then an ex-slave of his told him that the architects had arrived – a pre-arranged signal – , and he went off on the pretence of inspecting a house which was up for sale. He ran out through the rear of the palace to the agreed meeting-point. Another story has it that he pretended to be ill and told his confidants to use that as an excuse, if questions were asked.

He then quickly hid himself in a women's carriage, and made for the 3 guards' camp, but the bearers flagged and he got out and ran. He had to stop because his shoe came undone, and to avoid any further delay those with him

imperator consalutatus inter faustas adclamationes strictosque gladios ad principia devenit, obvio quoque non aliter ac si conscius et particeps foret adhaerente. Ibi missis qui Galbam et Pisonem trucidarent, ad conciliandos pollicitationibus militum animos nihil magis pro contione testatus est, quam id demum se habiturum, quod sibi illi reliquissent.

7] Dein vergente iam die ingressus senatum positaque brevi ratione quasi 1 raptus de publico et suscipere imperium vi coactus gesturusque communi omnium arbitrio, Palatium petit. Ac super ceteras gratulantium adulantiumque blanditias ab infima plebe appellatus Nero nullum indicium recusantis dedit, immo, ut quidam tradiderunt, etiam diplomatibus primisque epistulis suis ad quosdam provinciarum praesides Neronis cognomen adiecit. Certe et imagines statuasque eius reponi passus est et procuratores atque libertos ad eadem officia revocavit, nec quicquam prius pro potestate subscripsit quam quingenties sestertium ad peragendam Auream Domum.

Dicitur ea nocte per quietem pavefactus gemitus maximos edidisse 2 repertusque a concursantibus humi ante lectum iacens per omnia piaculorum genera Manes Galbae, a quo deturbari expellique se viderat, propitiare temptasse; postridie quoque in augurando tempestate orta graviter prolapsum identidem obmurmurasse:

Τί γάρ μοι καὶ μακροῖς αὐλοῖς;

8] Sub idem vero tempus Germaniciani exercitus in Vitelli verba iurarant. 1 Quod ut comperit, auctor senatui fuit mittendae legationis, quae doceret electum iam principem, quietem concordiamque suaderet; et tamen per internuntios ac litteras consortem imperii generumque se Vitellio optulit. Verum haud dubio bello iamque ducibus et copiis, quas Vitellius praemiserat, appropinquantibus animum fidemque erga se praetorianorum paene internecione amplissimi ordinis expertus est. Placuerat per classiarios arma transferri remittique 2 navibus; ea cum in castris sub noctem promerentur, insidias quidam suspicati tumultum excitaverunt; ac repente omnes nullo certo duce in Palatium cucurrerunt

raised him on their shoulders and saluted him as emperor. To a chorus of favourable acclamations of men with drawn swords, he finally reached the headquarters of the camp: all who met him on the way joined him as if they knew what was going on and supported him. Men were then sent to murder Galba and Piso, whilst Otho addressed the troops, and made just one promise to win them over – that he would be satisfied with whatever position that they decided to give him.

7] Later, as evening was drawing in, he went to the senate-house, and in a brief 1 account of events, he made out that he had been accosted in the street and forced to become emperor; he would comply, he said, because the proposal commanded general agreement. He then made for the palace. He was generally flattered and congratulated, but by the ordinary people he was hailed as Nero; nor did he give any sign of objecting to this. On the contrary, some have alleged that in his official letters and travel-documents sent to certain provincial governors, he actually added 'Nero' to his name. At any rate, he allowed Nero's statues to be set up again, and restored all of Nero's procurators and ex-slaves to their former jobs; indeed, the first official requisition which he signed as emperor was one for fifty million *sestertii* for the completion of the Golden House. The same night, it is said, he was terrified in his sleep and uttered terrible groans; his 2 servants came running in and found him lying on the floor by his bed. He tried every means to appease the spirit of Galba, by which he saw himself attacked and removed. The following day, he was taking the auspices when a violent storm blew up; he is said to have collapsed to the ground, uttering occasionally in Greek, "What have I to do with long pipes?"

8] At about this same time, the armies in Germany had sworn their allegiance 1 to Vitellius; when Otho heard this he proposed to the senate that a delegation be sent to inform them that an emperor had already been chosen, and to advise them that they should peacefully accept this. Despite this, he also sent letters and personal approaches to Vitellius suggesting that they should share power and that he would marry Vitellius' daughter. But when it became clear that war was inevitable, and that the generals and troops whom Vitellius had sent on ahead were already approaching, he received proof of the praetorians' loyalty to and support for him in an incident which nearly involved the destruction of the senatorial order.

It had been decided that some arms should be entrusted to the marines to 2 transport by ship; these were being handed out in the camp at night when some, suspecting treachery, became violent. Suddenly, all of them without a clear leader rushed to the palace demanding that all senators be put to death. Some

caedem senatus flagitantes, repulsisque tribunorum qui inhibere temptabant, nonnullis et occisis, sic ut erant cruenti, ubinam imperator esset requirentes perruperunt in triclinium usque nec nisi viso destiterunt.

Expeditionem autem inpigre atque etiam praepropere incohavit, nulla ne 3 religionum quidem cura, sed et motis necdum conditis ancilibus, quod antiquitus infaustum habetur, et die, quo cultores deum Matris lamentari et plangere incipiunt, praeterea adversissimis auspiciis. Nam et victima Diti patri caesa litavit, cum tali sacrificio contraria exta potiora sint, et primo egressu inundationibus Tiberis retardatus ad vicensimum etiam lapidem ruina aedificiorum praeclusam viam offendit.

9] Simili temeritate, quamvis dubium nemini esset quin trahi bellum oporteret, 1 quando et fame et angustiis locorum urgeretur hostis, quam primum tamen decertare statuit, sive impatiens longioris sollicitudinis speransque ante Vitelli adventum profligari plurimum posse, sive impar militum ardori pugnam deposcentium. Nec ulli pugnae affuit substititque Brixelli.

Et tribus quidem, verum mediocribus proeliis apud Alpes circaque 2 Placentiam et ad Castoris, quod loco nomen est, vicit; novissimo maximoque apud Betriacum fraude superatus est, cum spe conloquii facta, quasi ad condicionem pacis militibus eductis, ex inproviso atque in ipsa consalutatione dimicandum fuisset. Ac statim moriendi impetum cepit, ut multi nec frustra 3 opinantur, magis pudore, ne tanto rerum hominumque periculo dominationem sibi asserere perseveraret, quam desperatione ulla aut diffidentia copiarum; quippe residuis integrisque etiam nunc quas secum ad secundos casus detinuerat, et supervenientibus aliis e Dalmatia Pannoniaque et Moesia, ne victis quidem adeo afflictis ut non in ultionem ignominiae quidvis discriminis ultro et vel solae subirent.

10] Interfuit huic bello pater meus Suetonius Laetus, tertiae decimae legionis 1

of the tribunes tried to stop them, but these were pushed aside, and some were actually fatally wounded; so covered in blood as they were, they forced their way into the dining-hall, demanding to know where the emperor was. They did not calm down until they had seen him.

He started his campaign vigorously – indeed, one might say, over-hastily; 3 for he took no note even of religious considerations: the sacred shields had been removed and not yet returned to their proper place, and this from time immemorial had been held to be a very unlucky sign. Moreover, this was on the very day that the devotees of Cybele traditionally began their wailings and lamentations. In addition, the auspices proved most unfavourable; for a victim sacrificed to Dis the Father provided lucky signs, although in a sacrifice like this entrails which exhibited sinister signs were preferable. Indeed, the moment he made to leave the city he was held up by flooding of the Tiber, and later twenty miles out he found the road closed by collapsed buildings.

9] No-one was in any doubt that the proper course of action was to employ 1 delaying-tactics in the war, since the enemy were hard pressed by a shortage of food, and by their cramped position. Nevertheless, Otho exhibited the same haste as before; he decided to precipitate a battle at the first opportunity: it is possible that the prospect of longer delay worried him and that he hoped to settle the main issue before Vitellius' own arrival. Alternatively, he may have been unable to control the eagerness of his troops' demands for battle. In any case, he did not himself stay for the battle, but remained behind at Brixellum.

In three encounters, albeit minor ones, in the Alpine region, near Placentia 2 and at a place called Castor's, Otho's side gained the advantage. But in the last and most important battle – at Bedriacum, he lost out as a result of treachery; for his troops were lured out by the hope of talks which, it was thought, would specify peace-terms; unexpectedly, however, when they were exchanging greetings with the enemy, they were forced to fight for their lives.

With no second thoughts, Otho took a decision to commit suicide; many 3 believe – almost certainly correctly – that he could not bring himself to carry on a struggle for dominance which would cost so much in loss of men and materials. This is much more likely an explanation than that he despaired of victory or did not trust his troops. For still unharmed in reserve were the soldiers he had kept back with him for a second trial of strength, and reinforcements were on their way from Dalmatia, Pannonia and Moesia. Even those troops who had suffered defeat were not so disheartened as not to be prepared of their own free-will and without support to suffer any danger necessary to wipe out their earlier disgrace.

10] My father, Suetonius Laetus, was an equestrian tribune in the thirteenth 1

tribunus angusticlavius. Is mox referre crebro solebat Othonem etiam privatum usque adeo detestatum civilia arma, ut memorante quodam inter epulas de Cassi Brutique exitu cohorruerit; nec concursurum cum Galba fuisse, nisi confideret sine bello rem transigi posse; tunc ad despiciendam vitam exemplo manipularis militis concitatum, qui cum cladem exercitus nuntiaret nec cuiquam fidem faceret ac nunc mendaci nunc timoris, quasi fugisset, ex acie argueretur, gladio ante pedes eius incubuerit. Hoc viso proclamasse eum aiebat, non amplius se in periculum talis tamque bene meritos coniecturum.

Fratrem igitur fratrisque filium et singulos amicorum cohortatus, ut sibi 2 quisque pro facultate consuleret, ab amplexu et osculo suo dimisit omnis, secretoque capto binos codicillos exaravit, ad sororem consolatorios et ad Messalinam Neronis, quam matrimonio destinarat, commendans reliquias suas et memoriam. Quicquid deinde epistularum erat, ne cui periculo aut noxae apud victorem forent, concremavit. Divisit et pecunias domesticis ex copia praesenti.

11] Atque ita paratus intentusque iam morti, tumultu inter moras exorto ut eos, 1 qui discedere et abire coeptabant, corripi quasi desertores detinerique sensit: "Adiciamus," inquit, "vitae et hanc noctem," his ipsis totidemque verbis, vetuitque vim cuiquam fieri; et in serum usque patente cubiculo, si quis adire vellet, potestatem sui praebuit. Post hoc sedata siti gelidae aquae potione 2 arripuit duos pugiones et explorata utriusque acie, cum alterum pulvino subdidisset, foribus adopertis artissimo somno quievit. Et circa lucem demum expergefactus uno se traiecit ictu infra laevam papillam irrumpentibusque ad primum gemitum modo celans modo detegens plagam exanimatus est et celeriter, nam ita praeceperat, funeratus, tricensimo et octavo aetatis anno et nonagensimo et quinto imperii die.

12] Tanto Othonis animo nequaquam corpus aut habitus competit. Fuisse enim 1 et modicae staturae et male pedatus scambusque traditur, munditiarum vero paene muliebrium, vulso corpore, galericulo capiti propter raritatem capillorum adaptato et adnexo, ut nemo dinosceret; quin et faciem cotidie rasitare ac pane

legion, and took part in this war. Later on, he used to say that even before he became emperor, Otho had such a profound dislike of civil war that once when someone was talking at the dinner-table about the deaths of Brutus and Cassius he physically shook: he would not have challenged Galba had he not been confident that the issue could be settled short of fighting. Further, he was encouraged to take a poor view of human life by the example of an ordinary soldier; this man came with news of the army's defeat but nobody would believe him, and he was accused of lying or even having fled the field from cowardice. He fell on his sword at the emperor's feet. My father said that at this Otho cried out that he would no longer expose to danger such brave men who had served him so well.

So he gave a few words of encouragement to his brother, his nephew, and 2 each of his friends that they should all look to their own well-being; he embraced and kissed them and then sent them away; after this, he found somewhere private, and wrote two letters – one of consolation to his sister, the other to Nero's widow, Messalina, whom he had intended to marry, asking her to give due honour to his body and to remember him well. After this, he burnt all his other letters so that they should not do anyone any harm if they fell into the victors' hands. The money he had with him he distributed amongst his servants.

11] In this way, intent as he was on suicide, he put his affairs in order; whilst 1 he was still in the camp there was an outbreak of trouble and he discovered that those who were beginning to drift away were being captured and held as deserters; "let us", he said, "add this one further night to our lives" – these were his exact words – and he gave instructions that violent behaviour should not be shown to anyone. Until late into the night he left his bedroom-door open, so that anyone who wished could come and see him.

Then he quenched his thirst with a drink of cold water, took two daggers 2 and, testing the point of each, hid one under his pillow. Closing his door he slept soundly; about daybreak he woke up, and stabbed himself with a single blow below the left breast. Hearing his first groan his servants burst in; Otho first concealed the wound, but then died as he revealed it; out of respect for his instructions he was hastily given a funeral: he had lived for thirty-seven years and been emperor for ninety-four days.

12] In no way did Otho's physical appearance match this nobility of spirit: he 1 is said to have been on the short side, to have had bad feet and was bow-legged. But the care he afforded his body was like a woman's. His skin was plucked free of hair, and because of the thinness of the hair on his head he wore a wig that was so closely fitted that nobody could tell. It is also said that he shaved his face each

madido linere consuetum, idque instituisse a prima lanugine, ne barbatus umquam esset; sacra etiam Isidis saepe in lintea religiosaque veste propalam celebrasse. Per quae factum putem, ut mors eius minime congruens vitae maiore 2 miraculo fuerit. Multi praesentium militum cum plurimo fletu manus ac pedes iacentis exosculati, fortissimum virum, unicum imperatorem praedicantes, ibidem statim nec procul a rogo vim suae vitae attulerunt; multi et absentium accepto nuntio prae dolore armis inter se ad internecionem concurrerunt. Denique magna pars hominum incolumem gravissime detestata mortuum laudibus tulit, ut vulgo iactatum sit etiam, Galbam ab eo non tam dominandi quam rei p. ac libertatis restituendae causa interemptum.

day and wiped it with wet bread: he did this from the moment that he grew his first facial hair to avoid the growth of a beard. They also say that he was open in his frequent celebration of the rites of Isis, wearing the linen vestment which was used in that cult. It is my opinion that because of habits like these his death 2 was seen as completely inconsistent with his lifestyle, and for that reason excited greater surprise. Many of the soldiers who were present wept uncontrollably as they kissed the dead man's hands and feet, calling him an extraordinarily brave man and the best emperor ever; there and then, by his funeral-pyre they committed suicide. Many who were not at the scene heard the news and in their grief rushed at each other in suicide-pacts. In short, the majority of people who had vented bitter hatred on him whilst he was alive, praised him to the skies in death: as a result, it was commonly put about that he had murdered Galba not so as to win power for himself but to restore liberty and the republic.

VITELLIUS

1] Vitelliorum originem alii aliam et quidem diversissimam tradunt, partim 1
veterem et nobilem, partim vero novam et obscuram atque etiam sordidam;
quod ego per adulatores obtrectatoresque imperatoris Vitelli evenisse opinarer,
nisi aliquanto prius de familiae condicione variatum esset. Exstat Q. Elogi ad 2
Quintum Vitellium Divi Augusti quaestorem libellus, quo continetur, Vitellios
Fauno Aboriginum rege et Vitellia, quae multis locis pro numine coleretur, ortos
toto Latio imperasse; horum residuam stirpem ex Sabinis transisse Romam
atque inter patricios adlectam; indicia stirpis mansisse diu viam Vitelliam ab 3
Ianiculo ad mare usque, item coloniam eiusdem nominis, quam gentili copia
adversus Aequiculos tutandam olim depoposcissent; tempore deinde Samnitici
belli praesidio in Apuliam misso quosdam ex Vitellis subsedisse Nuceriae
eorumque progeniem longo post intervallo repetisse urbem atque ordinem
senatorium.

2] Contra plures auctorem generis libertinum prodiderunt, Cassius Severus 1
nec minus alii eundem et sutorem veteramentarium, cuius filius sectionibus et
cognituris uberius compendium nanctus, ex muliere vulgari, Antiochi cuiusdam
furnariam exercentis filia, equitem R. genuerit. Sed quod discrepat, sit in medio.
Ceterum P. Vitellius domo Nuceria, sive ille stirpis antiquae sive pudendis 2
parentibus atque avis, eques certe R. et rerum Augusti procurator, quattuor filios
amplissimae dignitatis cognomines ac tantum praenominibus distinctos reliquit
Aulum, Quintum, Publium, Lucium. Aulus in consulatu obiit, quem cum
Domitio Neronis Caesaris patre inierat, praelautus alioqui famosusque cenarum
magnificentia. Quintus caruit ordine, cum auctore Tiberio secerni minus

VITELLIUS

1] The accounts of the origin of the Vitellii vary, and indeed wildly so: some 1 say that they were an ancient, well-born family, whilst others regard them as a family recently emerged from obscurity – and even low-born. I should have been inclined to think that this difference of opinion reflected the stances of the flatterers and denigrators of the emperor, Vitellius, except that there were divergent views on the family's status at a considerably earlier stage.

Quintus Elogius, in a pamphlet addressed to Quintus Vitellius, who acted 2 as the quaestor of the Deified Augustus, asserts that the Vitellii were descended from Faunus, the king of the Aborigines, and Vitellia who in many places was treated as a goddess; their descendants, it was said, once held sway over the whole of Latium. This version continues that the remainder of the stock moved from Sabine country to Rome, and was there enrolled in the patriciate.

Traces of the family long survived in the name of the Vitellian Way which 3 ran from the Janiculan hill to the sea; and also in the *colonia* of the same name which the family had once claimed to defend against the Aequiculi with a force made up of their own members. Later, at the time of the Samnite war, a garrison had been sent to Apulia, and some of the Vitellii had settled at Nuceria. According to this, their descendants long afterwards returned to Rome and again took up their rank as senators.

2] A contrary version is frequently heard, and maintains that the family's 1 founder was a freedman: indeed, Cassius Severus and others say that this freedman was a shoe-repairer, whose son made a fortune out of deals in confiscated property and as a debt-recovery agent. He had a son by a prostitute who was the daughter of Antiochus, a baker, and this son attained equestrian status. This is, however, a matter of dispute, and can be left open.

In any case, Publius Vitellius' home-town was Nuceria: whether he came 2 from an ancient family or had parents and grandparents to cause him embarrassment, he was himself certainly of equestrian rank and a procurator in charge of Augustus' property. He left four sons, each of whom reached the highest positions in the state, and who all had the same name being distinguished solely by the forenames Aulus, Quintus, Publius and Lucius. Aulus Vitellius died during his consulship which he shared with Domitius Ahenobarbus, Nero's father: he was a man of great refinement and was well-known for the magnificent scale of his dinner-parties. Quintus lost his senatorial status at the time that Tiberius prompted a decision to identify and remove senators who

idoneos senatores removerique placuisset. Publius, Germanici comes, Cn. 3
Pisonem inimicum et interfectorem eius accusavit condemnavitque, ac post
praeturae honorem inter Seiani conscios arreptus et in custodiam fratri datus
scalpro librario venas sibi incidit, nec tam mortis paenitentia quam suorum
obtestatione obligari curarique se passus in eadem custodia morbo periit.
Lucius ex consulatu Syriae praepositus, Artabanum Parthorum regem summis 4
artibus non modo ad conloquium suum, sed etiam ad veneranda legionum signa
pellexit.   Mox cum Claudio principe duos insuper ordinarios consulatus
censuramque gessit. Curam quoque imperii sustinuit absente eo expeditione
Britannica; vir innocens et industrius, sed amore libertinae perinfamis, cuius
etiam salivis melle commixtis, ne clam quidem aut raro sed cotidie ac palam,
arterias et fauces pro remedio fovebat. Idem miri in adulando ingenii primus C. 5
Caesarem adorare ut deum instituit, cum reversus ex Syria non aliter adire ausus
esset quam capite velato circumvertensque se, deinde procumbens. Claudium
uxoribus libertisque addictum ne qua non arte demereretur, proximo munere a
Messalina petit ut sibi pedes praeberet excalciandos; detractumque socculum
dextrum inter togam tunicasque gestavit assidue, nonnumquam osculabundus.
Narcissi quoque et Pallantis imagines aureas inter Lares coluit. Huius et illa vox
est: "Saepe facias," cum saeculares ludos edenti Claudio gratularetur.
3]   Decessit paralysi altero die quam correptus est, duobus filiis superstitibus, 1
quos ex Sextilia probatissima nec ignobili femina editos consules vidit, et
quidem eodem ambos totoque anno, cum maiori minor in sex menses successisset.
Defunctum senatus publico funere honoravit, item statua pro rostris cum hac
inscriptione: PIETATIS IMMOBILIS ERGA PRINCIPEM.

were not suited to their rank.

Publius was on Germanicus' staff, and acted as accuser of Germanicus' 3 enemy and murderer, Gnaeus Piso, securing his condemnation. He reached the praetorship, but was then arrested amongst the accomplices of Sejanus and put under his brother's supervision; whilst there, he cut his wrists with a scribe's knife, but changed his mind not so much because he regretted his decision but due to his friends' entreaties. He allowed his wounds to be bound up and was nursed back to health, but died of an illness later whilst still in his brother's custody.

Lucius Vitellius reached the consulship and was subsequently put in 4 command of Syria: very skillfully he enticed Artabanus, the Parthian king, not just to negotiate, but even to pay ceremonial respect to the legionary standards. Later, with the emperor Claudius as his colleague, he held two more consulships and the censorship: indeed he even deputised for Claudius in government whilst the emperor was away on his expedition to Britain. He was a man of integrity and energy, though his reputation suffered greatly because of his affair with a freedwoman; indeed he was greatly taken by the use of her saliva mixed with honey as a medicine for his windpipe and throat: nor was this something he took privately and on rare occasions, but constantly and in public.

Lucius Vitellius was also a man inventive in flattery: he was the first to 5 establish the cult of Gaius Caesar as god: for on his return from Syria he would approach the imperial presence only with his head covered, turning himself in the correct directions and then falling prostrate before him. Claudius was obsessed with his wives and freedmen: to curry favour with this emperor Vitellius left no stone unturned. He asked Messalina as an outstanding favour to be allowed to take off her shoes; when she consented he removed her right shoe and always kept it between his toga and his tunics, kissing it from time to time. He kept golden statuettes of Narcissus and Pallas on his altar to the household gods. He it was who coined the famous expression, "May you do it often", when he congratulated Claudius on his celebration of the Secular games.

3] Lucius Vitellius died of a stroke the day after he had been arrested: he left 1 two sons, born to him by Sextilia, a lady of the highest reputation and of a good family: he lived to see them both reach the consulship. Curiously, both were consuls in the same year and between them occupied the office for the whole year, since the younger son succeeded his older brother for the second six months of the year. On his death, the senate honoured him with a public funeral and with a statue at the front of the Rostra which bore this inscription: "Of unswerving loyalty towards his emperor".

A. Vitellius L. filius imperator natus est VIII. Kal. Oct., vel ut quidam VII. 2
Id. Sept., Druso Caesare Norbano Flacco cons. Genituram eius praedictam a
mathematicis ita parentes exhorruerunt, ut pater magno opere semper contenderit,
ne qua ei provincia vivo se committeretur, mater et missum ad legiones et
appellatum imperatorem pro afflicto statim lamentata sit. Pueritiam primamque
adulescentiam Capreis egit inter Tiberiana scorta, et ipse perpetuo Spintriae
cognomine notatus existimatusque corporis gratia initium et causa incrementorum
patri fuisse.

4]   Sequenti quoque aetate omnibus probris contaminatus, praecipuum in aula
locum tenuit, Gaio per aurigandi, Claudio per aleae studium familiaris, sed
aliquanto Neroni acceptior, cum propter eadem haec, tum peculiari merito, quod
praesidens certamini Neroneo cupientem inter citharoedos contendere nec
quamvis flagitantibus cunctis promittere audentem ideoque egressum theatro
revocaverat, quasi perseverantis populi legatione suscepta, exorandumque
praebuerat.

5]   Trium itaque principum indulgentia non solum honoribus verum et
sacerdotiis amplissimis auctus, proconsulatum Africae post haec curamque
operum publicorum administravit et voluntate dispari et existimatione. In
provincia singularem innocentiam praestitit biennio continuato, cum succedenti
fratri legatus substitisset; at in urbano officio dona atque ornamenta templorum
subripuisse et commutasse quaedam ferebatur proque auro et argento stagnum
et aurichalcum supposuisse.

6]   Uxorem habuit Petroniam consularis viri filiam et ex ea filium Petronianum
captum altero oculo. Hunc heredem a matre sub condicione institutum, si de
potestate patris exiisset, manu emisit brevique, ut creditum est, interemit,
insimulatum insuper parricidii et quasi paratum ad scelus venenum ex conscientia
hausisset. Duxit mox Galeriam Fundanam praetorio patre ac de hac quoque
liberos utriusque sexus tulit, sed marem titubantia oris prope mutum et elinguem.

Aulus Vitellius, the emperor, who was Lucius' son, was born in the year 2 when Drusus Caesar and Norbanus Flaccus were consuls: his birthday was on September 24th, or, according to another version, on September 7th. The horoscope composed by astrologers so horrified his parents that his father spared no effort to prevent his son gaining any province so long as he was alive: his mother, for her part, hearing that he had been sent out to the legions and hailed as emperor, immediately mourned her son as a man struck a mortal blow. He spent his boyhood and early youth on Capreae amongst Tiberius' prostitutes; he was always known by the nickname, Spintria, and it was generally thought that his bodily charms marked the beginning and were the cause of his father's promotion.

4] For the rest of his life, too, he was corrupted by every kind of vice, and held a leading position at court: he was favoured by Gaius because of his passion for chariot-racing, and by Claudius because of his love of dice. These same enthusiasms found even greater favour with Nero, though for that emperor he performed a particular service. Vitellius was presiding at the Neronian games, and Nero dearly wanted to compete amongst the lyre-players, but though everyone was calling for him he did not dare to promise that he would perform. So he left the theatre; but Vitellius, on the pretext of acting as the emissary of an insistent people, called him back and gave him the opportunity of yielding to their prayers.

5] Thus by the favour of three emperors he won not only political honours, but also the highest priesthoods. After these, he secured the proconsulship of Africa and was put in charge of public works, though his enthusiasm for these, and his reputation, were divergent. He displayed great integrity in the province for two years without a break, for when his brother succeeded him he stayed on as his deputy. But in his post in Rome, he was said to have stolen some temple-gifts and treasures, and in the case of others he is said to have replaced gold and silver originals with tin and brass replicas.

6] He married Petronia, whose father was an ex-consul, and they had a son named Petronianus who was blind in one eye. Petronia named her son as her heir on condition that he was freed from his father's control: Vitellius freed him, and shortly afterwards, it is believed, murdered him, charging his son with intended parricide and alleging that because of his bad conscience on the matter he had drunk the poison he had prepared for his crime. Vitellius afterwards married Galeria Fundana whose father had risen to the rank of praetor; by her he had two children – a boy and a girl: the boy, however, stammered so badly that he was to all intents and purposes dumb.

7]   A Galba in inferiorem Germaniam contra opinionem missus est. Adiutum 1
putant T. Vini suffragio, tunc potentissimi et cui iam pridem per communem
factionis Venetae favorem conciliatus esset; nisi quod Galba prae se tulit nullos
minus metuendos quam qui de solo victu cogitarent, ac posse provincialibus
copiis profundam gulam eius expleri, ut cuivis evidens sit contemptu magis
quam gratia electum. Satis constat exituro viaticum defuisse, tanta egestate rei 2
familiaris, ut uxore et liberis, quos Romae relinquebat, meritorio cenaculo
abditis domum in reliquam partem anni ablocaret utque ex aure matris detractum
unionem pigneraverit ad itineris impensas. Creditorum quidem praestolantium
ac detinentium turbam et in iis Sinuessanos Formianosque, quorum publica
vectigalia interverterat, non nisi terrore calumniae amovit, cum libertino cuidam
acerbius debitum reposcenti iniuriarum formulam, quasi calce ab eo percussus,
intendisset nec aliter quam extortis quinquaginta sestertiis remisisset.

Advenientem male animatus erga principem exercitus pronusque ad res 3
novas libens ac supinis manibus excepit velut dono deum oblatum, ter consulis
filium, aetate integra, facili ac prodigo animo. Quam veterem de se persuasionem
Vitellius recentibus etiam experimentis auxerat, tota via caligatorum quoque
militum obvios exosculans perque stabula ac deversoria mulionibus ac viatoribus
praeter modum comis, ut mane singulos iamne iantassent sciscitaretur seque
fecisse ructu quoque ostenderet.

8]   Castra vero ingressus nihil cuiquam poscenti negavit atque etiam ultro 1
ignominiosis notas, reis sordes, damnatis supplicia dempsit. Quare vixdum
mense transacto, neque diei neque temporis ratione habita, ac iam vespere,
subito a militibus e cubiculo raptus, ita ut erat in veste domestica, imperator est

7]   Much to everyone's surprise, Galba appointed him as commander in Lower 1
Germany; it is thought, however, that he had the backing of Titus Vinius, then
the most powerful man in Galba's entourage, and who was a long-standing
friend of Vitellius because of the enthusiasm for 'the Blues' which they shared.
Galba, however, was on record as having said that none were more to be feared
than those who were obsessed with the thought of food, and that even Vitellius'
huge appetite could be filled with the endless resources of that province. Thus
it is obvious that the appointment of Vitellius was more an indication of the
contempt in which he was held than a sign of favour.

It is well known that when he was on the point of leaving for his province 2
he did not have sufficient resources for the journey; he was in such stretched
circumstances that he had to leave his wife and children in Rome, hiding them
away in an attic that was available at a small rent, so as to be able to let his own
house for the rest of the year. Further, he took a pearl stud from his mother's ear
and pawned it to meet the expenses of his journey. When he set off to leave, a
crowd of his creditors lay in wait for him and tried to stop him, amongst them
people from Sinuessa and Formiae whose public taxes he had embezzled. He
had recourse to frightening them with the threat of false accusations before he
could move them away: for one particular freedman was pushing his claim with
especial vigour: Vitellius instituted proceedings against this man alleging that
he had been kicked by him and refused to withdraw the accusation until he had
extorted fifty thousand *sestertii* from him.

When he had reached Germany, he found the army hostile towards the 3
emperor and ready for mutiny; but they greeted him joyfully and with hands
outstretched as if the gods had given as a gift this man whose father had been
consul three times and who was in the prime of life and had an easy and
extravagant disposition. This reputation which Vitellius had long enjoyed he
had enhanced by his recent behaviour; the whole length of his journey he had
kissed any common soldiers he had happened to meet, and was extremely
affable to mule-drivers and travellers he encountered in wayside inns: indeed,
he asked each and every one of them whether or not he had had breakfast, and
showed by belching that he had.

8]   When he entered the camp he refused no request at all and took it on his own 1
authority to remove the punishments of those in disgrace, to dispel defendants'
anxieties and to quash the sentences of those who had been condemned. Thus,
after hardly a month had passed, with no regard paid to what day it was or to the
time of day – for it was already evening – he was with no warning hailed by the
soldiers from his bedroom. Just as he was, in his indoor clothes, he was hailed

consalutatus circumlatusque per celeberrimos vicos, strictum Divi Iuli gladium tenens detractum delubro Martis atque in prima gratulatione porrectum sibi a quodam. Nec ante in praetorium rediit quam flagrante triclinio ex conceptu 2 camini, cum quidem consternatis et quasi omine adverso anxiis omnibus: "Bono," inquit, "animo estote! nobis adluxit," nullo sermone alio apud milites usus. Consentiente deinde etiam superioris provinciae exercitu, qui prior a Galba ad senatum defecerat, cognomen Germanici delatum ab universis cupide recepit, Augusti distulit, Caesaris in perpetuum recusavit.

9] Ac subinde caede Galbae adnuntiata, compositis Germanicis rebus, partitus est copias, quas adversus Othonem praemitteret quasque ipse perduceret. Praemisso agmine laetum evenit auspicium, siquidem a parte dextra repente aquila advolavit lustratisque signis ingressos viam sensim antecessit. At contra ipso movente statuae equestres, cum plurifariam ei ponerentur, fractis repente cruribus pariter corruerunt, et laurea, quam religiosissime circumdederat, in profluentem excidit; mox Viennae pro tribunali iura reddenti gallinaceus supra umerum ac deinde in capite astitit. Quibus ostentis par respondit exitus; nam confirmatum per legatos suos imperium per se retinere non potuit.

10] De Betriacensi victoria et Othonis exitu, cum adhuc in Gallia esset, audiit 1 nihilque cunctatus, quicquid praetorianarum cohortium fuit, ut pessimi exempli, uno exauctoravit edicto iussas tribunis tradere arma. Centum autem atque viginti, quorum libellos Othoni datos invenerat exposcentium praemium ob editam in caede Galbae operam, conquiri et supplicio adfici imperavit, egregie prorsus atque magnifice et ut summi principis spem ostenderet, nisi cetera magis ex natura et priore vita sua quam ex imperii maiestate gessisset. Namque itinere 2 incohato per medias civitates ritu triumphantium vectus est perque flumina delicatissimis navigiis et variarum coronarum genere redimitis, inter

as emperor and carried through the crowded streets; he held aloft the unsheathed sword of the Deified Julius which had been taken from the temple of Mars and presented to him by somebody amidst the first congratulations.

By the time he returned to his quarters the chimney had caught fire and 2 started to blaze in the dining room; everyone was shocked and anxious at what seemed to be a bad omen; but Vitellius said, "cheer up: a light is lighting our way"; and that was all he said to the soldiers. The army of Upper Germany had already deserted Galba in favour of the senate; they too now joined Vitellius. He readily took the title, Germanicus, which they offered him, but put off accepting that of Augustus and refused the title of Caesar for all time.

9] As soon as news reached Germany of Galba's murder, Vitellius made the necessary arrangements; he divided the army into two, one part of which he intended to lead himself, whilst the other was to be an advance force to engage Otho. As this latter force set out, it encountered a lucky omen; an eagle suddenly flew in from the right-hand side, circled the standards, and flew on gently in front of them as they began their march.

On the other hand, as Vitellius himself was moving off, the equestrian statues of him, which were in the course of erection in many places, all suddenly collapsed, their legs broken; what is more, the laurel wreath, which, according to strict observance of religious custom, he had placed on his head, fell off into a fast-flowing stream. Later, when at Vienne he sat on the dais dispensing justice, a cock perched first on his shoulder, and then on his head. The outcome corresponded with these portents; for he proved himself unable to retain by his own efforts the empire won for him by his deputies.

10] He was still in Gaul when he heard of the outcome of the battle of 1 Bedriacum and Otho's death; without delay, he passed a single decree disbanding all the existing praetorian cohorts, on the ground of their terrible conduct, and ordered them to hand over their arms to the tribunes. What is more, he found petitions addressed to Otho by one hundred and twenty praetorians demanding rewards for their services in murdering Galba; these soldiers, he ordered, should be found and put to death. This would have seemed an excellent example to set and an act suggesting that he would make a great emperor; unfortunately his behaviour in other respects was to prove to be more in accordance with the character he had shown in his earlier life than with the dignity expected of the imperial position.

For on his march into Italy he rode through cities as if he were triumphing 2 over them, and sailed along rivers in boats that were exquisitely decorated and garlanded with many different types of wreath; throughout, the most lavish

profusissimos obsoniorum apparatus, nulla familiae aut militis disciplina, rapinas ac petulantiam omnium in iocum vertens qui non contenti epulo ubique publice praebito, quoscumque libuisset in libertatem asserebant, verbera et plagas, saepe vulnera, nonnumquam necem repraesentantes adversantibus. Utque campos, in quibus pugnatum est, adit, abhorrentis quosdam cadaverum 3 tabem detestabili voce confirmare ausus est, optime olere occisum hostem et melius civem. Nec eo setius ad leniendam gravitatem odoris plurimum meri propalam hausit passimque divisit. Pari vanitate atque insolentia lapidem memoriae Othonis inscriptum intuens dignum eo Mausoleo ait, pugionemque, quo is se occiderat, in Agrippinensem coloniam misit Marti dedicandum. In Appennini quidem iugis etiam pervigilium egit.

11] Urbem denique ad classicum introiit paludatus ferroque succinctus, inter 1 signa atque vexilla, sagulatis comitibus ac detectis commilitonum armis.

Magis deinde ac magis omni divino humanoque iure neglecto Alliensi die 2 pontificatum maximum cepit, comitia in decem annos ordinavit seque perpetuum consulem. Et ne cui dubium foret, quod exemplar regendae rei p. eligeret, medio Martio campo adhibita publicorum sacerdotum frequentia inferias Neroni dedit ac sollemni convivio citharoedum placentem palam admonuit, ut aliquid et de dominico diceret, incohantique Neroniana cantica primus exsultans etiam plausit.

12] Talibus principiis magnam imperii partem non nisi consilio et arbitrio vilissimi cuiusque histrionum et aurigarum administravit et maxime Asiatici liberti. Hunc adulescentulum mutua libidine constupratum, mox taedio profugum cum Puteolis poscam vendentem reprehendisset, coniecit in compedes statimque solvit et rursus in deliciis habuit; iterum deinde ob nimiam contumaciam et

banquets were arranged, and he exercised no discipline whatever either over his household or over his soldiers, but treated all their looting and vandalism as a joke. They were not even satisfied with the banquets provided everywhere at public expense, but whenever the whim took them they freed slaves, and those who protested they beat up, often inflicting serious, even occasionally fatal, wounds.

He eventually reached the battle-field where the rotting corpses disgusted 3 some of those with him; his outrageous attempt to rally them is recorded in one preposterous utterance – "The stench of a dead enemy is wonderful, and better still if he was a fellow-citizen". Still, to palliate the terrible smell, he publicly drank an enormous amount of wine, and offered the same to everyone else. He showed the same tasteless vanity when he inspected the stone erected in Otho's memory, and said that it was a tomb worthy of the man; he further sent the dagger which Otho had used to kill himself to Cologne with orders that it should be dedicated to Mars. In addition, high up in the Apennines he even held an all-night celebration.

11] After a journey characterised by incidents such as these, he finally entered 1 Rome to the sound of a bugle, wearing his military cloak and carrying his sword: all around him were the insignia of the various military units, his entourage with their officers' cloaks and the ordinary soldiers with weapons drawn.

He showed himself increasingly impervious to every human and religious 2 scruple, for on the anniversary of the battle of the Allia – of all days – he took the post of chief priest, settled the magisterial elections for the forthcoming ten years, and made himself consul-for-life. Further, so that there should be no mistake over whom he chose as his model for government, he made funeral offerings to Nero in the middle of the Campus Martius with a great company of the states' priests present; at the ritual feast, he openly told a lyre-player who had won his favour that "he should play something from the master's repertoire", and when he began to play Nero's songs, Vitellius was the first to leap to his feet and applaud.

12] This was how Vitellius started, and he went on to conduct a large part of his reign listening to the advice and whims of the most worthless actors and charioteers, and was particularly reliant on the ex-slave, Asiaticus. Vitellius had had a passionate affair with Asiaticus whilst he was a young man; Asiaticus, however, had grown weary of this and had run away to become a seller of vinegar-drinks at Puteoli. Vitellius found him and put him in chains, but almost immediately set him free and gave him a privileged position amongst his favourites. The emperor again became very annoyed at Asiaticus' insolence and

furacitatem gravatus circumforano lanistae vendidit dilatumque ad finem muneris repente subripuit et provincia demum accepta manumisit ac primo imperii die aureis donavit anulis super cenam, cum mane rogantibus pro eo cunctis detestatus esset severissime talem equestris ordinis maculam.

13] Sed vel praecipue luxuriae saevitiaeque deditus epulas trifariam semper, 1 interdum quadrifariam dispertiebat, in iantacula et prandia et cenas comissationesque, facile omnibus sufficiens vomitandi consuetudine. Indicebat autem aliud alii eadem die, nec cuiquam minus singuli apparatus quadringenis milibus nummum constiterunt. Famosissima super ceteras fuit cena data ei 2 adventicia a fratre, in qua duo milia lectissimorum piscium, septem avium apposita traduntur. Hanc quoque exsuperavit ipse dedicatione patinae, quam ob immensam magnitudinem clipeum Minervae πολιούχου dictitabat. In hac scarorum iocinera, phasianarum et pavonum cerebella, linguas phoenicopterum, murenarum lactes a Parthia usque fretoque Hispanico per navarchos ac triremes petitarum commiscuit. Ut autem homo non profundae modo sed intempestivae 3 quoque ac sordidae gulae, ne in sacrificio quidem umquam aut itinere ullo temperavit, quin inter altaria ibidem statim viscus et farris frusta paene rapta e foco manderet circaque viarum popinas fumantia obsonia vel pridiana atque semesa.

14] Pronus vero ad cuiuscumque et quacumque de causa necem atque suppli- 1 cium nobiles viros, condiscipulos et aequales suos, omnibus blanditiis tantum non ad societatem imperii adlicefactos vario genere fraudis occidit, etiam unum veneno manu sua porrecto in aquae frigidae potione, quam is adfectus febre poposcerat. Tum faeneratorum et stipulatorum publicanorumque, qui umquam 2 se aut Romae debitum aut in via portorium flagitassent, vix ulli pepercit; ex quibus quendam in ipsa salutatione supplicio traditum statimque revocatum, cunctis clementiam laudantibus, coram interfici iussit, velle se dicens pascere

dishonesty and sold him on to a travelling trainer of gladiators. This time, on an occasion when Asiaticus had been kept back for the climax of a show, Vitellius secretly stole him back and when he had received his provincial appointment granted Asiaticus his freedom. Finally, at dinner on the first day of his reign, he gave Asiaticus the golden rings, although that same morning when everyone had been begging him to do this, he deplored in the strongest possible terms the idea that the equestrian order should be polluted in such a way.

13] But he was especially addicted to high-living and cruelty; he always had 1 three meals a day, and sometimes even four – breakfast, lunch, dinner and a drinking-session. He coped with these easily because of his practice of self-induced vomiting. Each day, he appointed different hosts for each meal, and none of them spent less than four hundred thousand *sestertii* on providing a single meal. The most notorious of all of these was the one hosted by the emperor's 2 brother to mark his arrival in Rome; the story goes that during the course of it, two thousand of the best fish were served, and seven thousand birds. Yet even this was outdone by the emperor himself at the dedication of that dish which because of its great size he used to refer to as the shield of Minerva, Defender of the City; for in it he blended the livers of scar-fish, the brains of pheasants and peacocks, the tongues of flamingoes and the guts of lampreys. These delicacies had been fetched by trieremes commanded by senior captains from places as far distant as Parthia and the Straits of Gibraltar.

Moreover, his appetite was insatiable, coarse and constant; he could not 3 hold it in check even when he was conducting sacrifice or travelling; amongst the very altars he would devour bits of flesh and spelt-cake which he seized almost on the point of their consumption in the holy fire. In the same way, at every wayside-tavern he snatched up meat that was still cooking, and even the half-eaten remnants of the previous day's meals.

14] He was always ready to punish, even execute, anyone for any reason at all; 1 men of noble birth, his equals and contemporaries, on whom he had used all kinds of bribery, only just stopping short of offering them a share in his power, these he killed by various criminal acts. In one case he personally put poison into a drink of cold water for which a man who was suffering from a fever had asked.

Rarely did he spare the life of any of the money-lenders, debt- or tax- 2 collectors who ever dared to demand of him debts incurred at Rome or tolls-en-route; he handed over one of these for execution just when he had come to offer the emperor his greetings, and then straightaway called him back. Whilst everyone was praising the emperor for his clemency, Vitellius ordered the man

oculos; alterius poenae duos filios adiecit deprecari pro patre conatos. Sed et 3 equitem R. proclamantem, cum raperetur ad poenam: "Heres meus es," exhibere testamenti tabulas coegit, utque legit coheredem sibi libertum eius ascriptum, iugulari cum liberto imperavit. Quosdam et de plebe ob id ipsum, quod Venetae factioni clare male dixerant, interemit contemptu sui et nova spe id ausos opinatus. Nullis tamen infensior quam vernaculis et mathematicis, ut 4 quisque deferretur, inauditum capite puniebat exacerbatus, quod post edictum suum, quo iubebat intra Kal. Oct. urbe Italiaque mathematici excederent, statim libellus propositus est, et Chaldaeos dicere, bonum factum, ne Vitellius Germanicus intra eundem Kalendarum diem usquam esset. Suspectus et in 5 morte matris fuit, quasi aegrae praeberi cibum prohibuisset, vaticinante Chatta muliere, cui velut oraculo adquiescebat, ita demum firmiter ac diutissime imperaturum, si superstes parenti exstitisset. Alii tradunt ipsam taedio praesentium et imminentium metu venenum a filio impetrasse, haud sane difficulter.

15] Octavo imperii mense desciverunt ab eo exercitus Moesiarum atque 1 Pannoniae, item ex transmarinis Iudaicus et Syriaticus, ac pars in absentis pars in praesentis Vespasiani verba iurarunt. Ad retinendum ergo ceterorum hominum studium ac favorem nihil non publice privatimque nullo adhibito modo largitus est. Dilectum quoque ea condicione in urbe egit, ut voluntariis non modo missionem post victoriam, sed etiam veteranorum iustaeque militiae commoda polliceretur. Urgenti deinde terra marique hosti hinc fratrem cum classe ac 2 tironibus et gladiatorum manu opposuit, hinc Betriacenses copias et duces; atque ubique aut superatus aut proditus salutem sibi et milies sestertium a Flavio Sabino Vespasiani fratre pepigit; statimque pro gradibus Palati apud frequentes

to be put to death in his presence saying that he wished to feast his eyes on the spectacle. When another man was being punished, Vitellius extended the sentence to the man's two sons – for having tried to intercede on their father's behalf.

One Roman knight shouted out when he was being bundled off to 3 execution, "you are my heir". Vitellius forced him to produce the pages of his will, and when he read that one of the man's ex-slaves had been named as his co-heir, Vitellius instructed that they should both be strangled together. He even put some ordinary people to death on the grounds that they had raised their voices against 'the Blues'; he thought that they dared to do this to show their contempt of him and because they cherished hopes of overthrowing him.

To no groups, however, was his behaviour more savage than it was to 4 jesters and fortune-tellers; as each was charged, Vitellius sentenced him to death, his case unheard. The emperor was angry because in response to his edict in which he instructed all astrologers to quit Rome and Italy before October 1st, a notice was put up saying, "The Chaldaeans proclaim that a great good will have been done if Vitellius Germanicus is no more by the same date".

He was even suspected of having had a hand in his mother's death on the 5 ground that he had forbidden her to be given food during an illness; this was because a woman of the tribe of the Chatti, in whom he placed as much confidence as he did in oracles, had prophesied that he would reign with stability for a long time, only if he outlived his parent. Another version has it that his mother was weary of what was going on and fearful for the future, and so asked her son for poison; he gave her it without question.

15] In the eighth month of his reign, the armies stationed in Pannonia and in the 1 Moesian provinces put aside their allegiance to him; at the same time overseas, the armies in Judaea and Syria also revolted and took an oath of allegiance to Vespasian; the former swore its allegiance in Vespasian's presence, the latter in his absence. So Vitellius omitted no act whatever of public or private generosity to hold the loyal enthusiasm of the rest. He conducted a levy in Rome, the terms of which were extremely generous, promising discharge to the volunteers when victory was achieved, and all the benefits available to veterans after regular service.

Later on, when the enemy was pressing Vitellius both with land and naval 2 forces, he entrusted naval affairs to a fleet commanded by his brother and manned by raw recruits and a band of gladiators; the land-threat was met by the same armies and generals who had been victorious at Bedriacum. But he was defeated in all quarters either by superior strength or by treachery, and so made

milites cedere se imperio quod invitus recepisset professus, cunctis reclamantibus rem distulit ac nocte interposita primo diluculo sordidatus descendit ad rostra multisque cum lacrimis eadem illa, verum e libello testatus est. Rursus 3 interpellante milite ac populo et ne deficeret hortante omnemque operam suam certatim pollicente, animum resumpsit Sabinumque et reliquos Flavianos nihil iam metuentis vi subita in Capitolium compulit succensoque templo Iovis Optimi Maximi oppressit, cum et proelium et incendium e Tiberiana prospiceret domo inter epulas. Non multo post paenitens facti et in alios culpam conferens vocata contione iuravit coegitque iurare et ceteros nihil sibi antiquius quiete publica fore. Tunc solutum a latere pugionem consuli primum, deinde illo 4 recusante magistratibus ac mox senatoribus singulis porrigens, nullo recipiente, quasi in aede Concordiae positurus abscessit. Sed quibusdam adclamantibus ipsum esse Concordiam, rediit nec solum retinere se ferrum affirmavit, verum etiam Concordiae recipere cognomen.

16] Suasitque senatui, ut legatos cum virginibus Vestalibus mitterent pacem aut certe tempus ad consultandum petituros.

Postridie responsa opperienti nuntiatum est per exploratorem hostes appropinquare. Continuo igitur abstrusus gestatoria sella duobus solis comitibus, pistore et coco, Aventinum et paternam domum clam petit, ut inde in Campaniam fugeret; mox levi rumore et incerto, tamquam pax impetrata esset, referri se in Palatium passus est. Ubi cum deserta omnia repperisset, dilabentibus et qui simul erant, zona se aureorum plena circumdedit confugitque in cellulam ianitoris, religato pro foribus cane lectoque et culcita obiectis.

17] Irruperant iam agminis antecessores ac nemine obvio rimabantur, ut fit, 1 singula. Ab his extractus e latebra, sciscitantes, quis esset – nam ignorabatur – et ubi esse Vitellium sciret, mendacio elusit; deinde agnitus rogare non destitit,

a deal with Vespasian's brother, Flavius Sabinus, guaranteeing him safe-conduct and a hundred million *sestertii*. Straightaway, he stood on the steps of the palace and told a crowd of soldiers that he was retiring from the responsi-bilities of power which he had unwillingly accepted. The crowd, however, shouted out in protest: so he postponed the matter, but at dawn next day he put on mourning-clothes and went to the speakers' platform and tearfully repeated his decision, this time reading from a text. Again, the crowd of soldiers and 3 civilians interrupted him, and begged him not to lose heart, each trying to outdo the other in their promises of every assistance. This time he plucked up his courage, and mounted a sudden attack on Flavius Sabinus and the other Flavian sympathisers; because of the unexpectedness of this, they fell back on to the Capitol hill, where the Vitellians defeated them by setting fire to the temple of Jupiter. Vitellius himself watched the battle and the fire from the safety of the house of the emperor Tiberius, where he carried on feasting. A little later, he was sorry for what he had done, and shifted the blame on to others; he convened a public meeting and swore on oath, compelling others to do likewise, that nothing was of greater importance than public peace.

Then he unbelted his dagger, and tried to offer it to the consul, and when 4 the latter refused to accept it, Vitellius repeated his offer to other magistrates and to senators one by one. All, however, declined the offer, and Vitellius left as if to deposit the dagger in the temple of Concord. But then some shouted out that he was himself the embodiment of Concord: at this he returned, declaring that not only would he retain his dagger, but would also take the surname, *Concordia*. 16] At the same time he advised the senate that they should send intermediaries, with Vestal Virgins in the group, to ask for peace or at least a truce for consultation. Next day, as he awaited a reply to this approach, he received news from a scout that the enemy-troops were closing on Rome. Immediately he hid himself in a litter, and with just two companions, his pastry-cook and chef, he secretly made for his family-house on the Aventine hill; from here his plan was to escape south to Campania. At this point, a vague rumour came to him that his peace-terms had been accepted, and so he allowed himself to be taken back to the palace. There he found everything deserted, and even those who were with him had slipped away; so he buckled on a money-belt full of gold, and took refuge in the porter's room, tying a dog to the door, and piling against it a bed and a mattress.

17] Even now, the advance guard of the Flavian army had broken into the 1 palace and, finding no opposition, was not unnaturally conducting a thorough search. He was dragged out by them from his hiding-place; but his captors did not recognise him and kept asking him whether he knew the whereabouts of Vitellius; he lied his way out of this encounter. But soon he was recognised and

quasi quaedam de salute Vespasiani dicturus, ut custodiretur interim vel in carcere, donec religatis post terga manibus, iniecto cervicibus laqueo, veste discissa seminudus in Forum tractus est inter magna rerum verborumque ludibria per totum viae Sacrae spatium, reducto coma capite, ceu noxii solent, atque etiam mento mucrone gladii subrecto, ut visendam praeberet faciem neve summitteret; quibusdam stercore et caeno incessentibus, aliis incendiarium et 2 patinarium vociferantibus, parte vulgi etiam corporis vitia exprobrante; erat enim in eo enormis proceritas, facies rubida plerumque ex vinulentia, venter obesus, alterum femur subdebile impulsu olim quadrigae, cum auriganti Gaio ministratorem exhiberet. Tandem apud Gemonias minutissimis ictibus excarnificatus atque confectus est et inde unco tractus in Tiberim.

18] Periit cum fratre et filio anno vitae septimo quinquagesimo; nec fefellit coniectura eorum qui augurio, quod factum ei Viennae ostendimus, non aliud portendi praedixerant quam venturum in alicuius Gallicani hominis potestatem, siquidem ab Antonio Primo adversarum partium duce oppressus est, cui Tolosae nato cognomen in pueritia Becco fuerat: id valet gallinacei rostrum.

repeatedly asked that he should be held for a while even in custody, on the grounds that he had vital information affecting Vespasian's safety. Finally, however, his hands were tied behind his back, and a noose put around his neck; his clothes were ripped, and, half-naked, he was dragged to the forum: along the whole length of the Sacred Way he was subjected to actions and shouting of the most abusive kind. His head was pulled back by the hair, as happens to criminals, and even his chin was kept up by the point of a sword held beneath it to force him to keep his face visible and not to lower his gaze. Some threw 2 rubbish and sewerage at him, whilst others called him 'Firebug' and 'Fatty'; indeed some of the crowd even mocked him for his bodily defects, for he was extremely tall, with a face flushed due to excessive drinking, and a protruding stomach. He was lame in one leg following a chariot-crash sustained when he had been acting as assistant on an occasion when Caligula had been driving. Finally he reached the Gemonian Steps where he was tortured with tiny dagger-cuts; after this slow death he was dragged by a hook, and thrown into the Tiber.

18] So Vitellius died, along with his brother and his son; he was fifty-six years old, and his death fulfilled the guess of those, who, following the omen which, as I have already mentioned, befell him in Vienne, suggested that it meant one thing only – that Vitellius would fall into the hands of a man of Gaul; for in actual fact he had been defeated by the Flavian leader, Antonius Primus, a native of Tolosa, who as a boy had been given the nickname, *Beccus*, which means 'cock's beak'.

Commentary

Life of Galba

Nero's death: on June 9th, A.D. 68, Nero committed suicide at Phaon's villa, some four miles from Rome; his remains were placed in the family-tomb of the Domitii. His three marriages produced only one child – Claudia, the daughter of Poppaea Sabina, who died in infancy in A.D. 63 (Tac. *Ann.* XV. 23,4).

family of the Caesars: the Julii and Claudii had between them comprised the "imperial family" from Augustus to Nero; up to Caligula's time, marriage-alliances and adoptions had formally made the emperors members of the *gens Julia*. Claudius, although not adopted as a Julian, took the name of Caesar; Nero was formally adopted by Claudius into the *gens Claudia*, although, through his mother, Agrippina, he had both Julian and Claudian blood-connections (see stemma in Shotter, 1989, xiii). Many saw Rome as having become something of a family-"heirloom" (Tac. *Hist* I. 16, 1–2), but Nero's memory remained popular with some, which led to appearances in subsequent years of "false Nero-figures" (Warmington, 1969, 167; Dio Chrysostom *Orat.* XXI. 9–10).

Livia, following her marriage to Augustus: Livia Drusilla had been married to the anti-Caesarian Ti. Claudius Nero; they had two sons – Tiberius and Nero Drusus. In 39 B.C., following the accommodation with Sextus Pompeius, Livia and many more of Caesar's opponents returned to Italy, now reconciled with Octavian; it was no doubt a combination of emotion and political opportunism that persuaded Octavian a year later to marry Livia, following a hastily-arranged divorce from Ti. Nero. The marriage was thought by many to have been scandalous owing to Livia's pregnancy at the time; many, too, regretted Livia's influence as Augustus' wife and as Tiberius' mother (Tac. *Ann.* I. 9–10; Syme, 1939, 229, 340f and 422f).

at Veii: an Etruscan town some nine miles north of Rome, which in the fifth and early fourth centuries B.C. had been one of Rome's closest rivals. Traditionally, a ten-year's war had been fought between the two cities from 406 to 396 B.C. (Livy V. 1ff; Ward-Perkins, 1961).

The latin omits *praedium* ("property") with *Veientanum* – as often.

an eagle flew: this story is told in considerable detail by the Elder Pliny (*Nat. Hist.* XV. 136).

Livia decided: in Pliny's version, the decision was taken by priests (*haruspices*); see also Dio Cassius XLVIII. 52.

even to-day: Pliny says that the villa was situated by the Tiber near to the ninth milestone on the *via Flaminia*. The name, *Ad Gallinas*, was attached to the important river-crossing site at Prima Porta, where remains, apparently of a villa, were found in 1879; this site has always been identified as the "villa of Livia" (Ashby and Fell, 1921, 142; Blake, 1947, 272). Nothing of it now survives.

There was a street on the Viminal in Rome, bearing the name, *Gallinae Albae* ("White Chickens").

The latin, *hodieque*, is a post-Augustan usage for *hodie quoque*.

those who triumphed: Pliny, too, says that the actual laurel-sprigs were replanted. For a brief description of the practice of triumphing, see Nicolet, 1980, 352ff.

the whole grove withered: the story is told also by Dio Cassius (LXIII. 29,3) and Victor (*Caes.* 5,17). A similar omen is said to have foretold the fall of Troy (Quintus Smyrnaeus XII. 517).

all the hens: the construction, *quidquid* with the genitive case (*quidquid gallinarum erat*), is a favoured usage of Suetonius (cf. *Otho* 10,2; *Vitell.* 10,1).

temple of the Caesars: the *aedes Caesarum* appears to have been the name applied later in the first century A.D. to the temple of the Deified Augustus, which was one of only two public building-projects carried out by Tiberius (Tac. *Ann.* VI. 45,2); for some reason – presumably the emperor's retirement to Capreae – it was left undedicated at the time of Tiberius' death in A.D. 37, and this function was completed by Caligula; it would appear to have been this temple which figures on a coin of A.D. 37 (*RIC* I^2. 36). It received major reconstruction under both Domitian and Antoninus Pius (see *RIC* III. (Antoninus) 973 of A.D. 157–8).

Problems surround our understanding of the building; for example, the temples featured on the coins of Caligula and Antoninus do not appear to be identical, though this may simply reflect changes made during its rebuildings. The precise site is still controversial, but the temple was probably situated in unexplored ground at the foot of the Palatine hill, near the Basilica Julia (see Platner and Ashby, 1929, 62–5; Blake, 1959, 13; Boethius and Ward-Perkins, 1970, 203). For contemporary references to the building, see Lugli, 1960, nos. 98–105.

even Augustus' sceptre: the statue of Augustus in the temple represented the *princeps* as a *triumphator*, in the triumphal toga (*toga picta* – see Pliny *Nat. Hist.* VIII. 195), carrying a laurel-branch in his right hand, and in his left the ivory-sceptre crowned by an eagle (Tac. *Ann.* IV. 26,4; Dion. Hal. III. 61; Val. Max. IV. 4,5; Juv. *Sat.* X. 43).

Section 2

by Galba: Galba's family-history, early life and career are discussed above in Introduction 4, whilst his campaign against Nero may be followed in Introduction 3.

had no connection at all: Plutarch (*Galba* 3,1) says that Galba was related to Livia, the wife of Augustus, whose favour he certainly enjoyed. A very tenuous connection did exist through Galba's step-mother, Livia Ocellina, and it is possible that Plutarch confused the two ladies.

of a most noble origin: all writers stress the *nobilitas* of Galba's family (Tac. *Hist.* I. 49,2; Victor *Caes.* 6,1; Juv. *Sat.* VIII. 5). For the concept of *nobilitas* during the republic and early principate, see Gelzer, 1969. The earliest member of the family to attain curule office was the Servius Galba who in 148 B.C. precipitated a rising amongst the Lusitanians.

such an old and great family: Suetonius uses the archaic word, *prosapia*, for "family" presumably as appropriate to such a context. Interestingly, Quintilian

(*Inst. Or.* VIII. 3,26) deprecates it as a tasteless word, the use of which should be avoided.

on his statues he always added: no such information has survived on any of Galba's statues or inscriptions.

great-grandson of Quintus Catulus Capitolinus: Galba's mother, Mummia Achaica, was Catulus' granddaughter, and Galba's great pride in the family-connection is singled out by Plutarch (*Galba* 3,1). Q. Lutatius Catulus was one of the most influential of the optimate-senators of the late republic and was consul in 78 B.C. Although a staunch defender of Sulla's constitution, he was firmly opposed to the corruption of many of Sulla's associates; in particular, he was amongst those who condemned the infamous governor of Sicily, Gaius Verres, in 70 B.C. A strong opponent of Pompey and Caesar, he tried to implicate the latter in the Catilinarian conspiracy of 63 B.C., perhaps annoyed at his defeat at Caesar's hands in the election for the post of *pontifex maximus* in the same year. Cicero regarded him as one of the most powerful figures in the politics of the late republic (*Brutus* 222). Catulus died in 60 B.C. (Cicero *Ad Att.* II. 24,4). For his career and influence, see Syme, 1939, 21ff. The *cognomen*, Capitolinus, derived from his role as a commissioner in charge of restoring the temple of Jupiter, initially after the fire of 83 B.C.; he retained the title despite Caesar's attempt to deprive him of it in 62 B.C., and his name remained on the temple until the destruction of A.D. 69 (see *Vitell.* 15,3).

family-tree: these consisted of the masked busts of the family-ancestors arranged in the *atrium* ("entrance-hall") of a Roman noble's house; these busts would be joined by painted lines to create a family-tree (Pliny *Nat. Hist.* XXXV. 6). For the *atrium* in the Roman house, see Boethius and Ward-Perkins, 1970, 312ff.

back to Jupiter: the creation of such fanciful origins to family-trees was normal practice amongst noble families, who hoped in this way to enhance their standing (*auctoritas*); in the same way, members of the *gens Julia* looked back to the goddess, Venus.

Pasiphae: Minos' wife was the daughter of the sun-god, which probably explains her attraction for the Sulpicii. The contemporary epic-poet, Silius Italicus (VIII. 468ff), connects the same genealogical legend with a Galba who commanded an Etruscan unit at the battle of Cannae (216 B.C.).

Suetonius uses the same antique form, *Minonis* (*Minois*), as in *Tib.* 70,3; the form is preferred also by Sallust.

Section 3

1   **distinctions:** the *elogia* were the inscriptions (*tituli*) which were appended to the busts (*imagines*) in the *atrium*.

the whole family's: that is, all of the Sulpicii; Galba's was just one branch of a *gens* which could boast at least nine more (e.g. Cornutus and Rufus).

Familiae must be a genitive dependent on *imagines et elogia*, as the verb, *attingere* is always in Suetonius followed by the accusative case.

surname of Galba: the name appears in Silius Italicus' account of the battle of Cannae (VIII. 468ff), though without a gentile name; however, the mention in that

passage of the Pasiphae-legend (above on 2) suggests that Galba was indeed a Sulpicius.

beseiged a Spanish settlement: presumably the Servius Galba mentioned below in 3,2.

galbanum: a resinous gum which was taken from a Syrian plant, and used as a snake-repellent (Pliny *Nat. Hist.* XII. 126).

The whole passage illustrates a relaxed use of verb-tenses on Suetonius' part – *succenderit......uteretur......visus sit* –, where imperfect and perfect subjunctives, as elsewhere in his works, appear to be interchangeable.

applied a compress: a *galbeus* appears to have been a kind of decorative bracelet, which by an extension of meaning was applied to a medicinal bandage, in which medications were wrapped in wool, and put around the arm like a bracelet.

exceptionally fat: since many Roman *cognomina* described physical characteristics, the use of a celtic word (meaning "obese") seems the most reasonable explanation of the origin of the name. For examples of the name amongst celtic people, see Livy XXIII. 26 (Spain) and Caesar *Bell. Gall.* II. 4,7 (Germany).

a type of insect: apparently the larva of the ash-borer; if this is correct, its use as a name can be compared with Cossus, another word referring to a larva living under the bark of trees (Pliny *Nat. Hist.* XI. 113). Such detailed etymological research is a characteristic of Suetonius.

2 **The earliest member:** in choosing Servius Galba (the consul of 144 B.C.), Suetonius ignores a number of earlier members of the family who achieved position – P. Sulpicius Galba Maximus, who was consul in 211 and 204 B.C., without apparently having held any junior offices (Livy XXV. 41 and XXVI. 1); C. Sulpicius Galba, who was recorded as a *pontifex* in 201 B.C. (Livy XXX. 39); Ser. Sulpicius Galba, aedile in 188 B.C. and *praetor urbanus* in the following year (Livy XXXVIII. 35); C. Sulpicius Galba, who was *praetor urbanus* in 171 B.C. (Livy XLII. 28), and possibly the father of the consul of 144.

ex-consul, Servius Galba: consul in 144 B.C. with L. Aurelius Cotta. Appian (*Hisp.* 60) says that he was the richest man of his day.

the greatest orator of his day: Cicero noticed his rhetorical excellence in a number of places (*Brutus* 21 and 33; *De Oratore* I. 40), comparing him favourably with such contemporaries as the Elder Cato, Scipio Aemilianus, and C. Laelius.

he treacherously slaughtered: following his praetorship in 150 B.C., Galba was given Hispania Ulterior as his province; he invaded Lusitania (Portugal), suffering a major reverse, which he determined to avenge. He did this by luring the Lusitanians into a trap by pretending to sympathise with their problems, and massacred them irrespective of age or sex. Viriathus was one of the few who escaped. The reaction to Galba in Rome was extremely hostile, and he was impeached in a ferocious speech by the Elder Cato, then 85 years old; Galba managed to escape conviction partly by bribery, and partly by playing upon people's sympathy for his position (Appian *Hisp.* 58–60).

thirty thousand: the figure is given as seven thousand by Valerius Maximus (IX. 6,2).

war with Viriathus: following the massacre, Viriathus conducted a guerilla-campaign, which was effective enough to tie up consular armies for a decade; it was not until the then-proconsul, Servilius Caepio, had him assassinated that the Lusitanians gave in (139 B.C.).

His grandson: Servius Galba was one of the earliest of Caesar's *legati* (57 B.C.), who served him with some success in the Alps (*Bell. Gall.* III. 1ff; Syme, 1939, 67 and 69).

following his defeat: Galba had been disappointed in his hopes of a consulship in 49 B.C., and had not subsequently been designated by Caesar (*Bell. Gall.* VIII. 50,4). For his insolence to Caesar, see Val. Max. VI. 2.

he joined the conspiracy: he was a cousin of Decimus Brutus and a friend of Cicero (*Ad Fam.* X. 30 and XI. 7), who makes it clear that, like many members of his family, he was financially well-off. Galba joined the conspirators, and Cicero later (*Phil.* XIII. 16) told Marcus Antonius that the worthy Galba (*fortissimus et constantissimus civis*) would use the same dagger on him that he had used on Caesar (Appian *BC* II. 113). Galba commanded a legion on the republican side at Mutina (Cic. *Ad Fam.* X. 30).

under the law of Quintus Pedius: in 43 B.C., the consul, Quintus Pedius, who was a nephew of Caesar's, proposed a law banishing those who had taken part in the conspiracy against Caesar (Vell. Pat. II. 69,5; *RGDA* 2). Pedius did not live out the consular year which he shared with Octavian, but died of shame at having to connive at the triumviral proscription-programme (Appian *BC* IV. 6). Nero's great-grandfather also fell victim to this law (Suet. *Nero* 3,1). Pedius' career is discussed briefly by Syme (1939, 128f).

3 **His grandfather:** C. Sulpicius Galba was certainly used by the Elder Pliny, and is cited by both Plutarch (*Rom.* 17) and Orosius (V. 23).

did not move beyond: for this use of *egredior*, which is common in post-Augustan latin, cf. Tac. *Ann.* III. 30,1.

rose to the consulship: Servius Galba was suffect-consul, probably in 5 B.C.

even hunchbacked: this physical deformity of Galba's is said to have been the subject of a joke by Augustus (Macrobius *Sat.* II. 4,8; cf. II. 6,4).

moderate speaker: see Macrobius (*Sat.* II. 6,3) for a higher estimate of his ability.

4 **Mummia Achaica:** she may well have been a daughter of the Mummius who was a *legatus* of Crassus during the Spartacus-revolt of 71 B.C., and who incurred Crassus' wrath by a precipitate battle which led to a serious defeat (Plut. *Crassus* 10). Syme (1939, 377) argues that the use of antique family-*cognomina* had become fashionable under Augustus; it was encouraged in the "restored republic" to stress family-links that went back into the early days of the republic. The *cognomen*, Achaicus, derived from the Lucius Mummius who conquered Greece in 146 B.C., and who was responsible for razing the city of Corinth to the ground.

of Catulus: see above on section 2.

Livia Ocellina: it is possible that her father was Lucius Livius Ocella, who is recorded as having been quaestor in Hispania Citerior (*CIL* VI. 246). The name, Ocella, is said by Pliny (*Nat. Hist.* XI. 150) to have derived from the smallness of his eyes.

Gaius, the elder: Gaius Galba was consul in A.D. 22 with Decimus Haterius (Tac. *Ann*. III. 52,1); Tacitus (*Ann*. VI. 40,3) records his death by suicide in A.D. 36 after Tiberius had refused to allow him to take part in the drawing of lots for provinces after he had become senior ex-consul. Tiberius' reason for this decision probably stemmed from the poverty mentioned here; the *princeps* presumably either knew that the poverty was a bad reflection on Galba's soundness or was in general fearful that poverty might have tempted Galba into corrupt practices.

when he was due: this refers to Galba's becoming senior ex-consul. The Augustan system, like Pompey's of 52 B.C., required an interval of five years between the tenure of office in Rome and participation in the drawing of lots for a province. In the case of consular provinces the interval was usually longer because the number of consuls in each year (*ordinarii* and *suffecti*) produced more candidates than vacancies; the potential field was, however, reduced by disqualifications or by candidates who declined to participate. Asia and Africa were the only senatorial provinces normally governed by ex-consuls.

Section 4

1 **Servius Galba.....was born:** for the difficulty in establishing the true year of Galba's birth, see above in Introduction 4. Essentially, the statement here is at odds with that in section 23 concerning Galba's age at the time of his death.

Marcus Valerius Messala: this is the son of M. Valerius Messala Corvinus, who was consul in 31 B.C., a firm supporter of Augustus, literary patron of Ovid and Tibullus, and whose marriage-alliances bound him strongly into the governing faction (Syme, 1939, 423). The son, Messala Messalinus, after his consulship, served under Tiberius in the Balkans in A.D. 6, and is described by Velleius as a man "whose spirit was mightier even than his pedigree" (cf. Dio LV. 29,1). His brother was Tiberius' friend, Cotta Messalinus, who was consul in A.D. 20. Tibullus (II. 5) composed a poem on the subject of the appointment of Messala Messalinus to one of the priestly colleges, as a *quindecemvir sacris faciundis*; on this priesthood, see below in 8,1.

Gnaeus Lentulus: it appears that Suetonius has mistaken the Lentulus who was consul in 3 B.C., whose *praenomen* was Lucius. Two holders of the *praenomen*, Gnaeus, were consuls in 18 and 14 B.C. Lucius Lentulus went on to become proconsul of Africa in A.D. 4–5.

near Tarracina: Suetonius here uses an alternative spelling (Terracina) for the town in Latium, some sixty miles south-west of Rome; in poetry, its ancient Volscian name, Anxur, was used. The connection of Galba's family with Tarracina is demonstrated by *CIL* I. 576.

towards Fundi: some twelve miles south of Tarracina and the next major stopping-place on the *via Appia*.

Petentibus is a dative of the person concerned, and is commonly used in this formula for expressing directions.

He was adopted: because she was not considered to be the head of a household, a woman could not adopt during her lifetime; this adoption must, therefore, have been contained in the will of Galba's step-mother, Livia Ocellina (see above in Introduction 4 and note on section 3,4).

and took Livius: no extant documents indicate Galba's use of the gentile name, Livius, with the *cognomen* Ocella – though see below for the use of Livius. It was common practice in the expression of a *cognomen* to use an adjectival form of the name itself (*Ocellare*) in agreement with *cognomen*.

He also changed: there is evidence (*CIL* I. 770–1) for Galba's use of the *praenomen*, Lucius, during his consulship in A.D. 33. The *praenomen* was derived from Lucius Livius Ocella, who is assumed to have been Ocellina's father (see above on section 3,4).

until he became emperor: officially Galba, as emperor, was styled "Servius Galba Imp. Caesar Augustus" (*ILS* 1988). However, documents from the east display a greater freedom; for example, on *CIG* III. 4947, he is Λούκιος Λίβιος Σεβαστός Σουλπίκιος Γάλβα Αὐτοκράτωρ (Lucius Livius Augustus Sulpicius Galba Imperator). Alexandrian coins style him Λουκ Λιβ Σουλπ Γαλβα καισ Σεβ αυτ (Lucius Livius Sulpicius Galba Caesar Augustus Imperator; see Milne, 1971, 9–10). This lends weight to Suetonius' assertion of his late use of his adoptive names; it may well not have been known in Egypt that on his acclamation he had dispensed with their use.

There is a well-known story: Tacitus (*Ann.* VI. 20,3) attributes the prediction to Tiberius and relates it to A.D. 33, the year of Galba's consulship; Dio (LVII. 19,4) also attributes the saying to Tiberius, but relates it to the occasion of Galba's engagement in A.D. 20. Josephus (*Ant. J.* XVIII. 6,9) also refers the statement to Tiberius, but provides no context.

to greet: the traditional *salutatio* of the early morning was restricted to the emperor's *amici*; those that attracted a wider gathering were held more occasionally.

pinched him on the cheek: it is not clear what gesture is involved, and some refer it to a practice of transferring a kiss from lip to lip by means of the index-finger (Apuleius *Met.* VI. 22; Suet. *Div. Aug.* 94,8; Servius on Virgil *Aeneid* I. 260).

when Tiberius: Dio (LVII. 19,4) also gives Tiberius' reason for sparing Galba, saying that Tiberius saw no danger to himself from a man who would not win power until old age, and adds that Tiberius respected what fate had decreed.

The use of *sed et* is common in Suetonius to express an accumulation of evidence.

"Then he can live": a similar sentiment is related by Julius Capitolinus (SHA, *Maximinus* 4) with reference to Caracalla's dismissal of a possible threat to himself from Maximinus.

2 **When his grandfather:** that is, Gaius Galba, the historian (see above on section 3,3).

sacrificing to avert: the latin verb, *procurare*, was a technical term for averting the evil consequences of portents, especially lightning. The full details of the averting of the evil effects of lightning-strikes (the *ars fulminum*) were learned by the Romans from the *libri fulgurales* of the Etruscans (see Seneca *Quaest. Nat.* I.I 32,2).

laiden with acorns: this is meant to indicate a late stage in the year, from which it was interpreted that power would come to Galba late in life.

"When mules have foals": a proverbial expression commonly used in the classical world (Herodotus III. 151; cf. Pliny *Nat. Hist.* VIII. 173; Juv. *Sat.* XIII. 64), and equivalent to our usage "pigs might fly".

Later when Servius Galba was contemplating: this could refer to any time after Vindex's initial approaches to provincial governors late in A.D. 67 (see Introduction 3) and until Galba's entry into the field in April, A.D. 68.

a mule happening to give birth: see also Dio LXIV. 1,3; for the assumed force of the portent, see Livy XXVI. 23 and XXXVII. 3.

shuddered at this: prior to this and other passages in Suetonius (e.g. *Vitell.* 10,3), the verb, *abhorrere*, is followed by *a* with the ablative case.

3   **when he came of age:** Dio (LVI. 29, 5–6) records that Galba's assumption of the *toga virilis* took place on January 1st in A.D. 14, and that it was subsequently observed that there was significance in the fact that the man who overthrew the last of the Julio-Claudians had "come of age" in the last year of Augustus' life.

he dreamed that: the same dream is related by Dio (LXIV. 1,2).

The construction of a present participle after *somniavit* is similar to that found with verbs such as *videre* and *audire*.

quickly: the word *ocius* commonly means "at once", though Cicero always retains a comparative force.

when he woke up: the use of *evigilare* in the sense of "wake up" is post-Augustan; in earlier latin, it has the force of "to be watchful".

he opened the hall-door: that is, the door leading from the *atrium* into the street. See below in 18,2 for a further mention of the statue – in connection with Galba's fall.

to Tusculum: the modern Frascati, where many members of the senatorial nobility had country-villas.

in a room of his house: the latin, *in parte aedium*, appears to need further specification; the reference might normally be to the *atrium* which housed the shrine to the family's gods. Later emperors kept a golden statue of Fortuna in their bedrooms (SHA, *Antoninus* 12).

all-night vigil: this kind of occasion was borrowed by Roman religion from the practices of eastern cults, such as the worship of Dionysus.

4   **Even when:** Suetonius employs a great variety of constructions with *quamquam*; the present example, using a descriptive ablative, finds a parallel in *Div. Tit.* 3,1.

The idea of *aetas constans* is the "stability" which comes with maturity.

obsolete national custom: we have no other references to this custom.

Section 5

1   **the liberal arts:** according to Cicero (*De Oratore* III. 127), these included geometry, music, poetry and other literature; it is clear from other references that rhetoric and the law were also included.

Suetonius prefers the use of the dative case after *attendere* to the more normal accusative.

into his marriage: the lax attitude to marriage had been a problem since the later second century B.C., and had attracted the attention of Augustus (Balsdon, 1969, 82ff; Jones, 1970, 131ff).

Lepida: this was probably Aemilia Lepida, the daughter of Manius Aemilius Lepidus (consul in A.D. 11). For an elucidation of the Aemilii Lepidi in the early principate, see Syme, 1955 and stemma IV in Syme, 1939. Contrary to much that

was written before Syme's clarification of the branches of the family, this Aemilia Lepida was not the "marriageable daughter" who provided the grounds for her father's excusing of himself from the lots for the proconsulship of Africa in A.D. 21 (Tac. *Ann*. III. 35,2); that Lepidus was Marcus, the cousin of Manius and consul in A.D. 6.

by any match: the word, *condicio*, used here of a marriage-arrangement, represents an abbreviation of *condicio uxoria*.

not even with Agrippina: Agrippina (the younger) was a daughter of Germanicus and Agrippina, and who was born at Cologne in A.D. 15 (Tac. *Ann*. XII. 27,1); in A.D. 28, she married Gnaeus Domitius Ahenobarbus (*Ann*. IV. 75,1; Shotter, 1989, 203), who is described by Suetonius (*Nero* 5) as "totally uncongenial". He reached the consulship in A.D. 32, and died seven years later. His death must have been followed almost immediately by Agrippina's banishment by her brother, Caligula. She was recalled by Claudius soon after his accession in A.D. 41, and married him in A.D. 49 (*Ann* XI. 5), making sure that her and Domitius' son, Nero, was adopted by Claudius as his successor. Agrippina's influence over her son as *princeps* was at first strong, but gradually waned; she was murdered by him in A.D. 59 (*Ann*. XIV. 1ff). According to Tacitus (*Ann*. IV. 53,3), Agrippina wrote an account of her family, which might conceivably have been the source of Suetonius' story here. Between the time of her recall from exile and her marriage to Claudius, she was married to the orator, Passienus Crispus, whom she is alleged to have murdered after he had left his property to his stepson, Nero (*Nero* 6). It is not clear when this attempted seduction of Galba took place; it is, however, noteworthy that it failed, in view of Agrippina's well-attested determination to get what she wanted (*Ann*. XII. 7,5); for her role as Nero's mother, see Warmington, 1969, 12ff.

at a meeting of married women: this refers to a religious guild which had existed from very early times, and which met on the Quirinal to celebrate certain festivals, and to mark the entry of a bride into the ranks of *feminae consulares* (Livy V. 25).

2   **always especially respectful:** Galba's respect was shown by his commemoration of her on his coinage in A.D. 68 (*RIC* I². pp. 226 and 240), which also helped to establish an idea of his connection with the family of Augustus and thus his claim to represent a legitimate continuation of the principate. Livia Drusilla was adopted under the terms of her husband's will into the *gens Julia* and given the name, Augusta (*Ann*. I. 8,2). Suetonius refers to her here as Livia Augusta, but elsewhere uses her correct adoptive name of Julia Augusta (*Cal*. 16,3). For her role, see Jones, 1970, 164ff.

he enjoyed great favour: according to Plutarch (*Galba* 3,2), Galba owed his consulship to her, though this is hard to accept in view of the fact that Galba's consulship came in A.D. 33, four years after Livia's death; further, Livia had had little contact with Tiberius since the latter's departure to Capreae in A.D. 26.

legatee: this is the first recorded use of *legatarius*, though the word is commonly employed by later juristic writers.

and left him: to make the amount intelligible, *centena milia* has to be understood with *quingenties* – that is, fifty million *sestertii*; the *sestertius* represented the largest element in the "small change" in the money-system, which was made up of

interrelated denominations of gold (AV), silver (AR) and orichalcum/copper (Æ).
Under Augustus, the system was:

1 aureus (AV)	=	25 denarii
1 denarius (AR)	=	4 sestertii
1 sestertius (Æ)	=	2 dupondii
1 dupondius (Æ)	=	2 asses
1 as (Æ)	=	2 semisses
1 semis (Æ)	=	2 quadrantes (Æ)

Thus, fifty million *sestertii* is here rendered as half a million *aurei*, there being one
hundred *sestertii* to each *aureus*.

because the sum was indicated: an expression in words was important, because
slight distinctions between symbols made a great difference to the amount involved.
In this case, fifty million *sestertii* was shown as HS⌐D⌐. whilst five hundred thousand
– Tiberius' preferred figure – was HS D̄.

reduced the sum: the use of *revocare* in the sense of "reduce" is without parallel;
redigere or *recidere* are normally employed by Suetonius.
With *quingenta* we should understand *sestertia*.

did not receive even that: Tiberius suppressed Livia's will and paid none of the
bequests (Dio LIX. 1,4). Caligula, however, is said by Suetonius (*Cal.* 16,3) to have
honoured the wills of both Livia and Tiberius.

Section 6

1   before the legal age: the lowest magistracy on the *cursus honorum* was the
quaestorship, which under Augustus' management was held at about the age of
twenty-five years, though two hurdles had to be passed before this, in the form of
the vigintivirate and military tribunate; in both of these, performance had a bearing
on the future career (Birley E., 1953, 197ff). The minimum-age for the praetorship
was normally thirty years, though this could be reduced by a year in respect of each
legitimate child of the candidate. The consulship would then follow at about thirty-
five, leaving many years of relative youth available for the important proconsular
posts. Thus, the consulship was less of an end in itself than a gateway to major
posts in the service of the *princeps*.

as praetor: during the republic most games and shows had been organised by the
aediles, though in 22 B.C. Augustus conferred this task (*cura ludorum*) upon the
praetors (Dio LIV. 2,3; Tac. *Ann.* I. 15, 3–5; Juv. *Sat.* XI. 193), who were given
grants from the treasury (*aerarium*) to perform the function.

in charge of: the word, *commissio*, is normally used of opening the games (cf.
Suet. *Div. Claud.* 21,1; *Nero* 23,1).

Floral games: the games in honour of Flora were one of a number of plebeian
festivals introduced around the time of the Punic wars. This festival was associated
with spring and the rebirth of wild nature, and was a holiday of unfettered
carousing; it included lewd theatrical performances and hunting in the *circus
maximus* (Wiedemann, 1992). The festival was formally instituted on an annual
basis in 173 B.C., under the control of the aediles, and its celebration eventually
spanned the period from April 28th until May 3rd (Ovid *Fasti* V. 371).

elephants walking on tight-ropes: Dio (LXII. 17,2) describes this kind of display as a speciality during Nero's reign (cf. *Nero* 11,2); the elephants were made to walk, carrying a rider, down wires which were extended from the top of the auditorium down to the arena; see also observations in Pliny (*Nat. Hist.* VIII. 3) and Seneca (*Ep. Mor.* 85,41).

governor of Aquitania: possibly in A.D. 31 or 32, just prior to his consulship – a similar sequence to that followed by Agricola (Tac. *Agr.* 9,1, where it is suggested that the governorship was seen as a preparation for the consulship). Aquitania (in south-west France) was one of the three imperial provinces in Gaul, along with Lugdunensis and Belgica. The fourth, Narbonensis, had been a province since the late second century B.C., and was handed over by Augustus to the control of the senate (Shotter, 1991b, 53f).

for almost a year: the latin, *anno*, is an ablative expressing duration of time.

he held the consulate: Galba was *consul ordinarius* in A.D. 33; that means that he gave his name to the year. It had been usual since Augustus' time for the *ordinarii* to resign after a number of months to make room for one or more pairs of replacement-consuls (*suffecti*).

succeeded Lucius (sic) Domitius: Nero was born Lucius Domitius, but his father, who was consul in A.D. 32, bore the *praenomen*, Gnaeus. Suetonius (or a later copyist) has made an error here. For Gnaeus Domitius, see above on section 5,1 and *Nero* 5.

by the father of the future emperor, Otho: Lucius Salvius Otho (on whom see below on *Otho* 1,2) was the *consul suffectus* who replaced Galba on July 1st, A.D. 33.

This was a portent: like many such coincidences, great significance was read into it after the event. We may compare Tacitus' comment (*Ann.* XV. 74,2) on the subsequent reaction to the fact that Nero dedicated to Jupiter *Vindex* the dagger that had been meant to kill him in the Pisonian conspiracy of A.D. 65.

2   **He was appointed by Gaius Caesar:** that is, Caligula, who reigned from A.D. 37 to 41. It is clear that the purpose of the appointment was to restore discipline amongst the legions of Upper Germany, following Gaetulicus' lax tenure. See Balsdon, 1934, 58ff and Barrett, 1989, 104f and 129ff.

to replace Gaetulicus: the sense clearly requires the mention of Gaetulicus' name in a lacuna between *Caesare* and *-lici*. Scholars are, however, uncertain of the length of the lacuna; the present text represents the minimal restoration. Gnaeus Cornelius Lentulus Gaetulicus was consul in A.D. 26. Despite his daughter's engagement to Sejanus' son, he survived Sejanus' downfall because of Tiberius' fear that he would turn the German legions on Rome, if threatened. He was extremely popular with his troops because of his lax discipline (Tac. *Ann.* VI. 30,2). It is unclear whether he was involved with Sejanus (Syme, 1958, i.384), though he protested his innocence and may have been protected by his father's influence with Tiberius; Gaetulicus' father became *praefectus urbis* in A.D. 33 (see Seneca *Ep. Mor.* 83,14; Dio LVIII. 8,3; Shotter, 1989, 177f). Caligula had Gaetulicus put to death in A.D. 39 as a result of his popularity with the army (Dio LIX. 22,5), and Suetonius (*Div. Claud.* 9) connects Gaetulicus with a conspiracy which apparently aimed to replace Caligula by his brother-in-law, Marcus Aemilius

Lepidus (Balsdon, 1934, 66ff). The seriousness of the situation is confirmed by the records of the Arval Brethren, noting the detection on October 27th, A.D. 39 of the "wicked plans" (*nefaria consilia*) of Gaetulicus against Caligula (*ILS* 229; Smallwood, 1967, 14). For the circumstances of Gaetulicus' conspiracy and Galba's possible part in his execution, see Barrett, 1989, 104ff. Caligula visited the Rhine in person, arriving either in time for or just after Gaetulicus' execution.

Gaetulicus was a noted composer of epigrams (Pliny *Epp*. V. 3,5), and probably a historian also (Suet. *Cal*. 8).

he issued an order: orders of movements were issued on wooden tablets (*tesserae militares*; Livy IX. 32,4).

inside their cloaks: the *paenula* was a sleeveless, leather, cloak with a hood, which was widely worn in bad weather (*Nero* 49).

"Learn, you soldiers.....": the verse is in trochaic metre, which was commonly used in soldiers' doggerel.

3　**over requests for leave:** unusually Suetonius constructs *interdicere* with an infinitive in preference to the more common *ne* with the subjunctive.

The purchase of leave from centurions amounted to something of a scandal in the army (Tac. *Ann*. I. 17,6), occasionally weakening legions to the point of disastrous ineffectiveness (*Ann*. XV. 9,2).

the enemy: Galba was victorious over the Chatti in A.D. 41 (Dio LX. 8,7), and his reputation as commander in Germany remained high (Plut. *Galba* 3,2; Tac. *Hist*. I. 49,4).

During all of this: Caligula's presence as a campaigner in Germany attracted universal ridicule in antiquity (Tac. *Hist*. IV. 15,2; *Germ*. 37,5; Suet. *Cal*. 44–7; Dio LIX. 21), though Persius (*Sat*. VI. 43f) records the emperor's announcement to the senate of a great victory over the Germans. It is unlikely that a full campaign would have been mounted as late in the year as November, and it is perhaps safest to assume that Caligula was enthusiastic in his participation in and support of Galba's manoeuvres aimed at the restoration of discipline following Gaetulicus' tenure and conspiracy (Balsdon, 1934, 76ff).

countless troops: elsewhere Suetonius (*Cal*. 43) refers to the gathering as the greatest number ever, whilst Dio (LIX. 22,2) puts the number at two hundred or two hundred and fifty thousand men.

field-manoeuvres: Vegetius (*De Re Mil*. I. 9) shows that the *decursio* consisted of covering a distance of twenty Roman miles at normal pace and twenty-four Roman miles at an accelerated pace. This was meant to be done in a time equivalent to about six-and-a-half hours. Vegetius calls such manoeuvres *campicursio*.

with his shield on his shoulder: Nero (*Nero* 7,2) is said to have performed in a similar fashion at the head of the praetorian guard to mark the commencement of his public career.

running alongside the emperor's chariot: this was normally taken as an act of public humiliation (Plut. *Lucullus* 21). Diocletian is said to have inflicted it on his Caesar and son-in-law, Galerius, following the latter's defeat at the hands of the Persians (Ammianus XIV. 11; Eutropius IX. 15), and Caligula is reported to have humiliated senators in this way (*Cal*. 27).

twenty miles: for the significance of the distance, see note (above) on *field-manoeuvres*; twenty Roman miles is equivalent to approximately 18.5 of our miles (or 29.5 kilometres).

Section 7

1 **when Gaius was assassinated:** Caligula was murdered at the Palatine games on January 24th, A.D. 41 by Cassius Chaerea and Cornelius Sabinus, both of whom were tribunes in the praetorian guard (*Cal.* 58).
Some such formulation as *capiendi imperii* has to be understood with *ad occasionem*.
circle of close friends: the *comites* were those of an emperor's friends (*amici*) who were chosen to accompany him when he went abroad or on campaign. The *amici* were admitted to his *salutationes* (see above on 4,1), and from them were chosen his close advisers (*consilium principis*; see Crook, 1955).
expedition to Britain: in A.D. 43; for Claudius' presence on that expedition, see *Div. Vesp.* 4,1. There is no other evidence for Galba's participation, which is clearly implied here.
without ballot: the normal procedure for proconsulships of Africa and Asia was for a ballot to be held from amongst senior ex-consuls. A parallel to the present occasion is to be found in the appointment, also to Africa, of Quintus Junius Blaesus by Tiberius (Tac. *Ann.* III. 35). On that occasion, because of the continuing war against the guerilla-leader, Tacfarinas, the senate had requested Tiberius – much against his will – to resort to the extraordinary procedure. Blaesus, too, held his appointment for two years.
proconsulship of Africa: the high quality of Galba's administration of Africa is mentioned by both Plutarch (*Galba* 3,2) and Tacitus (*Hist.* I. 49,4). The appointment, since the time of Augustus, had been set at one year, but was occasionally exceeded; Dio (LX. 25,6) mentions Claudius in this context.
he was given the job: inter-tribal conflict was a notorious problem in a province which was extremely sensitive because of its role in Rome's corn-supply. The Musulamii, under Tacfarinas, had defied Roman generals during the reign of Tiberius (A.D. 17–24), and had caused trouble again under Claudius (Victor *Caes.* 4). Similarly troublesome were the Garamantes and the Gaetuli. Tacitus (*Hist.* IV. 50) alludes to further difficulties in A.D. 70. The reorganisation to which Suetonius refers may be connected with the undoing of the arrangements of Caligula, who had put the legion in the province (III Augusta) under an imperial *legatus*, whilst confining the proconsul's responsibility to civil administration in Africa Vetus.
with great strictness: Tacitus (*Hist.* I. 49,4) refers only to Galba's *moderatio* in the post. The attention to detail remained a characteristic of Galba as *princeps*, though he then sometimes pursued the small issues at the expense of larger and more significant matters.

2 **what was left over:** the amount specified in the latin is a *modius*, which is approximately one quarter of a bushel; the price mentioned was around one third of a year's pay for a legionary soldier. For another example, see Pliny (*Nat. Hist.* VIII. 222).
concerning the ownership: *proprietas* had not been previously used of ownership.

Section 8

1 **the triumphal insignia:** since the time of Augustus, the honour of a full triumph had been restricted to members of the imperial family; successful generals were permitted to style themselves *triumphalis*, and to enjoy the symbols of the honour – the *toga picta*, the *tunica palmata*, the *aurea corona*, the *scipio eburnus*, and usually a statue. There was a general tendency during the first century A.D. for the honour to be handed around uncritically, and, by the time of Trajan, it had little value left.

three priesthoods: such honours were often coupled with the triumphal insignia (*Div. Vesp.* 4,2).

the Board of Fifteen: this ancient priesthood went back to the regal period, and had been increased to fifteen members by Sulla. As priests of Apollo, their duties included consulting the Sibylline Books (when the senate instructed that a consultation should take place), and organising the secular games and those that were sacred to Apollo (see Tac. *Ann.* XI. 11).

the Brotherhood of Titius: their origin was obscure, and different versions existed as to whether the Brotherhood was founded by Romulus or by the Sabine, Titus Tatius (Tac. *Hist.* II. 95,1 and *Ann.* I. 54,1). Historically, the priests preserved practices that were distinctly Sabine in origin. Augustus injected new dignity into the Brotherhood as part of his religious revival, becoming a member himself.

and of the priests of Augustus: this priesthood was introduced by Tiberius to organise the cult of the deified Augustus and the *gens Julia* (Tac. *Hist.* II. 95,1 and I. 54,1). There were originally twenty-one priests, together with Tiberius, Claudius, Drusus and Germanicus as supernumeraries. After Claudius' deification in A.D. 54, his cult was subjoined to that of Augustus, and the brotherhood entitled *sodales Augustales Claudiales*.

Suetonius here, as elsewhere, uses *item* as an alternative to *et*.

enrolled as a member: originally, the priests had controlled their own membership by co-optation; after 103 B.C., a process of election took place from a group nominated by the priests. Formally, those successful in the election were then co-opted. In the early principate, Augustus and Tiberius instituted a practice which was close to that governing the election of magistrates: the *princeps* provided a list of approved candidates (*nominati*) and singled out some whose "election" was required (*commendati*). The election-process from Tiberius' time was carried out in the senate and, as before, successful candidates were formally co-opted by the priestly bodies (Shotter, 1966, 328ff).

in retirement: it is not clear how voluntary this retirement was; for examples of enforced retirement, see Birley E., 1953. On the other hand, Vespasian seems to have *chosen* to retire between his consulship (A.D. 51) and proconsulship (A.D. 63), because of his fear of Agrippina (*Div. Vesp.* 4,2).

for a drive: the *gestatio* was a popular form of exercise at this time.

ten thousand aurei: expressed in latin as one million *sestertii* (see note above on 5,2).

There is some textual difficulty in the passage as *quam ut* would normally be preceded by *aliter*. It may have slipped out because of confusion with *iter*; alternatively, *iter* may itself represent a corruption of *aliter*.

town of Fundi: near Galba's birthplace (see above on 4,1).

Hispania Tarraconensis: one of the three Spanish provinces which resulted from Augustus' organisation; Tarraconensis and Lusitania were imperial provinces, whilst Baetica was left under the control of the senate.

was offered to him: the appointment was made in A.D. 60 before events in the mid-60s had greatly enhanced Nero's fears of members of the senatorial order. Plutarch specifically says (*Galba* 3,3) that the appointment was made because Nero had no fear of Galba, who was then 65 years of age.

2   **during it, the hair:** Dio (LXIV. 1,3) recounts the same prodigy, and provides the same interpretation of it.

in other words, he would succeed Nero: this has been regarded by some as an explanatory gloss in the manuscript.

in Cantabria: a mountainous area of northern Spain.

twelve axes: the ancient symbols of regal authority in Rome; during the republican period, twelve lictors, with rods and axes, attended the consuls and proconsuls. Augustus made this virtually a symbol of imperial authority by restricting the privilege to himself and the proconsuls of Asia and Africa. The number of lictors attending the *princeps* was increased by Domitian to twenty-four (*Dom.* 41,3).

Section 9

1   **for eight years:** that is, from A.D. 60 until 68, when he became emperor. The length of tenure as an imperial *legatus* was not fixed, but depended on the will of the *princeps*. Tiberius, for example, kept Poppaeus Sabinus in Moesia for twenty-four years, whilst Nero kept Otho in Lusitania for ten (*Otho* 3,2). On the other hand, after the civil war, Vespasian tried to limit tenure to about three years.

in an uneven fashion: Tacitus, on the other hand (*Hist.* I. 49,4), praised Galba's sense of justice in this appointment, which matched his behaviour in his earlier appointments. Plutarch (*Galba* 4, 1–2) provides a number of examples of how Galba tried to relieve provincials of the full load of hardships inflicted upon them by Nero's agents.

money-changer: *nummularius* was the post-Augustan word for a money-changer, banker and auctioneer; the usual word in earlier latin was *mensarius*.

Ex fide is commonly used in silver-age latin for "fraudulent", as the antithesis of *cum fide*.

versanti is used for the more common *tractanti*.

his hands chopped off: Domitian inflicted this punishment as a torture in his search for the co-conspirators of Antonius Saturninus in A.D. 89 (*Dom.* 10,5), whilst Claudius had it inflicted as a punishment for a forger in the courtroom itself (*Div. Claud.* 15,2). The punishment itself may be seen as consistent with a general Roman desire to match the penalty to the crime (Wiedemann, 1992, 70).

he might inherit the property: he had himself named as "second heir" (*secundus heres*), so that he might inherit if the principal heir did not or could not (Quintilian *Inst. Or.* VII. 6.9).

protested that he was a Roman citizen: during the republican period, Roman citizens were, in theory at least, protected from capital sentence and scourging by a lex Porcia (of 197 B.C.) and a lex Sempronia (of 123 B.C.); the latter provided wider use of the practice of appeal to the people in such cases (*provocatio*). One of

the primary accusations made against the infamous Gaius Verres was his treatment of men who were Roman citizens (Cicero *Verr*. V. 63). During the principate, probably as a result of a law of Julius Caesar, the right of appeal was transferred from the people to the emperor (Paul. *Sent*. V. 26,1); hence, the appeal made by Saint Paul to Nero against a sentence of scourging (*Acts* 22,25). The present instance, however, illustrates how, even under the principate, the power of a Roman governor remained arbitrary (Wiedemann, 1992, 68).

compensate the man: Verres had been similarly contemptuous in his behaviour by having his victim crucified by the Strait of Messina, so that he could "see Italy and his home from the cross".

Galba became idle and lazy: Galba's reaction was not uncommon amongst senior administrators during Nero's reign (see Tac. *Agr*. 6,3; *Ann*. XIV. 47,2). Tacitus (*Hist*. I. 49,3) says that Galba's behaviour was taken for wisdom when it was in fact due to idleness.

to account for his leisure-time: this clearly refers to the *dictum* of Cato the Censor, which was much admired by Cicero (*Pro Planco* 66), that members of the aristocracy should be as ready and able to account for their conduct off-duty as for when they were undertaking public business. Galba's ironic rejection of this Stoic rule may be regarded as his contribution to the "debate" which was in progress between the *princeps* and Stoic philosophers and senators (Warmington, 1969, 142ff).

2 **New Carthage:** the modern Spanish town of Cartagena; it was founded by the Carthaginians in 242 B.C., becoming a Roman town following its capture by Scipio Africanus in 210 B.C. Under the principate, it enjoyed the status of a *colonia* with the name, *Colonia Victrix Iulia Nova Carthago*.

conducting assizes: the Elder Pliny (*Nat. Hist*. III. 18) provides some detail on such arrangements in Tarraconensis; the province was divided into judicial districts (*conventus*), of which Tarraconensis had seven. The governor held the assizes in the chief town in each of these. Pliny adds that the seven districts of Tarraconensis contained 472 towns and villages.

that the Gallic provinces were in revolt: for a discussion, see Introduction 3 and Shotter, 1975. The news will have reached Galba in the second half of March, though he made no *public* move until April 2nd. Vindex's rebellion certainly did not command total support amongst the Gauls; Lugdunum (Lyons), because of the beneficence which it had received from Nero, refused to join. In fact, the centre of activities was the "native" town of Vienne; Vindex was supported probably by the Arverni, Sequani and Aedui, though the tribes nearer to the Rhine refused to help (Tac. *Hist*. I. 51,3).

a plea for help: it is not clear whether the governor of Aquitania was requesting Galba's help for or against Vindex. Although the unarmed province was governed by a Julius Cordus at the beginning of A.D. 69 (Tac. *Hist*. I. 76,1), it is not known if he had been a Neronian appointment; there is little doubt that Galba would subsequently have removed a governor who had been hostile to Vindex.

a letter from Vindex: Vindex had approached a number of governors by letter prior to the uprising (Plut. *Galba* 4,2); some had reported Vindex to Nero, but it is evident that many, like Galba, had done nothing – itself treasonable inaction (see

below in note on *instructions for Galba's death*). The letter which Vindex now wrote to Galba was more specific, presumably rehearsing Nero's crimes (as in the speech attributed to him by Dio – LXIII. 23), and giving Galba an appraisal of the situation, as a preliminary to inviting him to put himself forward as the movement's leader. Vindex, as a Romanised Gaul, could hardly have expected to carry alone an empire-wide credibility.

The "position" offered by Vindex (*ut humano generi assertorem ducemque se accommodaret*) is echoed in the large volume of coinage connected with the episode (see Kraay, 1949; Sutherland in *RIC* I². 197ff); in particular, notable coin-legends are SALVS HVMANI GENERIS, LIBERTATI, HERCVLES ADSERTOR, LIBERTAS RESTITVTA.

Verginius Rugus, the governor of Upper Germany, in retrospect claimed patriotic motives, as indicated on his epitaph which is quoted by the Younger Pliny (*Epp.* IX. 19,5), though the historian, Cluvius Rufus, put a rather different gloss on Verginius' conduct (Shotter, 1967).

With little hesitation: Plutarch (*Galba* 4, 3–4) says that he consulted with his friends and advisers, and that whilst some were (understandably) for caution, Galba's closest associate, Titus Vinius (*legatus* of legion VI in Tarraconensis), urged prompt action, perhaps utilising similar arguments to those later urged upon Vespasian by Licinius Mucianus (Tac. *Hist.* II. 76–7).

Principally, he argued that disloyalty was shown not just by those who revolted, but also by those who merely contemplated it.

The use of *recipere* for "accept" is less common than *accipere*.

his agents: that is, the procurator and his staff who in all provinces looked after the interests of the emperor, which were mainly in the form of properties comprising imperial estates. The procurator was an imperial appointee, who operated independently of the governor, even in imperial provinces, such as Tarraconensis. Plutarch (Galba 4, 1–2) describes unscrupulous activities on the part of Nero's agents which Galba was unable to prevent. A striking – and calamitous – example of the consequences of the independence of *legatus* and procurator is to be seen in the events in Britain before A.D. 59, which led to the rebellion of Boudicca.

instructions for Galba's death: it is unclear whether this is an example of the measures which Suetonius elsewhere (*Nero* 43,1) describes Nero as planning in the wake of the news of Vindex's rebellion. Alternatively, the *princeps* may have marked Galba out as one of those governors who had failed to report Vindex's earlier overtures.

at Clunia: one of the chief towns of the seven judicial districts in the province; Galba retired there after the debâcle at Vesontio which brought Vindex's rebellion to an end. He presumably awaited the imperial orders which inevitably came to failed conspirators, and was still there in June of A.D. 68, when news arrived of Nero's death and his own elevation to power. The name of the town appears on Galba's coinage, coupled with his own gentile name, Sulpicia (*RIC* I² (Galba), 469).

would arise in Spain: a similar prophecy concerning men from Judaea was taken to refer to Vespasian (*Div. Vesp.* 4, 5).

Section 10

1   **for manumission-cases:** the regular freeing of slaves in the courts: the process was
     full of symbolism with regard to current events, as the formal act was conducted by
     a *lictor* as *assertor libertatis*, a term associated with Vindex and Galba. Plutarch
     (*Galba* 5,1) directly relates the freeing of slaves to the freeing of the world from the
     despotism (*dominatio*) of Nero.
     Vacare with the dative case is regularly used of a judge making himself available for
     certain types of case.
     nearest of the Balearic Islands: the Balearics formed part of the *conventus* (see
     above on 9,2) of New Carthage in Tarraconensis, and were regularly used as a place
     of exile. The nearest of the islands (*Baliaris Maior*) is the modern Majorca.
     hailed as emperor: Plutarch (*Galba* 5,1) has a slightly different account, in that he
     has Galba hailed as emperor the moment he stepped on to the tribunal.
     the representative of the Roman senate and people: the use of the title, *legatus*,
     with this qualification, of course, represented a formal repudiation of his allegiance
     to Nero, since Galba's proper title was *legatus Augusti*. His motive is less clear; he
     may have thought that a refusal directly to accept the acclamations of his own
     sovereignty, or for that matter of anyone else, might have left him a margin of safety
     if the venture were to fail. On the other hand, there may have been a feeling of
     republicanism in the air, showing itself in a reluctance to ignore the right of the
     senate and people to decide upon the future. Two other protagonists in these events
     uttered similar sentiments – Verginius Rufus (Dio LXIII. 25, 1–2), and Clodius
     Macer (*RIC* I^2. p.215). The coinage of the civil war was full of republican echoes,
     including a re-issue of the type, showing the daggers and the cap of freedom, which
     had originally been struck in the aftermath of the assassination of Julius Caesar (*RIC*
     I^2. p.205).

2   **a cessation of public business:** a *iustitium* was a suspension of all business in a
     time of crisis; under the principate, the death of an emperor or a member of his
     family was regarded as such an occasion.
     Indicere or *edicere* were regularly used of "proclaiming" a *iustitium*.
     enrolled legions: Suetonius would appear to be in error in using the plural; there is
     no evidence that Galba raised more than one legion in Spain – VII Galbiana. It
     accompanied Galba to Rome, and was subsequently sent to Pannonia by Otho and
     reorganised as VII Gemina (Parker, 1928, 99f).
     auxiliaries: the auxiliaries were the successors of those troops who, during the
     republic, had fought alongside the legions as "allies" (*socii*). In the early principate,
     the auxiliaries were recruited from non-citizens, and disposed, usually under native
     commanders, in territories where they had been recruited, and using their traditional
     weaponry. After twenty-five years' service, auxiliary troops were discharged with a
     grant of Roman citizenship – unless this had previously been awarded for valour on
     the battlefield. After the war of A.D. 68–9, and particularly because of the rebellion
     of auxiliaries on the Rhine under Julius Civilis, Vespasian instituted changes which
     drew auxiliary-troops more formally into the regular command-structure.
     Auxiliaries were recruited into three types of unit – *alae* (cavalry), *cohortes*
     equitatae (infantry-units with a cavalry-attachment), and *cohortes peditatae*
     (infantry-units); these could be of quingenary strength (480–500) or milliary (960–
     1000). Under the principate, the auxiliaries were recruited in numbers

approximately equivalent to the total of those in the legions; thus, twenty-eight legions would imply an auxiliary force of around one hundred and fifty thousand troops (see Cheeseman, 1914; Webster, 1985, 141ff).

consisted of one legion: Tarraconensis was guarded by VI Victrix.

when he felt: Suetonius was especially fond of using *quotiens* – once with the indicative (its usual construction in classical latin), and at other times, as here, with the subjunctive.

3 **some young equestrians:** in the later republic and principate, the gold ring, given at public expense, was the token of membership of the equestrian order. Suetonius' point is that normally the type of service described here would precede membership of the equestrian order, and equestrians who undertook certain military duties had to sacrifice the status of the order until that service was completed. The distinction was referred to as the *ius anulorum* (Pliny *Nat. Hist.* XXXIII. 8).

volunteers: those referred to as *evocati* were generally veterans who came back into service on favourable terms, having a rank equivalent to that of centurion, and who were frequently organised into a *cohors praetoria*, or bodyguard of the *imperator*. It is made clear with the use of the word, *excubias*, that they were conceived as equivalent to those praetorians who were styled *excubitores*, and who represented an advance on the normal military guard who would attend a provincial governor.

through the provinces: Galba seems to have received active or passive support from most provinces; only Verginius Rufus (Upper Germany) and Clodius Macer (*legatus* of III Augusta in Africa) appear to have been hesitant (Plutarch *Galba* 6,1). Even then it is not clear what Verginius Rufus' "private" stance really was (Shotter, 1975, 65). The first provincial governor to declare for Galba was his "neighbour", Otho, in Lusitania (Suet. *Otho* 4,1; Plut. *Galba* 20,2). Galba's coin-issue, CONCORDIA PROVINCIARVM (*RIC* I². pp.234ff), expresses either Galba's wish or his confidence in its fulfilment.

calling upon people: the sentence contains a notable shift in construction (*variatio*) – *auctor.....conspirandi.....et ut.....iuvarent*.

common cause: the notion of *communis causa* is again suggestive of the republic.

4 **the town which:** the identity of this town is unknown; Tacitus (*Hist.* I. 65,2) refers to Vienne with similar words in the case of the Gallic part of the rebellion (see note on 9,2 above).

its setting carried an engraving: some striking gemstone-engravings are mentioned in ancient sources – for example, Pompey's (Dio XLII. 18,3), Galba's family's (Dio LI. 3,7), Sulla's (Pliny *Nat. Hist.* XXXVII. 8), Augustus' (Suet. *Div. Aug.* 50). See Henig (1974) for this subject.

a ship from Alexandria: Dio (LXIV. 1,2) indicates that there was more than one.

at Dertosa: this town, the modern Tortosa, was situated near the mouth of the river Ebro; according to Strabo (III. 160), it enjoyed the status of a *colonia*.

Section 11

the death of Vindex: the circumstances and timing of this are discussed in Introduction 3 and Shotter, 1975. Vindex appears to have committed suicide after the battle outside Vesontio (Besançon), in which, despite the evident intentions of

the commanders, the troops brought from Upper Germany overwhelmed Vindex's troops who in stature and experience at least were no match for their opponents. It was at this point that Verginius refused the offer of the throne that was made by his troops – a refusal born probably more of despair than of the positive resolve which he later claimed in his epitaph (Pliny *Epp.* IX. 19). The doubts led to disputes amongst contemporary writers, and Juvenal (*Sat.* VIII. 221) evidently saw it as a missed opportunity on Verginius' part. For Verginius' reaction, see John of Antioch (frag. 91, 10–25; text and translation of this are available in the Loeb edition of Dio, volume 8, pp.176–9).

panic-stricken by this: Plutarch (*Galba* 6,4) describes Galba's actions in more detail: he wrote to Verginius suggesting a pact to bring freedom to the Romans. After this, he retired to Clunia, presumably to await his fate at Nero's hands.

messengers: Plutarch (*Galba* 7) says that the freedman, Icelus, brought the basic news of Nero's death and Galba's succession, and that further details were added a little later by Titus Vinius, *legatus* of VI Victrix. Nero was outlawed on June 8th, and committed suicide the following day; we may assume that Galba would have received the news within a week.

Nero was dead: for a detailed account, see *Nero* 47–9; Nero was sentenced to a "traditional death" (*Dom.* 11,2), which is explained as being stripped, pinned down with a wooden fork, and then flogged to death.

everyone had sworn allegiance: this was a rather one-sided picture: some had in fact not yet taken the oath – for example, the German legions who presumably failed to understand why they were being asked to swear allegiance to a man whose cause they believed that they had destroyed. Others evidently had to be offered considerable inducements to accept the new *princeps* – for example, the praetorian guard, who had been bribed by their commander, Nymphidius Sabinus, to accept Galba. It was the praetorians' chief complaint against Galba that this "debt" was not honoured. The universality of Galba's acceptance is also brought into doubt by Tacitus (*Hist.* I. 6,1), who describes Galba's journey from Spain to Rome as *tardum iter et cruentum*, and details Galba's treatment of those he supposed to be his enemies.

that of "Emperor": a fuller account is provided by Dio (LXIII. 29,6). With the demise of the Julio-Claudians, of course, the name, Caesar, now became a title.

setting out on his march: Tacitus (*Hist.* I. 6,1) describes the journey as slow, and it appears to have taken from late June until September.

his general's cloak: the *paludamentum*, originally a cloak for all generals, was by this time restricted to the *princeps*, as supreme *imperator*.

with a dagger hanging: officers wore daggers either around their necks, or hanging from a waist-belt. The wearing of a *pugio* was traditionally an emblem of the proconsular authority, and thus in the context of the principate symbolic of the emperor's military role. Other military figures could not carry the *pugio*, unless given permission by the *princeps*; this was most commonly granted to the prefect of the praetorian guard. The symbolism contained in the wearing of the *pugio* is brought out clearly in Tacitus' description of Vitellius' abdication (*Hist.* III. 68,2), in which the *pugio*, the symbol of *ius necis vitaeque civium* ("the power of life and death over citizens"), was taken from him by the consul. Dio (LXIV. 3,4) says that

Galba was ridiculed because of the incongruity of a weak, old, man wearing such a large sword all the way from Spain to Rome.

He did not use: Suetonius employs *reciperare* for the more usual *repetere*.

those who had plotted against him: the roll-call of murders/executions was certainly larger; Tacitus (*Hist*. I. 6,1) mentions Cingonius Varro, the consul-designate and apparently an ally of Nymphidius Sabinus, and Petronius Turpilianus, joint-commander of the force which Nero had sent to northern Italy to block Vindex's and Galba's passage. Dio (LXIV. 3,2) says that many thousands of unarmed soldiers in and around Rome were butchered; Suetonius mentions (below in 12,2) the decimation of soldiers either from Nero's legion I Adiutrix or irregulars recruited from the navy. Besides these, we can include the "dismissal" of Verginius Rufus. Dio also adds (LXIV. 2,3) that assassinations were carried out by others in Galba's name, but without his knowledge (cf. *Hist*. I. 6,1). Further victims are listed by Otho (*Hist*. I. 37,3) – Obultronius Sabinus and Cornelius Marcellus in Spain, and Betuus Cilo in Gaul.

Nymphidius Sabinus: he was the son of Martianus, a gladiator, and Nymphidia, an ex-slave (Plut. *Galba* 9,2), though Nymphidius himself appears to have claimed Caligula as his father (Tac. *Ann*. XV. 72,4), and to have used as "evidence" his resemblance to that emperor. Nymphidius was made prefect of the praetorian guard following the conspiracy of Gaius Piso in A.D. 65, but deserted Nero when he judged his case lost, persuading the praetorians to declare for Galba. Unfortunately for him, the suspicious Galba preferred his own associates and replaced Nymphidius with Cornelius Laco (on whom, see Tac. *Hist*. I. 6,1). Nymphidius thereupon attempted a coup, but was killed by the praetorians themselves.

Fonteius Capito: he had been consul in A.D. 67, and *legatus* in Lower Germany since early in A.D. 68. Plutarch (*Galba* 13,3) and Suetonius assume his guilt of conspiracy against Galba; Tacitus, however (*Hist*. I. 7, 1–2), is more cautious, saying that whilst some believed him to have conspired, others thought that he was guilty only of gross corruption, and that the charge of conspiracy was trumped up by legionary *legati* who tried unsuccessfully to persuade him to involve his troops in the warfare of A.D. 68. Capito was, in fact, murdered by two legionary *legati*, Cornelius Aquinus and Fabius Valens, the latter of whom, thinking that Galba ill-appreciated this service, later deserted to Vitellius. Dio (LXIV. 2,3) has a story which, if true, might suggest that Capito tried to make a bid for power on his own account, hearing personally an appeal which had been made "to Caesar". At any rate, the legions of Lower Germany were reluctant to swear allegiance to Galba.

Clodius Macer: he was praetorian *legatus* of legion III Augusta in Africa. His motives in A.D. 68 are far from clear, though he was without doubt guilty of corruption. It appears that he made a move only after Nero's death; at the urging of Nero's mistress, Calvia Crispinilla, who went to Africa, he began to use his chief weapon, namely interference with the corn-supply to Rome (Tac. *Hist*. I. 7, 1; 73). It remains unclear whether he wished to see a re-establishment of the republic or, like Galba and Verginius Rufus, was using constitutional language to cloak ambition. Galba arranged his murder through the agency of the procurator, Trebonius Garutianus. Calvia Crispinilla retained favour under Galba, Otho and Vitellius, and into the Flavian period. Macer is said by Tacitus (*Hist*. II. 97,2) to

have raised a legion (I Liberatrix Macriana) and auxiliary cohorts, which were dismissed by Galba, but temporarily recommissioned by Vitellius (Parker, 1928, 106).

Section 12

1   **reputation for cruelty and stinginess:** these qualities are frequently mentioned (Tac. *Hist*. I. 49,3; I. 87,1). Otho's speech attacking Galba puts a credible gloss on these characteristics, by saying that Galba described as *severitas* and *parsimonia* what others called *saevitia* and *avaritia* (*Hist*. I. 37,4).

   some of the communities: Tacitus refers to some of these – for example, Lyons' revenues were appropriated to the *fiscus* (in contrast to the great honours done to neighbouring Vienne – *Hist*. I. 65,1); the Treveri, Lingones and other unspecified communities were lashed with tough edicts and suffered territorial confiscations (*Hist*. I. 53,3).

   Hispaniae and *Galliae* are put in the plural, because each area contained a group of provinces.

   razed their walls: this was not so much a reduction of their strategic capabilities, as a very public humiliation.

   some army-officers: the latin word, *praepositi*, is of uncertain significance. It could hardly be taken to refer to the more senior people whom Galba had executed, as their cases have already been cited (above in 11). Indeed, it is not clear whether Roman or local officials are indicated, though the context must suggest that they came from the Spanish and Gallic provinces. In this case, the names mentioned by Otho (*Hist*. I. 37,3) come to mind (see above, note on 11).

   imperial officials: Galba's strained relations with the procurators in Tarraconensis have already been mentioned (above in 9,2).

   Tarraco: that is, the chief town of Tarraconensis.

   he had melted down: that is, for the purpose of striking coins.

2   **he entered Rome:** Tacitus, too (*Hist*. I. 6,2), paints a picture of confusion and butchery as characterising Galba's arrival in Rome, which, according to Tacitus, was unusually full of troops.

   the oarsmen: there is some confusion surrounding the status of the various ex-oarsmen, because the accounts in our sources are not easy to reconcile in detail. In the last months of his reign, Nero had certainly brought to Rome a large number of oarsmen (*classiarii*) with the intention of forming them into a new legion – I Adiutrix Classica. The difficulty in the sources rests on the question of how far this process had developed before Nero's death, and thus on the status of the *classiarii* with whom Galba dealt so severely: had a legion already been formed, with further *classiarii* demanding this status? Or did the *classiarii* with whom Galba dealt include both the new legionaries and others who now demanded that status? The clear implication of Tacitus' references is that the former was the case, that Galba treated the unorganised *classiarii* badly and that this alienated those already formed into a legion. As a result, the *classiarii* as a whole declared for Otho (*Hist*. I. 31,3; I. 36,3), who offered prospects of legionary service to other *classiarii* as a way of winning the loyalty of the fleet (*Hist*. I. 87,1). On the other hand, Suetonius (in this passage) and Plutarch (*Galba* 15, 3–4) seem to suggest that Galba's harsh treatment

was meted out to those whom Nero had formed into a legion, but who had not yet received the formalities of eagle and standards (*aquila*; *signa*). Note that Dio (LV. 24,2) credits Galba with the formation of this legion.

to return to their original status: this important detail has Suetonius at variance with Plutarch, who says that Galba wanted to avoid making a decision, but was forced into brutal measures because the *classiarii* refused to accept his delaying-tactics.

eagle and standards: since the time of Marius' army-reforms (107 B.C.), these were the distinctive symbols of legionary status. The legion had one eagle (*aquila*), which was made usually of silver, though occasionally of gold. The *signum* picked out a maniple – that is, two centuries –, and was a silver-plated cross, from which hung silver discs (*phalerae*) and ribbons (see Maxfield, 1981, 28ff).

with a cavalry-charge: the incident took place at the Milvian bridge (Tac. *Hist.* I. 87,1); whilst Suetonius and Plutarch say that cavalry was used, Dio simply refers to Galba's "army". According to Tacitus (*Hist.* I. 6,2), many thousands were killed, whilst Dio puts the number at seven thousand. At any rate, this was regarded – not surprisingly – as a bad omen, and the contempt which Galba's old age had previously occasioned was turned to fear.

literally decimated: Tacitus (*Hist.* I. 37,3) has Otho use the word, "decimate", in referring to this incident. Polybius (VI. 38) explains the practice as being carried out in cases of dereliction of duty. All involved were reprimanded, and then approximately ten per cent of them were selected by lot for beating or even execution. The remainder were put on harsh rations and denied the protection of their camp. Although an ancient punishment (Livy II. 59), decimation had been used in Rome's more recent history by Crassus, Caesar, and Augustus (Suet. *Div. Aug.* 24,2).

a cohort of German soldiers: Augustus had originally had a bodyguard of Spaniards, but after Actium the personal bodyguard was almost always made up of Germans, except for a short period after the Varus-disaster of A.D. 9 (Tac. *Ann.* I. 24,3). These Germans were legally slaves, drawn from tribes who were Rome's subjects, such as the Batavi and Frisii, and did not have a military organisation equivalent to that of the legions and auxiliaries.

It had proved its great loyalty: as when the Batavian bodyguard killed a number of Caligula's assassins (*Cal.* 43 and 58,3).

multis experimentis fidelissimam is used in place of a relative clause.

but Galba disbanded it: there is no evidence that it was ever reconstituted after this.

Gnaeus Dolabella: the bearer of this famous name was probably the son of Publius Cornelius Dolabella, a rather uncongenial character, who was consul in A.D. 10; as proconsul of Africa, he achieved the final defeat and death of the guerilla-leader, Tacfarinas, in A.D. 24 (Tac. *Ann.* IV. 24–6). Gnaeus Dolabella was intimately bound up in the events of A.D. 68–9; he was related to Galba (*Hist.* I. 88,1), and his wife, Petronia, had once been married to Vitellius (*Vitell.* 6; *Hist.* II. 64,1). According to Plutarch (*Galba* 23,1), he had been considered as a possible candidate to succeed Galba, which probably explains Otho's decision to banish him (Plut. *Otho* 5,1). After Otho's suicide, Dolabella returned to Rome, but was put to death

by Vitellius on a charge of interfering with military loyalty (Tac. *Hist.* II. 63,1), which lends a certain credibility to Galba's suspicions of him.

near whose gardens: the gardens of Dolabella stretched from the Pincian hill – an area prominent for the estates of the powerful – to the *Campus Agrippae*, where the German bodyguard had its fort (Platner and Ashby, 1929, 266).

Tendere is used for "being encamped", because literally it refers to the act of putting up tents.

3   **whether they were true or false:** Suetonius has a preference for expressing questions of this sort, whilst suppressing the word of introduction (e.g. *dubium* or *incertum*).

his steward: an *ordinarius* (or *servus ordinarius*) was one who enjoyed a permanent appointment and exercised control over others in the household. The *dispensator* was in charge of the emperor's finances.

plate of beans: the word, *paropsis*, is sometimes used of the contents of a dish, or of the dish itself; in this case, the uncertainty is probably deliberate on Suetonius' part. Such precision of detail is typical of Suetonius' writing (cf. *Vitell.* 16, where he specifies the *types* of servants who remained with Vitellius during his attempted escape from the advancing Flavian troops).

Canus: a famous flautist mentioned by Martial (*Epig.* IV. 5,8 and X. 3,8) and by Philostratus (*Vit. Apoll.* V. 21). He is on record as having claimed to derive more pleasure from playing than did his audience from listening to him. He is described as *choraules* – that is, one who accompanied a chorus on the flute. Such players are said to have received good rewards (Martial *Epig.* V. 56).

five denarii: Plutarch, who mentions this same occasion (*Galba* 16,1), records that Galba paid Canus in gold, and made a point of the fact that the money came from his own, not from the state's funds. Dio (LXIV. 2,1), whilst not referring to this incident, says that Galba's presents were all in small change (*sestertii*), never in *denarii*. Galba's meanness may be contrasted with the lavishness of Vespasian (*Div. Vesp.* 19,1).

private purse: *peculiaris* is used for *proprius*, whilst *loculus* means any kind of container for valuable or important items.

Section 13

For these reasons: the latin, *non perinde gratus*, represents, as commonly in the post-Augustan period, an ellipse of the implied point of comparison.

theatrical show: the latin word, *spectaculum*, covered all types of show – in the circus, amphitheatre, stadium, as well as in the theatre. The context soon makes it clear what is meant here.

Atellan farce: this type of production derived its name from the town of Atella in Campania. The "plays" were originally improvised, and rather indecent, burlesque, which, by the first century B.C., had become formalised into one-act performances with four standard characters – Pappus, Dossennus, Bucco and Macco (old man, hunchback, fool and simpleton).

song: the latin, *canticum*, might be used either of a formal "song", or of those metrical sections which were delivered to musical accompaniment. It was common

for a slave to sing to the music, whilst the actor performed mimic gestures which suited the context.

Onesimus is back: this is the generally-accepted reading, and has the virtue of reference to Galba's meanness, being derived from the greek word for "sell". That part of the reference which mentions a return from the country will have alluded to the long period, first of retirement and then whilst governor of Tarraconensis, during which Galba had been absent from the heart of events in Rome.

completed the rest of it: audiences became familiar with lines, and they and the actors enjoyed political allusions which they contained. Cicero (*Ad Att.* II. 19,3) recalls an occasion during 59 B.C., when the triumvirate of Pompey, Crassus and Caesar was particularly unpopular; the audience rose to the contemporary aptitude of the line *nostra miseria tu es magnus*, seeing the last word as an allusion to Pompey's well-known *cognomen*.

Section 14

1 **He gained more favour:** the sentiment is close to that found in Tacitus' famous summary of Galba (*Hist.* I. 49,4) – *et omnium consensu capax imperii nisi imperasset* ("he was widely thought capable of ruling – until he tried").

although he provided: Suetonius always uses *quamquam* with the subjunctive, never with the indicative. The use of *documentum* followed by a personal genitive (*egregii principis*) is to be found also in Velleius Paterculus (II. 42).

level of approval far lower: Tacitus (*Hist.* I. 7,2) also makes the point that, having gained a bad reputation, it made little difference for the general estimation of Galba whether subsequent individual acts were good or bad. Further, it made little difference to people (*Hist.* I. 7,1; Dio LXIV. 2, 1–2) whether Galba was directly responsible for crimes or whether others carried them out because Galba could not exercise an effective check on them. This was true of acts perpetrated by Vinius, Laco, Icelus and numerous other freedmen.

2 **He was under the control:** Tacitus, too (*Hist.* I. 13,1), singles out for mention the influence of the same three men.

his "childminders": Aurelius Victor (*Epit.* 6) has the same reference to *paedagogi*; these, in the Roman education-system, were the slaves who exercised tutelage over children's behaviour and who accompanied them to and from school. Although the word came to mean any kind of "guide", Suetonius clearly has the specific sense in mind in this passage, as it highlights Galba's helplessness (or *mobilitas ingenii*). The word is also used in connection with Tigellinus' influence over Nero (Plut. *Galba* 17,2).

Titus Vinius: the career of Titus Vinius Rufinus is laid out by Tacitus (*Hist.* I. 48). His character is summarised (*Hist.* I. 6,1) with the simple description, "the most disreputable of men", though, in the fuller summary of Vinius' life, Tacitus describes him as "daring, clever, and sharp", adding that "depending on how he set out on an enterprise he pursued wicked or good ends with the same vigour". He was in other words the kind of unprincipled individual, rather like Mucianus and Antonius Primus on the Flavian side, who could make a decisive contribution in disturbed times. It was Vinius who proved to be the crucial influence upon Galba in persuading him to join Vindex (see above in 9,2). Vinius was born in A.D. 12 into a

family which had reached as far as the praetorship; a grandfather had attained the dubious distinction of appearing on the proscription-list of the second triumvirate in 43 B.C. Vinius himself served as a military tribune under Calvisius Sabinus in Pannonia during the reign of Caligula, but, having become involved in an affair with his general's wife, was convicted and imprisoned. He was released by Claudius and resumed his career, becoming praetor and then passing to the command of a legion. Despite suspicion of theft from Claudius himself, he became proconsul of Gallia Narbonensis, where his regime received commendation. After two praetorian posts, he could have expected to proceed to the consulship, but this did not happen; it is a mark of imperial – that is, Nero's – disfavour that he next appeared serving in another praetorian position – as *legatus* of legion VI Victrix in Tarraconensis under Galba's governorship. It was Galba's gratitude that won for him his ill-fated consulship for A.D. 69, in which he supported the claim of Otho to succeed Galba.

his aide: it is assumed from Plutarch (*Galba* 4,4) that this *legatio* was that of legion VI; as noted above, this would have represented a rather unusual career-progression, but might constitute proof of Vinius' lack of imperial favour. Alternatively, this *legatio* might have been a "private" one – as one of Galba's personally-chosen aides.

of limitless greed: Plutarch makes the same point (*Galba* 4,4), and says that Galba's protection of the notorious Tigellinus was bought through Vinius, for whom everything had its price (*Galba* 17,5; *Hist.* I. 72,2).

Cornelius Laco: our only knowledge of him derives from the events of Galba's principate. His crowning characteristic, according to Tacitus (*Hist.* I. 6,1), was inertia, and his contributions negative or mistaken; for example, he failed to warn Galba of the guards' sympathy with Otho (*Hist.* I. 26,2), and advised Galba to present himself to the soldiers (*Hist.* I. 33); he declined to go to Germany to appease Vitellius' supporters (*Hist.* I. 19,2), and supported the case of Piso Licinianus for the succession to Galba (*Hist.* I. 13,2). On Galba's assassination, Laco was *formally* sentenced to banishment, though Otho planned to have him removed permanently (*Hist.* I. 46,5). Plutarch (*Galba* 27,4) says that he was assassinated along with Galba.

judge's assistant: the job of an *assessor* was to use his legal knowledge to help the civil and military authorities when dispensing justice. The job would have required considerable expertise and presumably gave its holder a great deal of confidential information about individuals. The "job-specification" is given in the *Digest* (I. 22,1)

prefect of the praetorian guard: the holder of this highly sensitive and significant post was almost always of equestrian status – though a senator (Arrecinus Clemens) held it for a while at the beginning of Vespasian's reign (Tac. *Hist.* IV. 68,2), as subsequently did the *princeps'* elder son, Titus. Augustus had placed two men in charge of the 9000-strong guard, though subsequently there had for periods of time been one only. A vigorous guard-commander was a virtual kingmaker, as was the case of Lucius Aelius Sejanus under Tiberius. Nero's praetorian commanders had comprised a varied group – Seneca's friend, Afranius Burrus, the compliant Faenius Rufus, and the uncongenial and scheming Ofonius Tigellinus and Nymphidius Sabinus, the latter of whom preceded Laco in the post (see Durry, 1938).

Icelus: Galba's ex-slave had been imprisoned in Rome when news came of Galba's joining of Vindex's rebellion, but was released on Nero's death (*Nero* 49,4). He took to Spain the news of Galba's elevation (see below in 22), and received the gold ring which was the token of promotion to equestrian status, taking the name of Marcianus. Tacitus (*Hist.* I. 46,5) says that Otho ignored his equestrian status and had him put to death as an ex-slave.

awarded the gold rings: the token of equestrian status (see above on 10,3). He was the most influential of Galba's ex-slaves (Tac. *Hist.* I. 13,1; Plut. *Galba* 7,3). It is likely that his full name would have been Servius Sulpicius Marcianus.

highest post on the equestrian career-ladder: the two highest posts were the prefecture of the praetorian guard (held now, of course, by Laco) and the prefecture of Egypt (held by Tiberius Julius Alexander).

in a different kind of criminality: such complaints find a place in Otho's speech of denunciation (Tac. *Hist.* I. 37,5); indeed, Tacitus uses the verb, *grassari*, of Vinius in that speech.

was so used by them: Plutarch (*Galba* 13,2) puts such sentiments into the mouth of Nymphidius Sabinus. Tacitus (*Hist.* I. 7,2) makes the point that Galba, either because he could not concentrate on his job or for fear of delving too deeply, approved all kinds of criminal behaviour.

appeared inconsistent: actually, a long-standing characteristic, which he had shown in Spain (seee above on 9,1).

rather harsh and mean: Suetonius has already provided ample evidence of Galba's harshness; his meanness, too, is well-documented. Tacitus (*Hist.* I. 49,3) describes him as *pecuniae alienae non adpetens, suae parcus, publicae avarus*. An example of the combination of the two characteristics is to be seen in his refusal to pay to the praetorian guard the donative promised in his name by Nymphidius Sabinus (*Hist.* I. 5,2 – *legi a se militem, non emi* – "he said that he picked his soldiers, and did not buy them"). Tacitus makes a criticism of this stance on the ground that other actions of Galba's were not consistent with it; yet Galba issued a coin showing himself in rapport with his soldiers (*RIC* I² (Galba), 462ff).

chosen to be emperor: Galba himself in his adoption-speech to Piso Licinianus (*Hist.* I. 15–16) contrasted the way in which the Julio-Claudians had *inherited* power with the fact that he himself had been *chosen* (*Hist.* I. 16,1: *loco libertatis erit quod eligi coepimus*).

a man of his age: Galba was seventy-three years old.

illud aetatis is an adverbial accusative.

3 He condemned: no names can be added to those cited in Otho's speech (Tac. *Hist.* I. 37,3). We do not have sufficient information to be able to comment on the weight of evidence, although in the known cases the defendants appear to have suffered summary justice.

He rarely made awards of Roman citizenship: the cases on record come from the Gallic tribes of the Sequani, Aedui and Arverni in return for their support of Vindex (*Hist.* I. 8,1 and 51,4). It is *not* clear, however, how widely the distinction was conferred amongst those tribes – possibly simply amongst their aristocracies (Sherwin-White, 1973).

privileges given to those with three children: these derived from two pieces of Augustan legislation – the *lex Julia de maritandis ordinibus* of 18 B.C., and the *lex Papia-Poppaea* of A.D. 9. Part of Augustus' programme to encourage childbearing within regular marriage was his system of rewards to those who complied and tax-penalties to those who did not. Privileges included preferential treatment in office-holding and choice of provinces (Tac. *Ann.* II. 51). Emperors certainly extended the privileges of the *ius trium liberorum* to some who did not technically qualify for them: indeed, the younger Pliny persuaded Trajan to do so in Suetonius' own case (see Introduction 1).

one or two men: presumably from amongst those who did not formally qualify. Galba's apparent stinginess in this regard may have been part of a plan to secure an effective system of promotion in which men were not to be allowed to become complacent (see Birley E., 1953; Shotter, 1966).

when the jurymen: that is, those who supplied the juries for the standing-courts (*quaestiones perpetuae*), which were presided over by a praetor (Tac. *Ann.* I. 75,1). Under a law (the *lex Aurelia*), passed during the joint-consulship of Pompey and Crassus in 70 B.C., there were three panels (*decuriae*), drawn from senators, equestrians and *tribuni aerarii*. Augustus had three panels, probably all composed of equestrians, and added a fourth, made up of *ducenarii* – that is, from men who possessed half of the equestrian property-level. This fourth panel appears to have been used for smaller cases (*Div. Aug.* 32,3). Caligula added a fifth *decuria* to lighten the workload (*Cal.* 16,2). It is likely that the desire for a sixth panel sprang from the workload, which was probably made more heavy as a result of the work of the commission established by Galba to enquire into the financial irregularities of Nero's reign (Tac. *Hist.* I. 20; see below on 15,1).

concession given to them by Claudius: see *Div. Claud.* 23,1. There had long been complaints about the workload, and Augustus had provided breaks from service in November and December (*Div. Aug.* 32,3). Claudius extended the break, leaving a law-session which ran from spring until early autumn. Galba evidently reverted to the Augustan arrangements.

Beneficium was the normal word for a "benefit" conferred by an emperor.

Section 15

1 **senatorial and equestrian posts:** senators and equestrians between them had effectively made up the Roman civil service since the time of Augustus. The senatorial career-structure (*cursus honorum*) included the traditional offices of quaestor, aedile, tribune of the *plebs*, praetor and consul, together with legionary and provincial commands and a range of curatorships (see Birley E., 1953). The equestrian career had a number of provincial governorships (including Egypt), prefectures (for example, of the praetorian guard, the fire-brigade, the corn-supply), and the offices of financial procurators in the provinces and their staffs (see Stevenson, 1939, 94ff; Lintott, 1993).

a two-year tenure: tenures of different offices varied one from another, and changed at different periods. It was generally the case that emperors did not like public servants to become too established in a post, so that tenures of from one to three years were normal. However, some notable exceptions existed, such as Gaius

Poppaeus Sabinus who was left by Tiberius in charge of Greece and the Balkans for twenty-four years (Tac. *Ann.* I. 80, 1–3). Clearly, complacency in public servants would have been a great enemy of efficiency, and in any case many emperors will have felt more safe if they kept their functionaries on the move.

who did not want them or refused them: the logic, of course, was to eliminate the greedy and over-ambitious, and would have had the virtue of preventing such people acquiring office rather than relying on the ability to punish them afterwards (*Div. Vesp.* 16,2). Galba may have recalled the case of his brother who was prevented by Tiberius from taking part in the "draw" for provinces because he had squandered his fortune (see Tac. *Ann.* III. 52,1; VI. 40,3; also above on 3,4).

to cancel and recover: Nero's excessive liberality is well-attested (*Nero* 30,2; Tac. *Hist.* I. 20, where the sum of 2.2 billion *sestertii* is mentioned), as are Galba's attempts to recover it. Dio (LXIII. 14, 1–2) mentions one million *sestertii* given to the judges of the Olympic Games and four hundred thousand *sestertii* to the Pythian priestess, both of which sums were recovered by Galba. Such recovery was not unique, as Tacitus cites Tiberius' action in the case of gifts bestowed by Augustus on Gaius Silius (see *Ann.* IV. 20,1 and Shotter, 1989, 151).
Liberalitates is a use of abstract for concrete (*dona*), which can be paralleled in Tacitus (see Gerber and Greef, *Lexicon Taciteum*: s.v. *liberalitas*).

actors: the word, *scaenicus*, is used of stage-actors; Nero considered appearing as one (*Nero* 21,2), and is referred to as *ille scaenicus* (*Ann.* XV. 59,3).

athletes: *xystici* took their name from the covered area (*xystus*) in which athletes exercised in winter (Vitruvius V. 11). The word derives from the verb meaning "to make smooth", and may therefore refer to an area where the athletes scraped their bodies clean. The Greek allusion is particularly appropriate in Nero's case.

recovered from the purchasers: Tacitus does not mention this, though Plutarch does (*Galba* 16,2), and indicates that Vinius in particular made money from these activities.

in those cases where: *quando* takes a subjunctive because there is clearly a causal connection in the clause; Galba was acting in this severe fashion because of the implied extravagance of those concerned.

2   **retinue and ex-slaves:** the *comites* constituted the complete circle of advisers; the principal ex-slaves were Icelus and Halotus.
Addici is the regular word used of selling goods at auction.

tax-collection: according to Galba's coinage (*RIC* I² (Galba), 77ff), a 2.5 per cent tax of an unspecified nature was remitted under Galba. This *may* be connected with the remission of taxes to those Gauls who had supported Vindex (*Hist.* I. 51,4). The taxes included under the term, *vectigalia*, were tithes (*decumae*), pasture-tax (*scriptura*), customs-dues (*portoria*), the tax on inheritance and manumission (*vicesima hereditatum et manumissionum*), tax on the sale of slaves (*quinta et vicesima mancipiorum venalium*), and a sales-tax (*centesima rerum venalium*). Taxes were, of course, removed or added from time to time (e.g. *Div. Vesp.* 16,1). For the subject of taxation, see Lintott, 1993, 70ff.

letting off the guilty: the plural, *impunitates*, is not found earlier than this example.

When the people demanded: people clamoured for the death of Tigellinus in the circus and theatre (Tac. *Hist.* I. 72,3; Plut. *Galba* 17,4). This could be regarded as a

form of *populi furor* – a judgement of accused persons achieved by denunciation in a place of entertainment (Bauman, 1972, 214ff; Wiedemann, 1992, 167).

Halotus: a eunuch who acted as Claudius' food-taster (*Div. Claud.* 44), and who was corrupted by Agrippina in the plot to poison Claudius (*Ann.* XII. 66,5); he retained his influence with Nero.

Tigellinus: there is uncertainty over the precise forms of his names – Tigellinus or Tigillinus; similarly, it is not entirely clear whether his gentile name was Ofonius or Sofonius, though inscriptions have the former. One of the more notorious figures of Julio-Claudian politics, Tigellinus (a native of Agrigentum, in Sicily) first came to notice when banished by Caligula for intriguing with the emperor's sisters. It was due to Agrippina that, after the death of Burrus, he became prefect of the praetorian guard along with Faenius Rufus. He encouraged Nero in his deteriorating life-style (*Ann.* XIV. 51,6), and was, with Poppaea Sabina, the emperor's closest adviser (*Ann.* XV. 61,4), encouraging Nero's vicious reaction after the failed conspiracy of Gaius Piso in A.D. 65. He deserted Nero for Galba, and committed suicide when Otho succeeded Galba (*Hist.* I. 72,3).

Nero's agents: *emissarius* was particularly an undercover agent who provided information for accusations.

singled them out for protection: Tacitus (*Hist.* I. 72,2) and Plutarch (*Galba* 17,5) ascribe Tigellinus' survival to the influence of Vinius, though Dio (LXIV. 3,3) makes out that it was due to Galba's obstinacy in refusing to do what people demanded of him; otherwise, Tigellinus would have shared the fates of Locusta, Narcissus, Helius, Patrobius, and others of Nero's creatures.

procuratorship: this possibly indicates that Halotus was, like Icelus, given equestrian status to qualify him for such a post. Halotus is mentioned (*CIL* VI. 8833) as *Augusti libertus procurator*. There is no indication of where the post was located.

in an edict: Plutarch (*Galba* 17,4) gives the sense of the edict, that as Tigellinus was suffering from a terminal condition, people should not contaminate Galba's reign by needless bloodshed.

Section 16

1 **most strongly:** the use of *vel* to intensify the meaning is a favourite characteristic of Suetonius' writing.

the commanders: besides Nymphidius Sabinus, we know of the legionary *legatus*, Fabius Valens, and Aulus Caecina (quaestor in Baetica, but *irregularly* promoted by Galba, prior to the praetorship, to a legionary command), who were instrumental in persuading the German legions to accept Galba. It was the feeling entertained by Valens and Caecina that they had been insufficiently rewarded for this service that caused them to throw in their lot with Vitellius. (On irregular legionary commands, see Shotter, 1969).

an abnormally large donative: according to Plutarch (*Galba* 2, 1–2), the sums promised were thirty thousand *sestertii* to each praetorian, and five thousand each to the others. This would not have been far short of a billion *sestertii* in all – so large a sum that Nymphidius, who made the promise, may have expected that he could himself profit from the unrest which would inevitably follow, if Galba failed to pay

it. The sums paid as donatives had clearly undergone considerable inflation since Augustus' time (*Ann.* I. 8,3).

frequently boasted: all our sources mention or allude to this statement (Tac. *Hist.* I. 5,2; Dio LXIV. 3,3; Plut. *Galba* 18,2), which was generally thought to demonstrate high-mindedness on Galba's part.

in all parts of the empire: there is no indication that initially any troops were active against Galba other than the praetorians and the legionaries in the Germanies, although once the "infection" had started, it was difficult to stop (*Hist.* I. 26,1).

he would often remove: Tacitus (*Hist.* I. 20,3) supplies some names of tribunes who were removed – Antonius Taurus and Antonius Naso (from the praetorian guard), Aemilius Pacensis (from the urban guard), and Julius Fronto (from the fire-brigade).

suspected them: see *Hist.* I. 25,2. Galba failed to grasp that what he saw as the destruction of the cause of Nymphidius Sabinus was simply providing fuel for Otho. The *princeps* did not apparently understand the expectations of the men or the volatility of sentiment.

2 **the Upper German army:** the account of these events is given at greater length by Tacitus (*Hist.* I. 12). The Germanies were not provinces in the strict sense, but military districts consisting of a narrow strip of land on the western bank of the Rhine. In the Augustan arrangements, four legions had been assigned to each (see App. I), though in A.D. 68 there were four in Lower (northern) Germany, and three in Upper Germany. The Germanies were dissatisfied and unstable for a number of interrelated reasons. The Upper army, under the command of Lucius Verginius Rufus, reckoned that it had destroyed the cause of Vindex and Galba at Vesontio. After this, it had offered power to Verginius himself, and on his refusal had evidently preferred to resume its loyalty to Nero rather than transfer it to another candidate. Galba removed Verginius and replaced him with Hordeonius Flaccus, whose only distinction appears to have been gout (*Hist.* I. 9,1: *senecta ac debilitate pedum invalidum sine constantia, sine auctoritate*). The legions of the two Germanies did not want to accept Galba at first, but were persuaded with difficulty by junior officers – particularly Fabius Valens (of I Germanica in Lower Germany) and Aulus Caecina (of IV Macedonica in Upper Germany), who had been newly promoted by Galba from a quaestorship in Baetica. The commander of Lower Germany, Fonteius Capito, had been put to death on Galba's orders, and replaced by the future emperor, Vitellius, who, despite a distinguished lineage, was not an effective commander. *Esprit de corps* demanded some action, and since Hordeonius Flaccus could not be regarded as a candidate for power, the two armies looked to Vitellius, encouraged in particular by Valens and Caecina, who did not regard their earlier services to Galba as having been adequately recompensed; indeed, Galba had prosecuted Caecina for financial mismanagement. The army in Britain, which included one legion from the Rhine (II Augusta), supported the German legions, and threw its weight behind Vitellius.

Vindex and his Gallic mercenaries: such disparaging descriptions have sometimes been taken to indicate that Vindex's cause was connected with Gallic nationalism. But the use of such terms as *Galli* or *Galbiani* (*Hist.* I. 51,3) simply indicate the contempt in which the German legions held the Gallic provincials.

refusing on New Year's day: Tacitus (*Hist.* I. 12,1) gives a similar account, and adds later (*Hist.* I. 55,3) that the soldiers of legions IV and XXII (based at Mainz/Moguntiacum) overturned Galba's statues. Tacitus also says (*Hist.* I. 55, 1–2) that the legions of Lower Germany (I, V, XV and XVI) did take the oath, though there was some dissent (also Plut. *Galba* 22).

to anyone except the senate: this attitude, which echoed the stance adopted by Galba and Verginius Rufus in the spring of A.D. 68, recalled the old and defunct practice of the republic (*Hist.* I. 55,4; I. 56,2).

for the emperor who was created in Spain: the emergence of such rivalry between legionary groups was a significant factor in the events of this period; that it was recognised as such is clear from the appearance of such coin-legends as CONSENSVS EXERCITVVM (RIC I². pp. 268ff).

the praetorians should choose: a recognition of their "king-making" role, which had emerged clearly in the reigns of Caligula, Claudius, Nero and Galba.

Section 17

when Galba heard: according to Tacitus (*Hist.* I. 12,1), the news was conveyed to Rome by a letter from Pompeius Propinquus, the procurator of Belgica.

look down on him: the use of *despectus* for "contempt" represents a metaphorical extension of meaning which figures in post-Augustan latin.

he had no son and heir: both Tacitus (*Hist.* II. 1,1) and Plutarch (*Galba* 19,1) make this point, though it is in reality an indication of how far Galba was out of touch with the true pressures behind events.

the midst of his morning-callers: Suetonius makes the choice appear more casual than does Tacitus (*Hist.* I. 13–14), who indicates that an intense, though naturally, brief, power-struggle took place over the issue amongst Galba's closest advisers.

Piso Frugi Licinianus: Lucius Calpurnius Piso Frugi Licinianus was a son of Marcus Licinius Crassus Frugi (consul in A.D. 27) and Scribonia, who was a grand-daughter of Pompey's son, Sextus (Hadas, 1930). From an ill-fated family, he had brothers put to death by Claudius and Nero, and a third brother refused an offer of power made to him later by Antonius Primus (*Hist.* IV. 39,3). Piso Licinianus was born in A.D. 38, but because he had spent much of Nero's reign in exile (*Hist.* I. 48,1) he had not set out on the senatorial *cursus honorum*. He was killed at the same time as Galba.

a young aristocrat with a blameless reputation: all sources refer to his rectitude (*Hist.* I. 14,2; Plut. *Galba* 23,2; Dio LXIV. 5,1), though Tacitus points out the fact that some questioned whether such a sombre young man was a sensible choice in such a fluid situation.

to his property and name: there is no mention in Tacitus or Plutarch to any will made by Galba, or (therefore) to any reference to Piso in it. It is not clear whether *semper* is correct, and thus whether Galba really had a long-standing intention of posthumously adopting Piso. The adoption of Piso is mentioned by Galba in his speech (*Hist.* I. 15,1), and there is a reference to Piso in the *Acts of the Arval Brethren* (for January 10th) as Servius Sulpicius Galba Caesar (McCrum and Woodhead, 1960, no. 2). Tacitus (*Hist.* I. 15–16) put into Galba's mouth on this

occasion a highly significant oration which amounts to a "manual of statecraft" (Syme, 1958, i. 151–2).

took him to the praetorian guard's camp: Tacitus' account of the procedure is rather more detailed (*Hist.* I. 14); Galba summoned a council to elect an emperor (*comitia imperii*), which consisted of Vinius, Laco, Marius Celsus (consul-designate) and Ducenius Geminus (prefect of the city). Although there were in the minds of some alternative candidates (e.g. Otho or Dolabella), Galba made a choice – either his own or prompted by Laco and Icelus who were determined to oppose any choice of Vinius'; Galba then in the oration (mentioned above) formally adopted Piso. After some debate as to the appropriate place for a formal announcement – in the forum, the senate, or the guards' camp –, the latter was chosen (*Hist.* I. 17–18).

The camp of the praetorian guard was built at the prompting of Aelius Sejanus in A.D. 23, and was situated on the city-walls between the Viminal and Colline gates (Platner and Ashby, 1929, 106–8). Previously, the praetorian cohorts had been split up and barracked in various towns near to Rome. The change clearly enhanced the power of the prefect(s) (Tac. *Ann.* IV. 2,1).

no mention was made of a donative: Plutarch (*Galba* 23,3) says that this further example of Galba's parsimony aggravated the soldiers, whilst Tacitus (*Hist.* I. 18,3) indicates that the praetorians would have accepted Galba's choice of Piso, if only the emperor had shown a little generosity to them.

This gave Marcus Salvius Otho: Otho's career prior to these events is recounted in *Otho* 2–4. Plutarch (*Galba* 24,1) stresses the opportunity that the disaffection due to Galba's meanness afforded to Otho's agents.

within six days: the adoption took place on January 10th; Galba and Piso were murdered on January 15th. Tacitus (*Hist.* I. 48,1) refers to Piso as the "four-day Caesar".

Section 18

1   **a steady stream of significant omens:** such a list is a normal feature in all of Suetonius' accounts (see also *Otho* 8 and *Vitell.* 9).

in town after town: *oppidatim* is unique to this passage and *Div. Aug.* 59; Suetonius had a penchant for adverbs terminating in *-im* (Mooney, 1930, 613).

blow from the axe: larger animals were sacrificed using an axe (*securis*) or hammer (*malleus*), whilst the smaller ones had their throats cut with a knife (*culter*).

broke away: a sure sign of coming catastrophe (*Div. Tit.* 10,1; Ammianus XXIV. 6,17 of Julian).

one of his bodyguard: the *speculatores* were specially-chosen soldiers from the praetorian guard to make up a bodyguard for emperors.

the Palace: the name of the Palatine hill (*Palatium*) is often used for the imperial residence upon it. The long-standing (and "purpose-built") palace – the *domus Augustana* – was not constructed until the reign of Domitian (A.D. 81–96). In Galba's time, there were a number of imperial residences; Augustus' house (*Div. Aug.* 29,3) stood close to the temple of Apollo, his tutelary deity, and Tiberius built a new palace (*domus Tiberiana*) close to it, and "landscaping" the ground as it rose from the forum-valley onto the Palatine. A Neronian extension of this, known as the

domus transitoria, underlies Domitian's later construction. After A.D. 64, Nero's attention was taken up by the new and much-resented *domus aurea* (see Boethius and Ward-Perkins, 1970, 183ff).

an earth-tremor: there had also been one during Nero's final flight from Rome (*Nero* 48,2); the noise accompanying a tremor is often compared to a "bellowing" (*mugitus*). Central and southern Italy seem to have been particularly vulnerable to geological disturbance at this time; a major earthquake in Pompeii in A.D. 63 was followed, of course, in A.D. 79 by the devastating eruption of Vesuvius.

2   **he intended to adorn:** to dress statues of deities or other favoured objects with jewels was a common practice (see Pliny *Nat. Hist.* IX. 121; *Cal.* 55,3 for Caligula's treatment of his favourite horse, Incitatus).

statue of Fortuna: see above on 4,3.

Venus on the Capitolium: the only other reference to a shrine of Capitoline Venus is in *Cal.* 7, where Suetonius states that Livia dedicated there a statue of Germanicus' third son, who died in childhood, dressed as a Cupid. Other possible locations are the shrine of Venus Victrix and Venus of Eryx, dedicated in 215 B.C. (see Platner and Ashby, 1929, 551).

her gift to him: that is, the imperial power.

to avert the threatened calamity: sacrifice was the commonest method of expiation.

when he got there: each feature that he came upon was the opposite to what it should have been: there should have been a blazing fire attended by young men dressed in white; incense and wine should have been dispensed from ornate and rich containers.

Catinus was the flat dish from which the incense was thrown on to the pan.

3   **the garland fell from his head:** a similar sinister omen struck Vitellius (see *Vitell.* 9). Tacitus (*Hist.* I. 29,1) talks of Galba sacrificing to the gods of an empire which was "no longer his".

when he was taking the auspices: the chickens were released from their coop to be fed; a good appetite on their part was a good omen. Conversely, the worst omen was taken to be the chickens flying away – as happened to Gaius Hostilius Mancinus before the outset of the disastrous Numantine campaign in 137 B.C. (Val. Max. I. 6,7).

on the day of Piso's adoption: January 10th; both Tacitus (*Hist.* I. 18,1) and Plutarch (*Galba* 23,2) talk of atrocious weather on that day (*foedum imbribus diem, tonitrua et fulgura et caelestis minae ultra solitum turbaverant*). Plutarch specifically makes the point that heaven disapproved of the adoption.

camp-stool: the special stool provided on the dais for the commander-in-chief.

state-chair: the emperor had a *sella curulis* in the senate – a seat raised and placed between those of the consuls. It was first assigned to Augustus in 19 B.C. (Dio LIV. 10,5); it was a folding-chair with no back or arms, and its legs were curved. It is depicted on coins of Titus (see *RIC* II (Titus), 20).

Section 19

1   **he was sacrificing:** this was on January 15th. The story is told also by Dio (LXIV. 5. 2–3) and Tacitus (*Hist.* I. 27,1). Otho was present, and was nearly exposed to

Galba (Plut. *Galba* 24,3). Suetonius narrates the same incident later from Otho's viewpoint (*Otho* 6).

soothsayer: the *haruspex* was a practitioner of an Etruscan form of divination, in which the future was revealed from the entrails of sacrificed victims.

Not long after this: the force of Tacitus' point concerns Galba's prolonged sacrifices to the gods of an empire "no longer his" (*Hist.* I. 29,1), for Galba was still at sacrifice when the news arrived of Otho's acceptance by the praetorian guard.

The historic present, *cognoscit*, is a rare usage in Suetonius.

the praetorian camp: see above in note on 17.

many of his associates: Tacitus (*Hist.* I. 32ff) brings out the effect of the two lines of advice, and of the choice that Galba made. Vinius urged him to remain indoors, whilst Laco and Icelus were for his making an appearance before the praetorian guard.

he decided that he would simply stay: it is clear from Tacitus (*Hist.* I. 34,1) that this was *not* what Galba decided, for he sent Piso on *in advance* to prepare the ground for his own arrival. He thought that Piso would succeed because of his nobility and because he was an enemy of Vinius. Plutarch's version (*Galba* 25) is closer to Tacitus'.

formed from legionary soldiers: there were many of these in and around Rome, principally the soldiers of legion I Adiutrix (see above on 12,2); VII Galbiana, the legion which Galba had recruited in Spain, had by this time been sent to Pannonia, but it is possible that some of the soldiers from other provinces, who Tacitus (*Hist.* I. 6,2) says were in Rome at the time of Nero's death, were still there. These were detachments from the Germanies, Britain and Illyricum, which Nero had drawn together for an expedition against the Albani, and which, when the news about Vindex had broken, had been put under the command of Rubrius Gallus and Petronius Turpilianus for the purpose of defending Italy. Tacitus (*Hist.* I. 31,2) indicates that elements from Illyricum were quartered in the Porticus Vipsania (in the Campus Martius), whilst those from Germany were in the Atrium of *Libertas* (see Platner and Ashby, 1929, 56–7).

linen tunic: Tacitus (*Hist.* I. 35,1) talks of Galba putting on his *thorax* in preparation for going out into a crowd which he was led to believe was largely friendly. There are frequent references in antiquity to a tunic made of folds of linen; it appears to have been used by the Romans as a protection whilst hunting, rather than in warfare.

2   **false rumours:** that is, that Otho was dead; Tacitus (*Hist.* I. 34,2) and Plutarch (*Galba* 26,1) indicate that the rumour was probably the result of ignorance and wishful thinking, though there were some who thought it deliberately contrived to draw Galba out into the open.

the conspirators: Suetonius was the first to use *conspirati* in preference to the more common *coniurati*.

a few even rashly asserted: Tacitus' picture of confusion and ignorance (*Hist.* I. 35) is much more dramatically conceived than is the case with Suetonius' rather flat report; in particular, Tacitus catches the prevailing mood with *nemo scire et omnes adfirmare, donec inopia veri et consensu errantium victus....Galba.... .*

everyone else was converging on the Palace: Tacitus (*Hist.* I. 35,1) describes in some detail the different sections of society converging on Galba with the kind of bold talk typical of cowards – *in periculo non ausurus, nimii verbis, linguae feroces.*

so he left: according to Tacitus, he was carried in a litter, because he was too frail to withstand the surge of the crowd (*Hist.* I. 35,1).

to a solider who boasted: Tacitus (*Hist.* I. 35,2) names this soldier as Julius Atticus, a member of the bodyguard (*speculator*), who approached Galba brandishing his blood-stained sword as "proof" of the deed. Dio (LXIV. 6,1) and Plutarch (*Galba* 26, 1–2) supply versions, differing in detail, of what the soldier said to Galba. Plutarch calls the soldier a distinguished member of the praetorian guard.

"On whose authority?": whilst Suetonius gives these words without comment, Tacitus indicates that they were proof of Galba's integrity and sense of discipline (*Hist.* I. 35,2).

some horsemen: Tacitus' account (*Hist.* I. 40) shows Galba completely at the mercy of the surging crowd; he also makes the point that Otho ordered the charge because he believed that Galba's friends were arming the mob. Tacitus leaves his reader in no doubt as to the moral depths to which, by this act, Otho had sunk – *igitur milites Romani, quasi Vologaesum aut Pacorum avito Arsacidarum solio depulsuri ac non imperatorem suum inermem et senem trucidare pergerent....* .

scattering the crowds: the use of *paganus* ("peasant") reflects a post-Augustan shift of meaning to "civilian". The Flavian general, Antonius Primus, is reported (*Hist.* III. 24,3) to have used the word to taunt the praetorians, much as Julius Caesar had used *quirites* to address his soldiers.

they halted for a moment: there is no reference in any other source to this incident. Both Tacitus (*Hist.* I. 41,1) and Plutarch (*Galba* 26, 3–4) say that when the Othonians were spotted, Galba's own bodyguard set their allegiance aside and attacked him.

deserted by all: see note below on 20,1.

Section 20

1   **Some report:** there were clearly differing versions of Galba's last moments, depending upon whether the source was friendly or hostile (*Hist.* I. 41,2; Dio LXIV. 6,4; Plut. *Galba* 27, 1–3).

"My fellow-soldiers..": the words scan as a trochaic line, and appear to have been a quotation, presumably from a play.

he even promised a donative: of the other sources, only Tacitus (*Hist.* I. 41,2) mentions this offer.

strike him down: the latin words recall the formula for initiating a sacrifice – *hoc age.* This may help to account for Dio's assertion (LXIV. 6,3) that Galba was on his way to the Capitolium to offer sacrifice. The masking of political murder with religious formulae recalls the death of Tiberius Gracchus, tribune of the *plebs*, in 133 B.C. (Earl, 1963, 119).

none of those present: Tacitus (*Hist.* I. 43,3), Plutarch (*Galba* 26, 4–5) and Dio (LXIV. 6, 4–5) all mention the bravery of a centurion named Sempronius Densus; Plutarch and Dio have him defending Galba, whilst Tacitus says that it was Piso who was defended by him. There is some suggestion in Tacitus' language that the

historian may, as a teenager, have witnessed these events (....*aetas nostra vidit*). Piso was dragged by Otho's troops from the temple of Vesta in which he had taken refuge.

all who had been summoned: Marius Celsus had tried unsuccessfully to persuade the troops from Illyricum to help Galba, whilst two centurions were sent with similar purpose to the troops from Germany. Three tribunes were sent to the praetorian guard (*Hist.* I. 31).

a detachment from the German army: a *vexillatio* ("detachment") was frequently taken from a legion for service elsewhere – either in the province in which the legion was based, or further afield.

recent kindnesses: they were given rest by Galba when he found them in Rome exhausted, having been sent by Nero to Alexandria and then recalled when Vindex declared his rebellion (*Hist.* I. 31,3). Tacitus regarded the detachment from the German army as undecided between Galba and Otho, rather than as positively committed to Galba (*Germanica vexilla diu nutavere...*).

out of their ignorance: this assertion seems strange if these troops had been in the city for at least a matter of months.

2   **He was murdered:** Tacitus (*Hist.* I. 41,3) provides a number of names for the person who struck the blow. Plutarch (*Galba* 27, 1–3) gives the same names, together with one other – Fabius Fabullus.

by the Lacus Curtius: this was originally a swamp in the forum-area close to where the *rostra* (speakers' platform) were later erected. It lost its swampy character as a result of the draining of the forum-valley by means of the *cloaca maxima* during the regal period (Gjerstadt, 1962, 33; Platner and Ashby, 1929, 126–7). Three individuals are canvassed as the origin of the name – the Sabine leader, Mettius Curtius (Livy I. 12), Marcus Curtius who sacrificed himself there in 362 B.C. (Livy VII. 6), and Gaius Curtius who in 445 B.C. constructed a kerbing around the spot. The stories are given in some detail by Varro *Ling. Lat.* V. 148–150); by Galba's time, the Lacus Curtius was a religious area, thought to have a connection with the underworld, and into which people threw coins as offerings on the anniversary of the birth of Augustus (Platner and Ashby, 1929, 310–1).

an ordinary soldier: according to Plutarch (*Galba* 27,2), this was Fabius Fabullus.

since he could not: this grisly detail is given by Plutarch (*Galba* 27,3), but not by Tacitus.

took the head to Otho: according to Plutarch (*Galba* 27, 3–4), Otho's reaction was dismissive, saying that he would have preferred to have seen the head of Piso. Tacitus (*Hist.* I. 44,1) provides a striking account of Otho's joy when presented with this prize.

camp-servants: the *lixae* and *calonae* were camp-followers, and not formally part of the army; the former were freedmen, the latter slaves. For the incident, see also Tac. *Hist.* I. 49,1.

fixed it on a spear-point: Dio (LXIV. 6,5a) says that the head was carried to the senate-house, whilst Tacitus (*Hist.* I. 44,2) says that the heads of Galba and Piso were carried amongst the military emblems.

"My vigour....": these words were used both by Diomedes (*Iliad* V. 254) and by Odysseus (*Odyssey* XXI 426).

Patrobius Neronianus: as a freed slave of Nero, Patrobius took a *cognomen* from the name of his patron. Tacitus mentions (*Hist.* I. 49,1) that next day Galba's remains were found by Patrobius' tomb. Tacitus elsewhere (*Hist* II. 95,2) indicates that Patrobius was one of the most loathed of Nero's freedmen, and Dio (LXIV. 3,4) says that Galba punished Patrobius along with Narcissus, Locusta and "other scum"; they were led in chains around the city, and then put to death.

a hundred aurei: the gold *aureus* was equivalent to 25 *denarii* (100 *sestertii*). Plutarch (*Galba* 28, 2–3) gives details of these final acts that differ slightly: the head of Galba was *given* to the slaves of Patrobius, whilst Vinius' head was sold to his daughter for ten thousand *sestertii*, and Piso's given to his wife, Verania (*Hist.* I. 47,2).

into the place: this was apparently near the building called the *sessiorium*, evidently a place of execution near to the Esquiline gate (Platner and Ashby, 1929, 488). This action appears to comply with the notion that the spirit of a murdered person derived most comfort when his murderer was himself put to death near his own spot of execution or near his tomb.

Argivus: Tacitus (*Hist.* I. 49,1) and Plutarch (*Galba* 28,3) give the name as Argius. Plutarch also says that Argius buried the body by night, but that, with Otho's permission, it was taken away by the stoic philosopher and senator, Helvidius Priscus.

Ceterus is rarely used in the singular, prior to Suetonius.

Aurelian Way: this road led northwards from Rome, through Etruria to Pisa; it was later extended to Arelate (Arles) in Narbonensis. The road had been built in the second century B.C. (Potter, 1987, 133).

Section 21

medium height: medium height (*statura iusta*) was thought of as in the region of six Roman feet; a Roman foot was a little over 11.5 inches (Vegetius *De re mil.* I. 5).

Statura iusta is an ablative of quality, which is usual in such expressions, though Suetonius uses a genitive in an equivalent description in *Otho* 12,1.

completely bald: the adjective, *praecalvus*, is used only here; the *prae*-prefix almost certainly has intensifying effect, though "in front" has been proposed as an alternative meaning. See also Plutarch *Galba* 13,4.

and a hooked nose: although some have explained *adunco naso* as "having a turned-up nose", there is little doubt from Galba's coin-portraits that "hooked" – that is, Roman or aquiline – is the proper iterpretation.

by gout: *articularis morbus* is "gout" or possibly "arthritis".

unroll: *evolvere* is the normal word for this; *valere* with an infinitive is a construction from poetry, and is not found in prose before Livy, and only rarely after that.

On his right side: Suetonius sometimes uses the comparative adjective (*dexterior/sinisterior*) instead of the positive in such expressions (*Dom.* 17,1).

Section 22

colossal appetite: latin writers appear to prefer a descriptive genitive (*cibi plurimi*) when it is doing the work of a greek compound adjective.
The infinitive, *fuisse*, needs to be understood with *traditur*.
distributed to the table-servants: this is the sense usually accepted for a difficult passage which many, because of its difficulty, believe to be textually corrupt. It was normal practice for servants to be given the left-overs from a meal, and Suetonius' point may be that in Galba's case there were huge amounts to be distributed in this way. Others have thought that Suetonius' point was that the servants were instructed to collect other diners' left-overs and bring them to the gluttonous Galba.
table-servants: these slaves stood behind the diners as they reclined, and might either be provided by the host or brought along in their retinues by the diners themselves (see Hor. *Sat*. II. 8).
homosexual tendencies: the use of *pronior* with a genitive (*libidinis*) is very unusual, Suetonius preferring a range of constructions, including a dative, *ad* or *in* (Mooney, 1930, 615).
very strong: *praedurus* is a rare usage, found mostly in poetry and late prose.
Icelus: that is, one of his three advisers (see above on 14,2).
told him of: see also Plutarch *Galba* 7,2.

Section 23

was in his seventy-third year: for a discussion of the problems surrounding Galba's year of birth, see Introduction 4. Galba was born on December 24th, 5 B.C., though Suetonius earlier (in 4,1) indicates that it was in 3 B.C. (Tac. *Hist*. I. 49,2; Dio LXIV. 6,5). There is also a complication in that Plutarch (*Galba* 8,1) says that Galba was in his seventy-third year when he became emperor, a statement which receives some support from the Delphic warning to Nero (*Nero* 40) that he should beware of the seventy-third year.
nearly seven months: that is, from June 9th of A.D. 68 until January 15th in the following year. Dio (LXIV. 6,5) says that Galba reigned for nine months, but is taking his dating from Galba's declaration at New Carthage on April 2nd, A.D. 68 (see above on 10,1).
as soon as it was able: some doubt exists as to what precisely is meant here: Antonius Primus, the Flavian general marching from Pannonia into Italy, ordered Galba's statues to be re-erected (Tac. *Hist*. III. 7,2). Suetonius may, however, be referring to a decree passed between the time of the Flavian victory over Vitellius (December 20th, A.D. 69) and Vespasian's own arrival in Rome in the summer of A.D. 70. The eastern armies, under Vespasian (Judaea) and Mucianus (Syria), had successively accepted both Galba and Otho as emperor (*Hist*. II. 1–6).
the senate had decreed: in 158 B.C., the censors ordered that the senate and people were the only sources of authority for the erection of statues on the Capitolium or in the forum; in effect, that restricted the authority to the senate. In A.D. 45, Claudius restricted the honour to those sanctioned by the senate or, unusually, if a man had built or restored a public building (Dio LX .25,3). This latter rarely happened during the principate, and the last recorded case is the restoration of the *Basilica Aemilia* by Marcus Aemilius Lepidus in A.D. 22 (Tac. *Ann*. III. 72, 1–3).

in that part of the forum: that is, by the Lacus Curtius (see above in 20). People celebrated Otho's death by paying honour to Galba at this spot (*Hist.* II. 55,1).

reversed the decree: it appears that *abolere* is used of emperors making such a cancellation, though the proper word was *inducere*, if the senate reversed one of its own decrees (Cic. *De Domo* IV. 10).

sent assassins: Suetonius is the only source for this story, though in view of Galba's fears of possible rivals with strong armies, it is not altogether impossible (see above on 11). Nero had tried a similar plan to remove Galba (see above on 9,2).

to Judaea: Vespasian had been appointed to this command in A.D. 66 (see *Div. Vesp.* 4,5), and was not untypical of the Neronian emphasis on making military appointments from amongst man whose social credentials made them unlikely rivals to his own position (Chilver, 1957, 32).

Life of Otho

Section 1

1   **the town of Ferentium:** Ferentium is described by Tacitus as a *municipium* (*Hist.* II. 50,1), though he does not always use this term in a strictly technical sense. It was an Etruscan city, and ruins of it survive at Ferento, near Viterbo (Pallotino, 1974, 114f); it should not be confused with a town of the same name in Latium. Formally, Ferentium was made into a *colonia* by Augustus (Strabo V. 226), and possessed a noteworthy temple of Fortuna (Tac. *Ann.* XV. 53,3). The most impressive of the surviving buildings is the theatre (Boethius and Ward-Perkins, 1970, 114; 543; 562). When describing origins, Suetonius uses *ortus* with *a*, with *e*, or with a simple ablative.

from Etruscan kings: see Pallotino, 1974, 124ff. A similar type of origin was proposed by Horace for Augustus' confidant, Maecenas (*Odes* III. 29,1), and may have been a way of claiming respectability for men who socially were not notable. It would thus be parallel to the older practice of noble families who linked themselves with gods and legendary heroes (see above in *Galba* 2).

Marcus Salvius Otho: the gentile name is rare, and those who held it were generally undistinguished; the emperor's grandfather, mentioned here, may have been a relative of the Salvius who, as tribune of the *plebs* in 43 B.C., first sided with Marcus Antonius, and then with Cicero, and died as a result of the proscription-programme of the second triumvirate (Broughton, 1952, ii.340).

perhaps even: as often, Suetonius introduces this kind of proposition in the form of a double question, in which the first part has been suppressed.

influence of Livia Augusta: Galba, too, benefited from her patronage (see on *Galba* 1 and 5,2). Vespasian's son, Titus, benefited in a similar manner, being brought up in the household of Claudius alongside the emperor's son, Britannicus. Emperors could create senators in two ways (Birley E., 1953) – either bringing them in at the bottom of the ladder and thus making them compete through the stages of

the *cursus honorum*, or introducing them by the process of *adlectio* at a level commensurate with their ages.

he did not progress: Tacitus mentions this also (*Hist.* II. 50,1); similarly, Galba's grandfather did not move beyond the rank of praetor (*Galba* 3,3). Otho's grandfather is recorded on Augustus' coinage (*RIC* I^2 (Augustus), 429) as one of the three mint-officials (IIIVIRI AAAFF – *tresviri auro argento aere flando feriundo*) in 7 B.C. The three mint-officials formed a section of the lowest senatorial grade (the vigintivirate, or board of twenty), which young men held in their late teens; for the significance of the grade and its constituent sections of officials, see Birley E., 1953.

2 **His father was Lucius Otho:** Otho's father was *consul suffectus* in A.D. 33, the year in which Galba was *ordinarius* for the first six months (*Galba* 6,1). He is listed as *flamen et pro magistro* of the Arval Brethren in A.D. 39 (see Syme, 1980b, 3).

whose mother's family: she probably belonged to the *gens Titia*, for Otho's brother, Titianus, presumably followed contemporary custom, deriving his name from his grandmother's family.

influential connections: here and in *Nero* 35,4, Suetonius uses *propinquitates* for the more usual *necessitudines*.

and so like him: a similar story was told of the relationship between Augustus and his step-son, Nero Drusus.

Absimilis is only rarely used for *similis*, and then only when (as here) negatived.

a number of posts in Rome: that is, the posts of the senatorial *cursus honorum*.

proconsulship of Africa: Lucius Otho may well have succeeded Galba in this appointment and, like him, may have had extraordinary powers in the military field (*Galba* 7,1).

some extraordinary commands: unless these included the manner of tenure of the proconsulship of Africa, there is no indication of their nature or location.

in Illyricum: although, in 27 B.C., Illyricum had constituted a single senatorial province, it was later in the Augustan period (c. 10 B.C.), because of the unsettled nature of the area, divided into two imperial provinces – Pannonia and Dalmatia.

during Camillus' rebellion: sometimes referred to as Furius Camillus Scribonianus or as Lucius Arruntius Camillus Scribonianus; his ancestry was distinguished and, in political terms, potentially dangerous. He was a son of Marcus Furius Camillus (consul in A.D. 8), but was adopted by Lucius Arruntius (consul in A.D. 6); both his natural and adoptive fathers were distinguished senators under Augustus and Tiberius. Camillus achieved success against the African guerilla-leader, Tacfarinas, and is described as a man of moderation (Tac. *Ann.* II. 52,9); Arruntius, moderate and constructive over a long period, eventually committed suicide shortly before the death of Tiberius, allegedly despairing of the principate (*Ann.* VI. 47,2 – 48,5). The mother of Camillus Scribonianus was the daughter of Sextus Pompeius and Scribonia. He was consul in A.D. 32, and was appointed by Caligula to be governor of Dalmatia; although his command was extended by Claudius, in A.D. 42 he raised a "republican" rebellion against the emperor which, although popular amongst members of the senatorial and equestrian orders, failed to gain a following amongst the troops. Two legions – VII and XI – were given the title, *Claudia Pia Fidelis*, for their loyalty to the emperor during the rebellion.

Tacitus (*Hist.* II. 75) says that Camillus was murdered by a soldier, whilst Dio (LX. 15,3) claims that he died by suicide.

regretted their complicity: see *Div. Claud.* 13,2.

rebellion against Claudius: Suetonius here has a unique usage of *defectio adversus* rather than the normal *defectio ab.*

in front of his headquarters: the *principia* was the headquarters-building of a fort or fortress, as opposed to the *praetorium*, which was the official residence of the unit-commander. Presumably, this punishment took place in the "cross-hall" (or *basilica*) of the *principia* in front of the commander's dais. It was normal practice for punishments which were intended to degrade the individual to take place there, whilst executions were carried out outside the fort.

had been promoted: Tacitus (*Hist.* II. 75) says that Camillus' assassin, Volaginius, was promoted *e gregario ad summa militiae.*

3   **the treachery of a member of the equestrian order:** equestrian conspiracies are mentioned by Suetonius (*Div. Claud.* 13), Dio (LX. 18,4, referring to A.D. 43) and Tacitus (*Ann.* XI. 22,1, referring to A.D. 47). It is probable that the present reference is to the latter case, for which Lucius Otho was made a patrician by Claudius during his censorship (A.D. 47–8).

a statue on the Palatine hill: as often, *Palatium* is used of the whole hill. Tigellinus and Cocceius Nerva were accorded a similar honour by Nero (*Ann.* XV. 72,2) in the wake of the Pisonian conspiracy in A.D. 65. Augustus permitted the erection in the forum of statues of prominent achievers (Dio LV. 10,3); it is clear that the process described here is as in *Galba* 23 – that although emperors decided who should be given such honours, the formality of senatorial authorisation still had to be sought.

made him a patrician: see Tac. *Ann.* XI. 25, 3–4 for Claudius' additions to the patriciate during his censorship. In the early republic, patrician (that is, aristocratic) families exercised total control over political activity, though new patrician families could be created by the *comitia curiata* (an ancient assembly of the *populus*), as happened to the Sabine leader, Attus Clausus (Appius Claudius), in 505 B.C. As a result of the "struggle of the orders", patricians gradually came to share more of the republic's burdens and privileges with wealthy plebeians. Because of this, some patrician families lost much of their influence in the late republic, although a conscious effort was made by both Julius Caesar and Augustus to revive the patriciate. Like Claudius, they recognised it as a social distinction and as an honour for services rendered, and may also have hoped to use it as a core of an "emperors' faction" in the senate. Emperors were able to create patricians either through holding the censorship (as Claudius did), or by the censorial function that was inherent in other powers that they held.

that Otho was a man: a similar compliment was paid by Augustus to his step-son, Nero Drusus (*Div. Claud.* 1,5).

he would not wish: *optare* was used of the kind of hopes that were dreamed of, whilst *sperare* was used when referring to hopes that might be reasonably fulfilled.

Albia Terentia: Tacitus (*Hist.* II. 50,1), without naming her, refers to her *genus inpar nec tamen indecorum*. The reference to her as "well-born" (*splendida*) probably marks her family out as significant amongst equestrians.

Lucius Titianus: his full name was Lucius Salvius Otho Titianus (see above in 1,2 for the likely significance of the name, Titianus). He was consul in A.D. 52 (*Ann.* XII. 52,1, where he is named *Salvius Otho*, although elsewhere Tacitus calls him *Salvius Titianus*). He was proconsul of Asia in A.D. 63–4, with Agricola as his quaestor; Tacitus (*Agr.* 6,2) described him as "totally greedy" in his conduct of that appointment. He became consul for a second time with his brother in A.D. 69; Otho first of all put him in charge of the city when he himself went north to meet Vitellius, but shortly afterwards called for him to command the army. He was defeated at the battle of Bedriacum, but was pardoned by the victors (*Hist.* II. 60,2 – *pietate et ignavia excusatus*).

a younger one: that is, the future emperor.

his father's surname: that is, Otho.

still in childhood: Roman girls were regarded as marriageable from about the age of thirteen, though there were a few examples of earlier marriages – for example, that between the eleven-year-old Messalina and the sixteen-year-old Nero.

Drusus: he was born in c. A.D. 7, the second son of Germanicus and Agrippina, who, with his elder brother, Nero, was designated heir to Tiberius, following the death in A.D. 23 of Tiberius' only son, also named Drusus (*Ann.* IV. 4,1 and 8,6–8). He was evidently an uncongenial young man whom Sejanus was able to corrupt against other members of his family. He was condemned for treason, and kept in prison until finally starved to death in A.D. 33. On his death, he was violently attacked by Tiberius as *exitiabilis in suos, infensus reipublicae* (*Ann.* VI. 24,1). For fuller discussions of Drusus and his role, see Shotter, 1974a and 1989, 21.

was engaged: it is unclear whether Drusus married Lucius Otho's daughter, but by A.D. 30 he was married to the profligate Aemilia Lepida (*Ann.* VI. 40,4), who helped to blacken her husband in Tiberius' eyes.

Section 2

1 **Camillus Arruntius:** he and Domitius Ahenobarbus were consuls in A.D. 32 (*Ann.* VI. 1,1); on Camillus, see above on 1,2. Gnaeus Domitius Ahenobarbus was the father of the emperor, Nero, and husband of Agrippina, the daughter of Germanicus. He became proconsul of Sicily, and was regarded as guilty of a great many crimes: he was saved from prosecution by the death of Tiberius, and died himself in the same year (A.D. 37). Elsewhere, Suetonius (*Nero* 5) described him as "irremediably atrocious".

From his earliest youth: see Tac. *Hist.* I. 13,3; Plut. *Galba* 19,2.

often beaten: the *flagrum* was made of knotted rope, in which the knots often concealed pieces of metal. Its use was properly reserved for the beating of slaves.

in the habit of wandering the city: a common and long-standing "pastime" amongst younger members of Rome's aristocratic familes (Juv. *Sat.* III. 278ff). It is said that Nero was a "practitioner" (*Nero* 26; *Ann.* XIII. 25,1), as were Caligula, Vitellius and Lucius Verus, the co-emperor of Marcus Aurelius.

in a stretched-out cloak: since the *sagum* was a soldier's cloak, it is likely that this pastime had a military origin.

2 **she was elderly:** the adjectival use of *anus* is largely restricted to poetry and post-Augustan prose.

because of the similarity: the friendship of Nero and Otho is remarked upon by all sources (Tac. *Hist.* I. 13,3; *Ann.* XIII. 45,4; Dio LXI. 11,2; Plut. *Galba* 19,2). The proximity of character between the two led to Otho being called *Nero Otho* by some (*Hist.* I. 78,2).

seduced each other: there are a number of references to the impropriety of the relationship between Nero and Otho (Juv. *Sat.* II. 99; Martial *Epig.* VI. 32,2).

condemned for extortion: the word *repetundae* is regularly used of extortion itself, though properly *res repetundae* were the monies sought as a refund by injured parties. The offence of extortion was covered by the earliest-established of Rome's permanent courts – by the *lex Calpurnia* of 149 B.C. The penalties had been frequently modified in the period since the establishment of the court, and were in the first century A.D., broadly governed by a *lex Julia* passed by Caesar during his first consulship in 59 B.C., and amounted to a fine established at approximately four times the level of the loss involved together with sacrifice of rank (*Div. Iul.* 43). Many emperors took the offence very seriously (*Tib.* 32,2), though Juvenal suggests of a later case that even when prosecutions were successful provinces rarely received any refund (*Sat.* I. 49–50).

Damnatus is rarely used with an ablative expressing the offence itself; the normal construction is either *de* with an ablative, or an ablative of the charge, followed by *crimine*.

full restoration: *restitutio* is the technical term for restoration following penal disqualification. Tacitus (*Hist.* I. 77,3) provides a list of men restored to senatorial status by Otho, who had lost their ranks following extortion-convictions in the reigns of Claudius and Nero.

Section 3

1   **He became the confidant:** Suetonius uses the same term, *particeps secretorum*, which Tacitus employed to describe the role of Sallustius Crispus under Augustus and Tiberius (*Ann.* I. 6,6). It presumably indicates one who had been admitted to the "inner circle" (*amici principis*), rather than referring to a specific post in the household.

As often in post-Augustan prose, *secretum* is used as a noun.

on the day which Nero: for the planning and execution of the murder of Nero's mother, Agrippina, in A.D. 59, see Tac. *Ann.* XIV. 1–13. Tacitus does not mention Otho's involvement in Nero's planning – indeed he records that Otho had been sent to Lusitania as governor in A.D. 58 (*Ann.* XIII. 46,5). The period selected by Nero was the festival of the *Quinquatrus*, held in honour of Minerva between March 19th and 23rd; it is likely that Vindex chose the anniversary of the festival to raise his rebellion against Nero in A.D. 68 (Shotter, 1975, 64). Nero's plots against his mother (described by Suetonius in *Nero* 34) were decidedly bizarre: following Nero's *alleged* discovery of his mother's plotting against himself, he first planned that a ceiling would collapse on her, then that she would drown in a collapsible boat; and finally, failing these, he had her stabbed in such a way as to make the deed appear like suicide. There are considerable differences of detail between the accounts of Tacitus and Suetonius. It has been suggested that there may have been an earlier attempt upon Agrippina's life, in which Otho had participated; Nero's

relations with his mother began to become strained from the early months of his reign in A.D. 54.

The gerundival dative of purpose (*necandae matri*) is especially common in the writings of Tacitus and Suetonius.

to avert suspicion: Tacitus indicates (*Ann.* XIV. 4,6) that Agrippina was suspicious and for that reason was taken to meet Nero by litter rather than by boat (cf. Dio LXI. 12, 2–3, who has a different version).

for its genial atmosphere: Tacitus (*Ann.* XIV. 4,7) also refers to the geniality of the occasion (*comitas*); also Dio (LXI. 13,1), who mentions a sequence of dinners over several days.

Poppaea Sabina: she was a daughter of Titus Ollius, who died as an associate of Sejanus; he had reached the rank of quaestor at that stage (*Nero* 35). Poppaea took the name of her maternal grandfather, Gaius Poppaeus Sabinus, consul of A.D. 9, and who was left as *legatus* of Moesia for twenty-four years until his death in A.D. 35 (Tac. *Ann.* I. 80). Poppaea married Rufrius Crispinus, an equestrian, who had been a prefect of the praetorian guard under Claudius (*Ann.* XI. 1,3), until removed in A.D. 51 by Agrippina's influence in favour of Afranius Burrus (*Ann.* XII. 42,1). Crispinus was exiled to Sardinia in A.D. 65 because of his part in the Pisonian conspiracy (*Ann.* XV. 71,8), and committed suicide the following year (*Ann.* XVI. 17, 1–2). Nero is said to have hated him because of his connection with Poppaea, and to have arranged, or even personally carried out, the murder of the son of Poppaea and Crispinus (see *Nero* 35; also Sen. *Octavia* 744–7). For a sketch of Poppaea, see *Ann.* XIII. 45; she died in A.D. 65 as a result of Nero's brutality to her during pregnancy (*Ann.* XVI. 6), and was subsequently deified (*Ann.* XVI. 21–2).

mistress of Nero: the chronology and nature of the relationship between Nero, Otho and Poppaea are obscure: Tacitus (*Hist.* I. 13,3), Plutarch (*Galba* 19, 2–5) and Dio (LXI. 11, 2–3) suggest that she was Nero's mistress first, and that Otho became involved as a "cover" when Nero needed to hide his passion from his mother. Tacitus later (in *Ann.* XIII. 45–6) shows that she was initially attracted to Otho, but used this relationship to penetrate Nero's court. In any case, this *ménage à trois* became excessively complicated, and Otho was removed to Lusitania in A.D. 58 – which in effect saved his life.

taken her from her husband: see above for the details of this (s.v. note on *Poppaea Sabina*).

Otho became so infatuated: so, too, Plutarch (*Galba* 19,4); Tacitus shows (*Hist.* I. 78,2) that Otho retained his infatuation with her memory even when he was emperor.

2 **he locked the doors:** Tacitus (in the *Annals*) and Plutarch contradict Suetonius' version in detail by saying that it was Poppaea, rather than Otho, who barred the doors.

the return of the property: the latin, *depositum reposcere*, is a metaphor from property-dealing.

was sent to Lusitania: Lusitania, originally part of Further Spain (*Hispania Ulterior*), was made into a separate imperial province by Augustus. Its chief town was the Augustan *colonia* of *Emerita Augusta* (Mérida).

The use of *seponere* implies a virtual exile.

under the guise of the governorship: Tacitus (*Hist.* I. 13,3) uses similar vocabulary – *specie legationis seposuit.* In the *Annals*, Tacitus describes how this "promotion" came at the end of a series of snubs: first, Otho was personally ignored by Nero, then struck off the list for *official* invitations, and finally sent to Lusitania. According to Plutarch (*Galba* 20,1) Seneca was the architect of Otho's promotion, and his intention was to protect him from Nero's jealousy.

more severe punishment: that is, execution (Plut. *Galba* 19,5).

the whole farce: the metaphorical use of *mimus* to describe any kind of farcical activity is post-Augustan (cf. *Cal.* 45).

in the following verse: normally the word, *distichum*, is used of an elegiac couplet, but examples show that it could be applied to a couplet in any metre.

under pretence of promotion: according to Plutarch (*Galba* 20,2), Otho's awareness of the real reason for his promotion was the cause of his "decision" to behave moderately in Lusitania and thus avoid attracting unwelcome attention (cf. *Hist.* I. 21,1). His administration of the province was generally praised (*Hist.* I. 13,4; *Ann.* XIII. 46,5); Tacitus' description (*Hist.* I. 22) points a contrast in Otho's behaviour between periods of sound activity and of self-indulgent idleness.

as an ex-quaestor: Otho's standing on the senatorial *cursus honorum* was significantly junior to that normally required for the governorship of Lusitania.

for ten years: that is, A.D. 58–68; such lengthy tenures were not normal in the early principate (see note above on *Galba* 9,1).

Section 4

1   **was the first to join:** so, too, Tacitus (*Hist.* I. 13,4); both Tacitus and Plutarch (*Galba* 20,2) present Otho as a vigorous supporter of Galba, who supplied many of Galba's needs and remained close to him throughout the journey to Rome.

from Seleucus, the astrologer: Tacitus (*Hist.* I. 22,2) and Plutarch (*Galba* 23,4) give the astrologer's name as Ptolemaeus and stress the strength of influence of his predictions upon Otho (cf. Juv. *Sat.* VI. 557ff). According to Tacitus (*Hist.* II. 78,1), Seleucus was the name of Vespasian's astrologer.

Astrologers were called *mathematici* because of the complexity of the calculations which they undertook; not surprisingly, they were *officially* unpopular, and had over the years been the subjects of a number of expulsion-orders – in 139 B.C., 33 B.C., A.D. 16, 52, and later by Vitellius in A.D. 69 and Vespasian in A.D. 70. Tacitus (*Hist.* I. 22,1) refers to them as "unreliable men who will always survive banishment-orders".

outlive Nero: here Suetonius uses a dative after *superstes*; elsewhere (*Tib.* 62,3), he uses the genitive.

further promised: the meaning is not entirely clear; the word, *repromittere*, is usually taken to mean "to promise in addition", though its normal sense, as a technical term of business, was "to promise in return (for something)". The difficulty has led to attempts to alter the text.

2   **used every opportunity to show attention:** the conscientiousness of Otho in this connection, both with groups and individuals, is frequently noted (*Hist.* I. 23,1; I. 36,1; Suet. *Galba* 14,2; Plut. *Galba* 20).

whenever he entertained: this is mentioned by Tacitus (*Hist.* I. 24) and Plutarch (*Galba* 20, 3–4); Tacitus further states that it was organised through the agency of Maevius Pudens, an associate of Tigellinus.

an aureus: the Roman gold coin (see on *Galba* 20,2).

man on guard-duty: it was usual practice for one praetorian cohort at a time to guard the emperor at home or at other places. Emperors gave their guards the food-allowance (*sportula*), and it is this that Otho appears to have made up for Galba.

a man who had gone to law: Tacitus (*Hist.* I. 24,2) recounts this incident and gives the soldier's name as Cocceius Proculus.

The role of *arbiter* was to decide a dispute which had been referred by the agreement of both parties concerned; the sale was conducted with full attention to the formalities (*emancipare*).

the only man deserving to succeed Galba: cf. the similar opinion that had been generally held of Galba before his accession (*Hist.* I. 49,4).

Section 5

1 His hope had been: For Galba's reasons for choosing Piso Licinianus, see on *Galba* 17. Otho hoped that his service to Galba in A.D. 68 would have put him at the head of Galba's list of choices; he also hoped to utilise the influence of Titus Vinius (on whom, see on *Galba* 14,2), to whose daughter, Crispina, he was engaged (*Hist.* I. 13,2; Plut. *Galba* 21), and the support of soldiers and civilians who looked to Otho as a "second Nero".

Galba's preference for Piso: the reasons are given by Plutarch (*Galba* 21,1) as deriving from Galba's care for the state; this is born out by the oration which Tacitus put into Galba's mouth on the occasion of the adoption of Piso (*Hist.* I. 15–16). As Tacitus relates the incident, Galba's perception of the delicate balance between the principate and *libertas* required the handling of a man of aristocratic background and impeccable character (Shotter, 1978a, 248f).

dispelled that hope: *decidere* is normally used with a preposition rather than, as here, an ablative of separation.

partly by resentment: this resentment is articulated in Plutarch (*Galba* 23,3–4) and Dio (LXIV. 5,1–2).

by his massive debts: Plutarch (*Galba* 21,2) puts Otho's debts at the Greek equivalent of two hundred million *sestertii*; Tacitus (*Hist.* I. 21,1) does not mention a figure, but refers to the lifestyle which led to the debt.

he fell in battle: the forum was not only the traditional political heart of Rome, but it was also the place where most financial business was transacted, including that which dealt with insolvency.

The use of *cadere ab* is a poetic alternative for *interfici ab*, which is rarely found in prose; *cadere sub* is similarly uncommon. The presence of the two unusual constructions with *cadere* suggests that the words used by Suetonius do represent a genuine recorded comment of Otho's.

2 stewardship: a highly influential financial post in the imperial household (see on *Galba* 12,3); corrupt practices in obtaining such posts were by no means unusual (see *Div. Vesp.* 23,2).

The figure, *decies sestertium* (one million *sestertii*), is an abbreviation of *decies centena milia sestertium.*

five guardsmen: for the *speculatores*, see on *Galba* 18,1. According to Tacitus (*Hist.* I. 25,1), the plot was first revealed to Onomastus (a freedman), and then to two soldiers, Barbius Proculus and Veturius; it then spread more widely.

he gave: the force of the verb, *repraesentare*, is of handing over cash on the spot; *dena sestertia.....quinquagena* means an initial sum of ten thousand *sestertii*, followed by fifty thousand more; the first figure represents around two years' pay for a guardsman, the second ten years'.

-though not many: Tacitus (*Hist.* I. 27,2) and Plutarch (*Galba* 25,1) indicate that the first salutation of Otho as emperor was carried out by only twenty-three soldiers, though others joined as Otho made his way to guards' camp. Even so, the slowness of the response brought Otho close to withdrawing from the enterprise (Dio LXIV. 5,3).

they were confident .... that: the use of *fiducia* (and similar words) followed by an accusative and infinitive construction is frequent in Suetonius.

Section 6

1 **His intention had been:** this is the only example in Suetonius of the use of the poetical expression, *animus fert.*

immediately after Piso's adoption: in fact, Piso was adopted on January 10th, and he and Galba were murdered on January 15th. There is no other mention of this particular plan of Otho's; only Tacitus (*Hist.* I. 26,1) says that there was a plan-of-action timed for January 14th, but that this came to nothing.

to burden with guilt: in view of the arguments laid out later in his suicide-message (*Hist.* II. 47), this reasoning on Otho's part is entirely plausible.

then on duty: *statio* here refers to the *period* of duty, though it can also mean the *place* of duty, and the *duty* itself. One cohort of the guard took on this role of bodyguard at a time.

when Caligula was murdered: the murder in January, A.D. 41 is attributed to Cassius Chaerea and Cornelius Sabinus, tribunes in the duty-cohort. Earlier in the reign, the two praetorian tribunes had been accused of involvement in a failed conspiracy (*Cal.* 56 and 58).

when Nero was deserted: Nero attempted (unsuccessfully) to persuade officers of the guard to accompany him on his flight from Rome (*Nero* 47).

omens: Seleucus warned Otho of the force of specific omens; the passage is not meant to imply that a religious "feast-day" was involved; *religio et Seleucus* is a form of hendiadys.

The notion of "taking away" (*eximere*) a day, and thus "wasting" it, is common.

2 **near the temple of Saturn:** this temple which, according to tradition, was dedicated in 497 B.C., stood near the road leading up on to the Capitolium from the forum. It was (and still is) an impressive structure, and had undergone a full restoration during the Augustan period (*Div. Aug.* 29; see Platner and Ashby, 1929, 463–5).

at the golden milestone: see also *Hist.* I. 27,2. This milestone had been erected in the forum in 20 B.C. by Augustus in his role as *curator viarum.* It was supposedly

the starting-point for measuring distances on all Roman roads in Italy (Plut. *Galba* 24,4), although these distances were in fact measured from the city-gates. According to the elder Pliny (*Nat. Hist.* III. 66), it was the starting-point of a survey of Rome which was set in train by Vespasian.

to pay his respects: that is, at the *salutatio*, a notoriously vulnerable occasion for leading figures.

received with a kiss: this practice had presumably been introduced from the east, and was an honour extended to the imperial entourage (*amici principis*) and to senators. To withhold the kiss or to offer it in a perfunctory manner was a clear sign of imperial disfavour (Dio LIX. 27,1 of Caligula; *Nero* 37,3; Tac. *Agr.* 40,3 of Domitian). Some emperors, to demonstrate their power and superiority, offered a hand or even a foot to be kissed, and Pliny lavishly praises Trajan for refusing to do this (*Panegyric of Trajan* 23-4).

whilst Galba was at sacrifice: Otho was the only senator present on this occasion (*Galba* 19,1).
The construction, *interesse* with a personal dative, is very rare; the normal usage was *interesse* with an impersonal dative (e.g. *sacrificio*), or *adesse* with a personal dative.

an ex-slave of his: according to Tacitus (*Hist.* I. 27,1), this was Onomastus. On the imperial palace, see note above on *Galba* 18,1.

through the rear of the palace: Tacitus specifies that Otho gained access to the Velabrum and thence to the forum through the *domus Tiberiana*, a building which amounted to a "structural landscaping" of the north-west slope of the Palatine.

agreed meeting-point: the neuter singular of the past passive participle (*constitutum*) is frequently used as a substantive.

pretended to be ill: Tacitus (*Hist.* I. 27,2) implies that Otho did carry out this pretence when he says that Otho left the *domus Tiberiana* supported by Onomastus. Suetonius on the other hand shows his disbelief in this version by having said that Otho *ran* out (*proripuit se*) through the rear of the palace.

3 **hid himself:** this was possible because the vehicle was a closed sedan (cf. *Vitell.* 16). The chair was probably fashioned after the *cathedra*, or special women's chair. The sedan could be open or closed, and women normally (out of modesty) closed the curtains.

shoe came undone: shoes (*calcei*) were fastened with leather straps.

raised him on their shoulders: the propriety of the latin word, *succollare*, stems from the fact that its normal usage is to describe the *lecticarii* putting the chair-poles on their shoulders.

saluted him as emperor: according to both Tacitus (*Hist.* I. 27,2) and Plutarch (*Galba* 25,1-2), it was at this point that Otho's nerve nearly broke because of the small number of his backers. These accounts suggest that the positive behaviour – raising Otho on their shoulders and saluting him – was entirely that of the soldiers who were determined not to allow Otho to back out. The "drawn swords", to which Suetonius refers, were intended to intimidate opposition, but also to prevent Otho's escape.

reached the headquarters: Tacitus (*Hist.* I. 28) says that a tribune named Julius Martialis, who was on duty at the gate, opened it in the general confusion; the

soldiers then, seeing Otho and perhaps imagining him to be more strongly supported than he was, joined his cause.

joined him: both Plutarch and Tacitus indicate that the number of Otho's supporters approximately doubled on the way from the forum to the guards' camp – that is, from the original twenty-three.

men were then sent: cf. *Galba* 19,2. Tacitus (*Hist.* I. 43,2) gives the names of Sulpicius Florus, who was a member of a cohort drawn from Britain, and Statius Murcus, a guardsman.

made just one promise: Tacitus (*Hist.* I. 37–8) puts an elaborate oration into Otho's mouth; it may be that Suetonius' version represents an implied criticism of Tacitus'.

Demum is used for *solum* or *tantum*.

Section 7

1   **as evening was drawing on:** although Suetonius uses *vergere* only here, this expression, and others relating to age or season, were quite common in post-Augustan writers (see Furneaux, 1896, i.71 for the variety of expressions used by Tacitus to convey this idea).

he went to the senate-house: Tacitus (*Hist.* I. 47,1) indicates that this formality had a gruesome aspect in view of what had happened (Plut. *Galba* 28,1–2).

Tacitus says that the senate was convoked by the *praetor urbanus* as both consuls (Galba and Vinius) were dead.

in a brief account: *ratione* represents a correction of the manuscripts' *oratione*, which seems well-taken in view of the general use of *rationem ponere* meaning "to give an account".

forced to become emperor: Dio (LXIV. 8,1) also gives this "self-defence" of Otho's, which went as far as suggesting that he had tried to resist the soldiers' enthusiasm. As noted above (on 6,3), Tacitus has a version suggesting that it was fear which brought Otho close to backing out.

Rapere appears to be used of "making" an emperor, because of the soldiers' practice on a number of occasions of carrying off their chosen candidate.

made for the palace: see also Tacitus (*Hist.* I. 47,2), who fills in some detail of Otho's journey through a forum still littered with bodies to the Capitolium, and then to the Palatine.

he was hailed as Nero: see also Plut. *Otho* 3,1; Dio LXIV. 8,2. Tacitus (*Hist.* I. 78,2) says that he was hailed as *Nero Otho*, and actively encouraged this association with the memory of his former friend.

Some have alleged: Plutarch (*Otho* 3,1–2) states that the name of *Nero* was added to that of *Otho* on official documents sent to Spain, adding that the practice proved unpopular and was rapidly discontinued. Plutarch indicates that his source for this was the historian, Cluvius Rufus (see Introduction 5), who had been appointed by Galba as governor of Tarraconensis (*Hist.* I. 8,1; Townend, 1964).

travel-documents: *diplomata* consisted of two tablets "hinged" together; there were two main types – travel-documents and discharge-certificates for soldiers. The former were valid only during the lifetime of the emperor in whose name they were issued.

provincial governors: *praesides* was a general term applied to provincial governors, and did not distinguish between different types of governor or province.

he allowed Nero's statues: it was normal for the statues of unpopular figures to be thrown down after their deaths (see Juv. *Sat.* X. 58–81 on the reaction to the fall of Sejanus in A.D. 31). For Otho's action, see Plutarch (*Otho* 3,1) and Tacitus (*Hist.* I. 78,2).

procurators and ex-slaves: there is not a great deal of information as to who these individuals were. Suetonius (*Galba* 20,2) records the execution of one, Patrobius. Dio (LXIV. 8,3) mentions Otho's use of Sporus and other (unnamed) courtiers, whilst Tacitus (*Hist.* I. 76,3) gives the name of Crescens, who honoured Otho's accession. Others, such as Helius, Polyclitus and Doryphorus, are known to have been dead by this time; Epaphroditus (*Ann.* XV. 55,1) survived to be of service to Domitian, and so may have been one of those reinstated by Otho.

of the Golden House: the *domus aurea* was built by Nero after the fire of A.D. 64 (*Nero* 31) to replace the earlier *domus transitoria*. It consisted of a residence in a large landscaped estate, which aroused a great deal of hostility because of its style, size and scope (*Ann.* XV. 42); its "crowning glory" was a statue, one hundred and twenty feet in height, of the emperor as "Helius-Apollo". It is likely that a principal objection to the structure lay in the fact that it resembled less a town-house than one of the lavish villas to be found on the coast of the Bay of Naples; indeed, a "cameo"-painting on a wall of the house of Lucretius Fronto in Pompeii depicts a villa with a sun-court similar to that in the *domus aurea*. Architecturally, one of the significances of the structure was the way in which it adventurously abandoned a strictly rectilinear approach (see Boethius and Ward-Perkins, 1970, 214–6 and McKay, 1975). Although Otho continued its construction, his successors did their best to obliterate it and its memory: Vespasian built his great amphitheatre on the site occupied by the statue of "Helius-Apollo" (*colossus*), whilst Trajan had many of its passages filled in with rubble to strengthen it sufficiently to act as foundation-material for the great bath-house (*thermae*), which he built on its site.

2 **It is said:** *dicitur* is followed by a changing construction – immediately by a nominative and infinitive, showing that *dicitur* is there used personally, and later by an accusative and infinitive, where the sense of *dicitur* has changed to an impersonal usage.

terrified in his sleep: Caligula (*Cal.* 50,3) and Nero (*Nero* 46) are both said to have suffered from terrifying nightmares – presumably as a sign of their guilt. This story is told also by Dio (LXIV. 7,2).

to appease the spirit of Galba: the spirits of victims of murder (*manes*) did not rest until their attackers had paid the penalty.

collapsed to the ground: such a collapse was a very unlucky sign; Marcus Crassus and his son are both said to have fallen at the doors of a temple of Astarte in Syria, a sign which presaged the disaster at Carrhae in which they lost their lives (Plut. *Crassus* 17).

muttering occsionally: the rare verb, *obmurmurare*, normally carries the sense of "murmuring *against*" someone or something; here, the force of the *ob-* compound appears to imply intensity or frequency (cf. *obverberare*).

What have I to do...?: Dio (LXIV. 7,1) gives the words in a slightly different form, and explains them as indicating somebody doing something for which he was unfitted, though some have interpreted this as applying to the attempts to atone by sacrifice rather than to do the job of emperor.

Section 8

1   At about the same time: having shown reluctance to swear to Galba on January 1st, the German armies had proclaimed Vitellius on January 3rd (Tac. *Hist.* I. 52,1; see Introduction 3, and note above on *Galba* 16,2).

Suetonius was the first to apply the adjective, *Germanicianus*, to the German army (see also *Div. Vesp.* 6,2).

Vitellius: for Vitellius' career, see Introduction 4; these events are given at greater length in *Vitell.* 7. Vitellius seems to have arrived in Germany to replace the murdered Fonteius Capito at around the beginning of December, A.D. 68.

he proposed to the senate: presumably employing the *ius primae relationis*, which will have been a feature of the *lex de imperio*, the passage of which in Otho's case is specifically mentioned by Dio (LXIV. 8,1). For a fragment of this law, as it was passed in the case of Vespasian, see *ILS* 244 (a translation is available in *Lactor* No. 8: *Inscriptions of the Roman Empire, A.D. 14–117*, Doc. 55).

that a delegation be sent: technically, the message to be carried by this delegation was appropriate, since the rebellion on the Rhine was directed against Galba, who had now been removed. These envoys were replacements for a group sent originally by Galba to inform the German armies of the adoption of Piso Licinianus, and recalled by Otho (*Hist.* I. 74, 2).

he also sent letters: Tacitus (*Hist.* I. 74,1) also mentions these approaches, as does Plutarch (*Otho* 4,2), though pointing out that when Otho gained confidence as a result of statements of support from Mucianus (Syria) and Vespasian (Judaea), the tone of his correspondence with Vitellius became less conciliatory.

they should share power: of the other sources, only Dio (LXIV. 10,1) mentions this offer.

marry Vitellius' daughter: no other source mentions this proposal. Vitellius' daughter was of marriageable age (*Hist.* III. 78,1), and was engaged to D. Valerius Asiaticus (*Hist.* I. 59,2). It is unclear whether this marriage took place, though later in the year, Vitellius is said to have contemplated a marriage between his daughter and the Flavian general, Antonius Primus (*Hist.* III. 78,1). Vespasian (*Div. Vesp.* 14) is said to have arranged a good marriage for her, though the name of the husband is not mentioned.

whom Vitellius had sent on ahead: although the German legions provided the main thrust of Vitellius' support, he was joined also by commanders in Gaul and by the British legions. The troops had been divided into two groups, both of which made for Italy ahead of Vitellius himself. One group, under Caecina, took the direct route over the Alps, whilst the other, under Fabius Valens, took a more circuitous route through Gaul to gather money and support (see Introduction 3 and note below on *Vitell.* 9).

in an incident which nearly involved: Tacitus (*Hist.* I. 80,1) and Plutarch (*Otho* 3, 3–8) give versions of this incident, the details of which are far from clear, partly

because of a possible corruption in Suetonius' text. The incident involved a seventeenth cohort – (whether or not of the urban guard is unclear) –, which was stationed at Ostia and summoned to Rome. Plutarch seems to say that the mutiny took place in Ostia, whilst Tacitus and (apparently) Suetonius locate it in the camp of the praetorian guard in Rome, at the moment when arms were being handed out to this cohort, presumably to be taken to the Tiber, loaded on board ship, and taken back (*remitti*) to Ostia. The mutiny seems to have occurred amongst the praetorians, rather than amongst the soldiers of the seventeenth cohort, thinking that these arms were being removed for use *against* Otho. The armouries of the praetorians' camp contained arms for all the cohorts stationed in the vicinity of Rome.

2   **rushed to the Palace:** Otho was entertaining senators and their wives to dinner (*Hist.* I. 81,1). It appears from Tacitus (*Hist.* I. 80,2) that the mutineers came on horseback to the Palace, which would tend to confirm the identification of them as praetorians. The praetorian cohorts had a cavalry-attachment, whilst the urban cohorts did not.

that all senators be put to death: Suetonius here represents this as a determined attempt on the part of the praetorians to attack senators; Tacitus' version (*Hist.* I. 82,1) suggests a much more confused scene, in which the anger of the praetorians veered irrationally from one objective to another in rapid succession.

these were pushed aside: Tacitus (*Hist.* I. 82,1) names two officers, Julius Martialis and Vitellius Saturninus, who were injured. There is no mention in Tacitus' or Plutarch's accounts of fatalities amongst the officers at the Palace, though some had been killed earlier at the camp of the praetorians (*Hist.* I. 80,2).

until they had seen him: Tacitus (*Hist.* I. 82,1) says that Otho threw convention on one side, and stood on a couch to address them; with entreaties and tears he restored some measure of calm, though more thorough-going measures were put in place the following day (*Hist.* I. 82, 2–3).

Suetonius' account of the incident is much shorter than those of Tacitus and Plutarch; far from shedding light on Otho or his circumstances, the biographer succeeds only in obfuscating the incident to the point where the issues involved are largely beyond recovery.

3   **he started his campaign vigorously:** according to Tacitus (*Hist.* I. 89,3), there were two reasons for this – the realisation of the effect of tardiness upon Nero's efforts to save himself, and the fact that Caecina had already crossed the Alps.

Suetonius is said to have regarded the form, *incohare* ("begin"), as more correct than *inchoare*.

he took no notice even of religious considerations: Tacitus (*Hist.* I. 89,3) gives a similar account.

the sacred shields: there were twelve of these, of which eleven were copies of the original one which is said to have fallen from heaven on March 1st during the reign of Numa Pompilius. Each year, on March 1st, which was taken as the opening of the campaigning-season, the shields were taken from the chapel of Mars (*sacrarium Martis*) by the priests of Mars (*salii*); they were carried around Rome for a month and returned to the chapel at the end of March.

a very unlucky sign: see Livy (XXXVII. 33) for Scipio's observance of the religious propriety.

on the very day: Suetonius gives the date as March 24th, whilst Tacitus (*Hist.* I. 90,1) puts it as the 14th; the *acta* of the Arval Brethren (*ILS* 241) appear to support Tacitus' date.

devotees of Cybele: the cult of Cybele had been introduced into Rome in 205 B.C., though the goddess did not receive the formality of a temple in Rome until Augustus built one on the Palatine. The celebration of Cybele's festival (*Megalesia*) was held between April 4th and 10th, until Claudius introduced another festival specifically connected with Cybele's grief at the loss of Attis; this was celebrated between March 22nd and 27th. March 24th was called the "Day of Blood" (Ferguson, 1970, 26–31).

the auspices proved most unfavourable: it is significant as an indication that Suetonius did not rely heavily on the account of Tacitus that the biographer omits a number of unfavourable signs which Tacitus lists (*Hist.* I. 86).

Dis the Father: the Greek god, Pluto, whose worship in Rome seems to have obtained prominence during the first Punic war. Even so, little is said of the cult by surviving writers.

in a sacrifice like this: this peculiarity of sacrifices to Dis is not mentioned elsewhere, and is thought by some to have been invented because of Otho's fate.

by flooding of the Tiber: described in detail by Tacitus (*Hist.* I. 86,2) and Plutarch (*Otho* 4,5), the latter of whom says that the river-level reached on this occasion was the highest on record. It was held that flooding of the Tiber was a sign of imminent disaster (Pliny *Nat. Hist.* III. 55). The problem was natural, and Augustus appointed a group of *curatores* to look at causes and solutions, though flooding in A.D. 15 led to the senate's consideration (and rejection) of a proposal to divert some of the Tiber's tributaries (Tac. *Ann.* I. 76, 1–3).

twenty miles out: on the *via Flaminia*, which followed the Tiber-valley through Etruria and across the Apennines to Ariminum (Rimini) on the Adriatic coast.

found the road closed: Tacitus (*Hist.* I. 86,3) talks of this and other natural disasters being interpreted as signs of impending doom.

Section 9

(For the topography of events described in this section, see map 3 (p.xvii) and Wellesley, 1975, 74ff).

1   **the proper course of action:** the fact that Suetonius inevitably does not develop the full historical context leaves his reader in some difficulty in understanding the sequence of events. The balancing arguments were that delay on Otho's part would certainly have worsened for Vitellius' troops the two considerations mentioned by Suetonius (shortage of food and space for deployment); delay would also have allowed for the arrival of reinforcements for Otho's cause from the Danube. On the other hand, speed would have allowed Otho to capitalise upon the undoubted enthusiasm of his supporters and prevent the growing sense of disillusionment on their part, and the suspicion that the "professional" commanders, who advocated delay, may have had treacherous intentions. Further, a speedy campaign would have allowed Otho's troops to take on separately the two parts of Vitellius' army; once joined, this army numbered approximately one hundred thousand men. In the Othonian "high command", delay was advocated by Suetonius Paulinus, Marius

Celsus and Annius Gallus, whilst Otho himself, his brother, Titianus, and Proculus, the prefect of the praetorian guard, were inclined towards a speedy strike (*Hist.* II. 30ff).

a shortage of food: one of the arguments passed by Suetonius Paulinus in his well-constructed advocacy of delay (*Hist.* II. 32).

the prospect of a longer delay: Otho is shown by Tacitus to have felt angrily frustrated by the delaying-tactics (*Hist.* II. 40). Plutarch (*Otho* 9,3), on the evidence of Otho's secretary (Secundus), indicates that Otho's nerve was breaking, and that it was essentially his inexperience and effeteness which blinded him to rational considerations. There was also a version, mentioned and rejected by Tacitus (*Hist.* II. 37,1), that in the view of the armies neither leader was worthy of this kind of sacrifice.

before Vitellius' own arrival: according to Tacitus, Vitellius had just set out from Germany with his remaining troops (which included an eight-thousand strong levy from Britain), when he heard of the death of Otho (*Hist.* II. 57).

to settle the main issue: *profligari* is clearly (unusually) an impersonal usage.

unable to control: there may have been two opposing reasons for the troops' eagerness; there was on the one hand on Otho's side clearly a zeal which was based upon personal loyalty to Otho, and which caused suspicion of the advocates of delay. At the same time, however, some of the praetorians probably wanted to be done with the fighting at the earliest possible opportunity, so that they could return to their comfortable life in Rome. It was generally imagined by Otho's troops, probably because of the mutual antipathy and contempt that existed between praetorians and legionaries, that a swift victory would be theirs.

remained behind at Brixellum: Brixellum (modern Brescello) was situated to the south of the river Po, and thus represented a rearward position with regard to the emerging battle-line. Otho's decision was urged on him by his brother and Proculus, and not opposed by the other commanders, so that he should not be exposed to danger. The decision was a mistake (*Hist.* II. 33,2), because it deprived Otho's troops of the presence of a leader to whom their sense of personal attachment was great (Dio LXIV. 12), and because it also involved the departure from the scene of the impending battle of the keenest of Otho's troops, who formed his bodyguard. Dio (LXIV. 10,2) suggests that Otho's reason for his withdrawal *may* have lain in his unwillingness to *witness* civil war (which, in view of Otho's ousting of Galba, Dio regards as a hollow reason). On the other hand, it may have been due to a desire on Otho's part to leave the organisation of the battle itself to the senior commanders and, by distancing himself from the scene, to be in a position to exercise a more effective overall control of the campaign. Brixellum was also in a commanding position for the line of the *via Aemilia* to Rome, and the road from the Danube.

2   **in the Alpine region:** see Tac. *Hist.* II. 12. Otho sent some troops on to the procuratorial province of *Alpes Maritimae* to secure it and neighbouring Narbonensis which was supporting Vitellius. Otho's troops defeated those raised in *Alpes Maritimae* and detachments of Valens' army in Narbonensis, but withdrew rather than capitalise on the victory.

near Placentia: the modern Piacenza, on the south bank of the river Po; Othonian troops, led by Vestricius Spurinna, defended it successfully against an assault

launched by Caecina across the river from Cremona, and followed it with a successful, though small-scale, raid on Cremona. The troops on Otho's side thought that it should have been followed up with a full-scale assault and interpreted the failure by Otho's generals to do this as a sign of their treachery (*Hist.* II. 17–23).

at a place called Castor's: the place was called *Locus Castorum*, because of a temple there dedicated to Castor and Pollux. It has been suggested that *locus castorum* might mean "place of beavers", and represent a translation of the celtic name, *Bebriacum (Bedriacum/Betriacum)*. The encounter is described by Tacitus (*Hist.* II. 24–6; cf. Plut. *Otho* 7), who places *Locus Castorum* as twelve miles east of Cremona on the *via Postumia*, in the direction of Bedriacum, where the main Othonian forces were now concentrated, hoping for Danubian reinforcements. They gained an advantage over Caecina's troops, which for some reason Paulinus let slip by not chasing the Vitellians back to Cremona and defeating them. Again, Otho's troops thought that they saw the signs of treachery in this failure.

at Bedriacum: the proper form of the name is uncertain, but may have been *Betriacum*; it was situated between Cremona and Verona (*Hist.* II. 23,2). It has given its name to two battles – that between Othonians and Vitellians in April, and in October that between Vitellians and Flavians. This battle was actually fought nearer to Cremona on the road from Bedriacum (*Hist.* II. 42); there was little in the outcome, though the dispirited Othonians fled to Bedriacum and surrendered there the following day.

as a result of treachery: it is not clear whether the reason was treachery, or the understandable confusion of civil war. At any rate (*Hist.* II. 41), two of Otho's officers came to try to talk to Caecina; however, Vitellius' troops interpreted this as a trap, and in their turn the Othonians (by treachery or chance) were taken by a rumour that the Vitellians were now deserting. At this, the Othonians tried to talk, but were "answered" by a Vitellian attack.

3   to commit suicide: see *Hist.* II. 46ff.

a struggle for dominance: Tacitus, although unable to condone or even understand Otho's murder of Galba, which he regarded as destructive of the whole concept of personal loyalty, nonetheless in no way doubted the sincerity and nobility of Otho's suicide (*Hist.* II. 50,1: *duobus facinoribus, altero flagitiosissimo, altero egregio....*).

still unharmed in reserve: that is, the troops which he had with him at Brixellum.

and reinforcements: see Tac. *Hist.* II. 44–6. Earlier, Tacitus says (*Hist.* II. 11,1) that VII Galbiana and XIII Gemina from Pannonia, and XI Claudia and XIV Gemina Martia Victrix from Dalmatia were coming to reinforce Otho, and that an advance-group of two thousand men from each had been sent on; some at least of these were present at Bedriacum. Further, III Gallica, VII Claudia and VIII Augusta were on their way from Moesia, and had reached Aquileia when they received the news of Otho's suicide.

Even those troops who had suffered defeat: Tacitus (*Hist.* II. 46, 1–2) shows that Otho's troops were not so disheartened that they were not prepared to fight on; Plutarch (*Otho* 15, 1–2) comments on the amazing level of personal loyalty to Otho on the part of his troops, which serves to explain their utter despair when they heard of his death (*Hist.* II. 51), and their anxiety to put matters right with their opponents.

Section 10

1 My father, Suetonius Laetus: it is generally thought that *Laetus* is more likely to have been the paternal *cognomen* than *Lenis*, which figures in the majority of manuscripts.

in the thirteenth legion: one of the legions that had come from Pannonia in Otho's support; it had been in Pannonia since the early days of Claudius' reign. Its defeat at Bedriacum was at the hands of V Alaudae, though it primarily blamed its own commander (Vedius Aquila) for this. Vitellius disgraced it by making it build amphitheatres at Cremona and Bononia (*Hist.* II. 67,2) before returning it to Pannonia. Because of this, it readily embraced the Flavian cause and stored up a terrible vengeance for Cremona later in the year (*Hist.* III. 32,1).

Later...: as often, *mox* is used for *postea*.

the deaths of Brutus and Cassius: the assassins of Julius Caesar met their deaths in 42 B.C. at the battle of Philippi at the hands of Marcus Antonius and Octavian (see Shotter, 1991b, 14ff); both committed suicide.

challenged Galba: *concurrere* followed by *cum* normally means "to join battle with". As this did not happen in Otho's displacement of Galba, the verb more appropriately means in the present passage "oppose" or "challenge".

by the example of an ordinary soldier: Dio (LXIV. 11) tells the story in the same way, whilst Plutarch (*Otho* 15,3), placing it in the context of his version that Otho was on the point of "deserting" his troops, interprets the soldier's suicide as an attempt to dissuade the emperor.

Otho cried out: both Plutarch (*Otho* 15, 3–6) and Dio (LXIV. 13) put into Otho's mouth a speech made to those who were urging him to continue the struggle. Tacitus (*Hist.* II. 47) puts Otho's sentiments in the context of a speech to his more intimate supporters.

2 his brother: for Titianus, see above on 1,3; he was pardoned by Vitellius (*Hist.* II. 60,2).

his nephew: Lucius Salvius Otho Cocceianus was spared by Vitellius, but put to death by Domitian for celebrating his uncle's birthday (*Dom.* 10,3). The year of his death is unknown, though it is possible that there was a connection with the appearance of a "false Nero" in A.D. 88 (*Hist.* I. 2,2). The sources have broadly similar accounts of the final meeting between Otho and his nephew, though Plutarch (*Otho* 16,2) includes the point that the emperor had entertained the idea of adopting his nephew.

each of his friends: so too Tacitus (*Hist.* II. 48,1).

two letters: *bini* is used for "two", because *codicilli* had in effect no singular. These were small wooden "frames" in which was placed a thin layer of wax, into which a message could be written with a stylus. Numbers of these have been found in recent years at Chesterholm – Roman *Vindolanda* – in Northumberland: over the years, the wax perishes and messages can be "recovered" from the impression left by the stylus on the wood beneath the wax (Bowman and Thomas, 1983, 32ff). Alternatively, a message might be written in ink on papyrus, wood or vellum.

exarare is a metaphor from "ploughing" applied to the action of the stylus (cf. *Nero* 52).

to his sister: see above on 1,3.

Nero's widow, Messalina: Statilia Messalina had a distinguished lineage: her grandfather had been consul in A.D. 11, and her father in A.D. 44. Her father's grandfather was the orator, Messala. Nero married her in A.D. 66, after murdering her husband, Vestinus Atticus, consul of A.D. 65 (Tac. *Ann.* XV. 68, 3–5; Suet. *Nero* 35), ostensibly for involvement in the Pisonian conspiracy of A.D. 65 (Warmington, 1969, 136–40).

he burnt all his other letters: Tacitus (*Hist.* II. 48) specifies that the letters involved were those which showed enthusiasm for Otho and/or disrespect to Vitellius.

he distributed amongst his servants: Tacitus (*Hist.* II. 48,1) says that this distribution was carefully managed (*parce nec ut periturus*), and Plutarch (*Otho* 17,1) shows that far from being lavishly uncritical, the donations took account of the nature and quality of service each recipient had rendered. Plutarch places the distribution later in the sequence of events, as Otho prepared himself for suicide (see below in 11).

Section 11

1   **he put his affairs in order:** see also Tacitus (*Hist.* II. 49,1) and Plutarch (*Otho* 16,3), who talk of the same violence being offered by "loyalists" to those whom they regarded as "deserters".

   who were beginning: the frequentative, *coeptare*, is used only here by Suetonius, presumably with the intention of conveying the lack of organisation in a situation where people were making their own individual decisions.

   were being captured: most prominent amongst these was Lucius Verginius Rufus, who had withdrawn from active participation in the events after the battle of Vesontio in the previous year (see Introduction 3). Following his dismissal by Galba (Shotter, 1967), Verginius had been made suffect consul by Otho, since the *ordinarii* (Galba and Vinius) had been killed in January. Verginius was plainly unwilling to risk further major involvement, and escaped after Otho's suicide, when the distraught troops asked first that he should become emperor, and then that he should try to negotiate a pardon for them with Vitellius' side (*Hist.* II. 51). As Tacitus narrates it, the incident hardly put Verginius in a favourable light.

   "Let us", he said: these words are nowhere else quoted; Suetonius not infrequently captures the real or imagined last words of emperors (e.g. *Nero* 49,1 and *Div. Vesp.* 23,4 and 24). The biographer is insistent on the accuracy of his quotation (*his ipsis totidemque verbis*), which may indicate the existence of contrary versions.

   he gave instructions: both Tacitus and Plutarch show that Otho did this in no half-hearted fashion.

   could come and see him: such objective genitives (*sui*) after *potestas* are not uncommon.

2   **Then he quenched:** Suetonius' description is very matter-of-fact, particularly when compared to Tacitus' description (*Hist.* II. 49,2), which is prefaced by one of the historian's most striking expressions for "the onset of evening" (*vesperascente die*, which is also used in *Ann.* I. 65, 9). In both Tacitean passages the objective appears to be to capture the notion of "struggle" on the part of the chief participants.

took two daggers: Nero also tested two daggers (Suet. *Nero* 49,2; cf. Suet. *Dom.* 17,2).

closing his door: *adopertus* (for *clausus*) is instanced only once – in Ovid (*Met.* I. 173) – prior to the present passage.

he slept soundly: Plutarch (*Otho* 17,2) agrees with Suetonius on this detail, though Tacitus is less positive (*Hist.* II. 49,2) – *noctem quietam, utque adfirmatur, non insomnem egit.*

at about daybreak: the use of *circa* of time (as distinct from place) is post-Augustan.

and stabbed himself: Dio (LXIV. 15,1) has none of the "serenity" of Otho's preparation, and represents the suicide as an "act of violence". Whilst Suetonius and Dio indicate simply that Otho stabbed himself, Tacitus and Plutarch both say that the emperor fell upon his sword. At the same time, Plutarch's account includes further enquiries which Otho supposedly made at that late stage concerning the well-being of his followers.

his servants burst in: Tacitus (*Hist.* II. 49,3) says that slaves and freedmen rushed in, together with Plotius Firmus, prefect of the praetorian guard.

he was hastily given a funeral: Tacitus (*Hist.* II. 49, 3–4) gives some detail of the funeral, including the genuine and intense grief felt by those of his partisans who attended. The funeral was rapidly carried out, at Otho's own request, to avoid the kinds of indignity inflicted upon Galba's corpse (*Galba* 20,2). Details of Otho's tomb are given in *Vitell.* 10,3 (see also Tac. *Hist.* II. 49,4 and Plut. *Otho* 18,1); it is evident that Otho's epitaph made no claims, true or false, for the dead emperor.

he had lived thirty-seven years: Suetonius' statement that Otho was in his thirty-eighth year is incorrect; he was born on April 28th, A.D. 32, so that he was a few days short of thirty-seven when he died (Tac. *Hist.* II. 49,4). Dio (LXIV. 15,2) says that Otho was eleven days short of his birthday.

for ninety-four days: precision is hard to achieve, since the exact date of Otho's death is not known. Dio (LXIV. 15,2) says that the duration of his reign was ninety days, Josephus (*Bell. Iud.* IV. 9,9) ninety-two. Tacitus (*Hist.* II. 55,1) says that the news of Otho's death reached Rome during the celebration of the *ludi Cereales* (April 13th–19th). If the news arrived towards the end of that period, then Otho's death could be placed around April 15th/16th, the latter of which would represent the ninety-second day of his reign.

Suetonius may have arrived at his calculation from the date of Otho's formal accession (*dies imperii*: January 15th) to that of Vitellius, which is said in the *acta* of the Arval Brethren to have been on April 19th – that is, immediately following the receipt *in Rome* of the news of Otho's death.

Section 12

1 **match this nobility:** *competit* for *competivit*; the verb is usually followed by a dative, but occasionally by the ablative.

on the short side: Otho's *modica statura* can be compared with Galba's *iusta statura* (*Galba* 21).

had bad feet: it is not precisely clear what the problem was; *pedatus* is normally used of plants rather than people.

bow-legged: if *scambus* is correct, it represents a "latinisation" of a Greek word; the idea is normally expressed by *varus*. The manuscript have *cambus*, which has been explained as a Gallic word, which in later times was used as a *cognomen*.

like a woman's: according to Juvenal (*Sat.* II. 99), Otho carried a mirror with him on campaign.

free of hair: cf. *Div. Iul.* 45; the practice was despised by traditionalists (Juv. *Sat.* VIII. 16 and 114; XI. 157).

wore a wig: the latin, *galericulum*, was the diminutive of *galerum*; originally, it referred to an animal-skin with the *original* hair still attached. It subsequently came to mean a cap with human hair (*Nero* 26,1). For Otho's hair-style, see *RIC I²*, plate 29. Thin hair was not uncommon in Rome, and may have been due to excessive use of the curling-tongs.

shaved his face: regular shaving was introduced in the third century B.C. The frequentative verb, *rasitare*, is post-Augustan in use.

with wet bread: Juvenal mentions this amongst the effeminate habits of Otho (*Sat.* II. 103–8); in *Sat.* VI. 461–2, Juvenal refers to cosmetics as *Poppaeana*; it is possible that Otho picked up some of his effeminate habits during his association with Poppaea Sabina (see above on 3,1).

avoid the growth of a beard: after the first shave, young Roman men normally remained clean-shaven or kept a well-trimmed beard. After the age of about forty, most Roman men were clean-shaven. The shaving of the first beard (*lanugo*) was a day of celebration, in which the shaved beard was dedicated to a god; Nero, for example, dedicated his to Jupiter Capitolinus (*Nero* 12).

rites of Isis: the worship of the Egyptian goddess was introduced into Rome early in the first century B.C. Like many foreign cults, its rites were secret, and the cult therefore fell under suspicion, and attempts were made to suppress it. Augustus tolerated it outside Rome, but in a notorious incident in A.D. 19, involving immorality and corruption, Tiberius closed the cult-centre in Rome and crucified the priests. The cult was *officially* tolerated in Rome from Flavian times, but had clearly on the basis of this passage received unofficial support prior to this (see Ferguson, 1970, 106ff). The linen-vestment described here was worn by the priests. There was an impressive temple to the goddess in Pompeii (Boethius and Ward-Perkins, 1970, 291–2).

2 **It is my opinion:** the subjunctive (*putem*) expresses a modest statement of opinion.

inconsistent with his lifestyle: the contrast was attractive to epigrammatic writers ("nothing in his life became him like the leaving of it") – see Dio LXIV. 15,2; Martial *Epig.* VI. 32; Tac. *Hist.* II. 31,1. The contrast was not, of course, precise, since all sources produce much evidence of Otho's ability to discipline himself when circumstances demanded (Tac. *Hist.* I. 22,1).

It is probable that the dative, *maiori miraculo*, is to be preferred to the ablative.

wept uncontrollably: both Tacitus (*Hist.* II. 49, 3–4) and Plutarch (*Otho* 17,3) describe the wild and desperate displays of grief by those present. Although the circumstances may have enhanced the emotions of Otho's followers, there can be little doubt of the deep and genuine personal affection which they felt; for many of them, this soon transferred itself into a bitter hatred of Vitellius.

committed suicide: see Tacitus (*Hist.* II. 49,4); Dio (LXIV. 15,2) talks of them killing each other in their grief.

in their grief: *prae* tends to be used in this sense only in early and post-Augustan latin.

whilst he was alive: Plutarch (*Otho* 18,2) makes the same point.

he had murdered Galba: this "popular" interpretation is not accepted by our main sources (above in 6,3; Tac. *Hist.* II. 50,1).

to restore liberty and the republic: this emotive, but vague, notion of abolishing the principate and returning to the government of the senate and people was talked about on a number of occasions during the Julio-Claudian period. Augustus is said (*Div. Aug.* 28) to have twice contemplated it; it was raised in the aftermath of Caligula and Nero (*Galba* 10,1). There was also a tendency to ascribe support for the idea to popular figures – Claudius' brother, Nero Drusus (*Div. Claud.* 1,4) and Drusus' son, Germanicus (Tac. *Ann.* I. 33, 3–4). A realistic assessment of the relationship between the principate and the republic is put by Tacitus into the mouth of Galba on the occasion of the adoption of Piso Licinianus (*Hist.* I. 15–16; for discussions, see Shotter, 1978a and 1991a, 3299ff).

Libertas was a word of many meanings (Wirszubski, 1950), but in the context of the politics of the republic tended in practice to mean the *freedom* of the nobility to glorify themselves and their families through public service with *no interference* (*dominatio*). The word was always a potent symbol in the unseating of a tyrannical emperor (*RIC I²*(Galba), 37).

Life of Vitellius

Section 1

1   **some say:** this difference of view is reflected in two later writers who will have picked up their opinion from earlier sources; Aurelius Victor (*Epit.* 8,1) refers to Vitellius' *familia nobilis*, whilst Eutropius (VII. 18,1) says that the family was *honorata magis quam nobilis*.

the flatterers and denigrators: Tacitus, in the preface to the *Histories* (I. 1, 1–2), makes the same point that the interest of posterity in discovering the truth was lost because, whilst an emperor was alive, writers flattered him, and once he was dead he became an object of often violent criticism. Tacitus adds that a particular aspect of this problem was that the views of the "critics" carried a false sense of objectivity. *Variatum esset* is an impersonal usage, not uncommon in Suetonius (e.g. *Div. Claud.* 11,1).

2   **Quintus Elogius:** there can be no certainty in the text here, and a writer of this name is not otherwise known. Some textual commentators have regarded it as unlikely that a name has been lost and have preferred something on the lines of *extatque elogi.....libellus*, which is interpreted as referring to a genealogical pamphlet (*Galba* 3,1), composed to "improve the ancestry" of a family. If, on the other hand, a name has been lost, the most attractive suggestion – by virtue of

causing least disturbance to the text – is to assume a reference to a freedman of Quintus Vitellius, who was manumitted with the name of Quintus Vitellius Eulogius. This *cognomen* is attested, and it would be an entirely appropriate task for such a person to draw up a flattering genealogy for his former master.

Quintus Vitellius: on him, see below in 2,2.

quaestor of the Deified Augustus: the task of a *quaestor Caesaris* was to perform specific tasks for the emperor, such as reading his speeches in public. The title amounted to commendation for the office (see Shotter, 1966), and indicated that such a man had performed well in his earlier posts – the vigintivirate and military tribunate – and was regarded as a promising candidate later on for high office. "Commended" candidates were included on the complete list of candidaes for election, but their positions were *not* contested (see Tac. *Ann*. I. 14,6–15,2 for a discussion of the conduct in Tiberius' reign of the elections for praetorships).

from Faunus: an ancient Italian god of the countryside who achieved "national" status with the establishment in 196 B.C. of a cult-centre in Rome and an annual festival-date (December 5th). This "promotion" was probably responsible for much of the legend that grew around Faunus; he was viewed as the Roman equivalent of Pan, as one of the legendary kings of Rome, as king of the Aborigines (Dion. Hal. I. 31), and as a deity of wisdom and prescience.

of the Aborigines: they were regarded as the original inhabitants of Latium, who had been restricted to that area by the hostile activities of the Sabines. Legend connected them with the foundation of Rome by Aeneas and his Trojans (Sallust *Cat*. 6). The name was taken to derive either from *ab origine* ("from the beginning"), or from the Greek word for "mountain" (*oros*; ὄρος).

Vitellia: we have no other reference to the worship of Vitellia; the name was thought to have the same origin as *Italia*, meaning "land of cattle".

enrolled in the patriciate: Livy (II. 4) mentions two Vitellii who were amongst a group of young nobles who conspired to reinstate the last king, Tarquinius Superbus, after his expulsion (traditionally in 509 B.C.). They failed, and the family lost its patrician status; their sister, Vitellia, is said to have been married to the Brutus who founded the republic. There is no further suggestion in republican times of patrician status for the family.

3   **The Vitellian Way:** the route of a *via Vitellia* is not known; the Janiculan hill was on the eastern side of Rome, and outside the early limits of the city.

colonia of the same name: the town of Vitellia was on the borders of Latium and the tribal territory of the Aequi (Livy II. 39 and V. 29). It was lost to the Aequi in 393 B.C., and its subsequent history is not known. Pliny (*Nat. Hist*. III. 69) refers to it as a city of Latium that no longer survived.

the Aequiculi: an alternative name for the Aequi, who lived in the hills of central Italy in the valley of the river Anio. They had a reputation for producing sturdy warriors (Virgil *Aen*. VII. 746–7), and were one of Rome's toughest opponents in the fifth and fourth centuries B.C., not being finally defeated until 304 B.C. (Livy IX. 45). There is no other reference to this family-enterprise on the part of the Vitellii.

at the time of the Samnite war: Rome fought three wars against these hill-people – 343–1 B.C., 327–04 B.C., and 298–0 B.C. The second of these is meant here, and

involved in 321 B.C. the defeat of a Roman army at the Caudine Forks, which lived on as one of the greatest disgraces ever inflicted upon a Roman army.

Nuceria: this Apulian town was known more usually as *Luceria*, and should be distinguished from towns in Campania and Umbria which also bore the name, Nuceria; its modern name is Lucera. Tacitus (*Hist*. III. 86,1) has it as the family's town-of-origin. Luceria was the only Apulian town to remain loyal to Rome in the second Samnite war. It was the Roman effort to relieve the consequent siege of the town that led to the ignominious defeat at the Caudine Forks (Livy IX. 12–15). In 314 B.C., the Romans made it into a *colonia*, with a plantation of two thousand five hundred Roman citizens (Livy IX. 26).

Section 2

1. **Cassius Severus:** his writings were notoriously scurrilous, and his style bitter and abusive (see Tac. *Dial*. 26; Quint. *Inst. Or.* X. 1,116). He attacked members of the aristocracy in Augustus' time, and was banished to Crete, probably in A.D. 12 (Tac. *Ann*. I. 72,4). Augustus was so incensed that he altered the *lex Julia maiestatis* (treason-law) to include scurrilous pamphlets, breaking with a tradition in which the law had confined its attention to treasonable *actions*. Cassius Severus continued his writings in exile, and in A.D. 24 (Tac. *Ann*. IV. 21,5), his exile was made harsher and he was sent to the barren island of Seriphos: he died there, apparently in A.D. 34.

   shoe-repairer: the word, *veteramentarium*, is used only here; the description is meant to contrast a shoe-*repairer* with more "honourable" trades, such as shoe-*making*.

   deals in confiscated property: the word, *sectio*, is thought to have derived from *secare* ("cut"), and refers to the practice of such people deducting money from sales to cover commission and liabilities attaching to such properties.

   debt-recovery agent: that is, by purchasing debts from the state, and then recovering them from debtors, with commission. Literally, a *cognitor* was one who appeared in court in the place of or representing another party.

   Antiochus: there is no other mention of him. *Furnaria* is a post-Augustan usage, with which *ars* has to be understood; the term refers to the baker's oven. A similar "charge" had been made about Augustus' ancestors (see *Div. Aug.* 4).

2. **In any case:** the latin, *ceterum*, indicates a resumption following a digression.

   Publius Vitellius: nothing is known of this Vitellius, though Dio (LI. 22,4) mentions a Quintus Vitellius, perhaps a brother of this Publius, who, though a senator, fought publicly as a gladiator in 29 B.C. (see Wiedemann, 1992, 102ff). *Nuceria* is an ablative of origin.

   a procurator in charge: in Augustus' time, property was probably divided between that which belonged to the state, which was held in the *aerarium Saturni*, and that which belonged to the emperor (*res Caesaris*). It was under Claudius that a division of the emperor's property took place, so that his *public* money was thereafter called *fiscus*, and his private resources *patrimonium*.

   the highest positions: the term, *amplissimae dignitatis*, clearly means office in the *cursus honorum*, as *amplissimus ordo* is regularly used to mean the senate.

the same name: it was unusual for members of the aristocracy under the principate to have only two names (*praenomen* and gentile name); indeed, the practice of adoption occasionally led to the most complex nomenclatures.

during his consulship: he was *consul suffectus* in A.D. 32, taking up office on July 1st.

shared with Domitius Ahenobarbus: on Domitius, see above on *Otho* 2,1. In strict usage, Suetonius' observation that Aulus Vitellius entered the consulship with Domitius is incorrect, since the consuls who opened the year were Domitius and Camillus Scribonianus (*Otho* 2,1; Tac. *Ann.* VI. 1,1). Unusually, in A.D. 32, only one of the *consules ordinarii* (Scribonianus) was required to resign at the end of June. Probably because of his recent marriage to the younger Agrippina (Tac. *Ann.* IV. 75), Domitius Ahenobarbus was permitted to retain office for a full year, and thus was the incumbent consul when Vitellius took over on July 1st.

great refinement: *praelautus* is used only by Suetonius, and demonstrates his liking for adjectives intensified with the *prae-* prefix. *Alioqui* is a post-Augusten word which can signify contrast ("otherwise") or addition ("besides").

Quintus lost: he is mentioned in 1,2 for the promising start to his senatorial career, signified by imperial commendation for the quaestorship. Tacitus (*Ann.* II. 48,3) shows that Quintus Vitellius was one of a group of senators who had fallen on hard times because of extravagance and whom Tiberius either removed from the senate or allowed to resign. It is possible that the significance of the unusual expression (*caruit ordine*), rather than the normal *motus est ordine*, is intended to indicate that Vitellius was one of those who were given the relative privilege of being allowed to resign. The episode also demonstrates that a favourable career-assessment early on did not *guarantee* continued success; this had to be earned, and emperors needed to be able to keep careers under review (*Ann.* II. 36, 4–5; Shotter, 1966). Tiberius was a careful manager of the public purse, and although he did sometimes give financial assistance to senators who had fallen into difficulty, he investigated such cases very closely to ensure that extravagance was not the cause (e.g. *Ann.* I. 75, 5–7; II. 37–8). For similarly tough treatment of Galba's brother, see above on *Galba* 3,4.

Tiberius prompted a decision: the phrase *auctore Tiberio* indicates that Tiberius made a formal proposal; this he would have done by virtue of the *censoria potestas* ("censorial function") which resided in his *imperium*.

3 **Publius was on Germanicus' staff:** Publius Vitellius was a *legatus* of Germanicus in Germany in A.D. 15 (*Ann.* I. 70), and distinguished himself by his bravery in leading the second and fourteenth legions to safety; he was subsequently entrusted with the Gallic census in A.D. 16 (*Ann.* II. 6,1). He accompanied Germanicus on his ill-fated eastern mission, and is thought to have been proconsul of Bithynia in A.D. 18; it is uncertain whether he had already held the praetorship or whether this was an extraordinary appointment, as was Otho's in Lusitania (see above on *Otho* 3,2). After Germanicus' death at Antioch in A.D. 19, a charge of poisoning was brought against Gnaeus Piso, the legate of Syria; Vitellius took part in the prosecution of Piso, and is said by Tacitus to have spoken very effectively (*Ann.* III. 13,3). Following Piso's suicide during the trial, Vitellius and the other accusers were rewarded with priesthoods (*Ann.* III. 19,1).

Germanicus was the son of Nero Claudius Drusus and Antonia (Kokkinos, 1992), and thus the elder brother of the emperor, Claudius. He married Augustus' granddaughter, Agrippina, and Augustus required Tiberius to adopt him as his own son and successor. The relationship between Tiberius and Germanicus, described by Tacitus in some detail in *Ann.* I–III, was never good during Germanicus' German and eastern commands; when Germanicus died in A.D. 19, it was widely assumed that Gnaeus Piso had poisoned him, but on instructions from Tiberius and Livia (see Shotter, 1968 and 1971).

Gnaeus Piso: Piso was a long-standing friend of Tiberius, and shared the consulship with him in 7 B.C. As governor of Tarraconensis under Augustus, he made himself very unpopular with the provincials; he was noted for his frank outspokenness (*Ann.* I. 74, 6–7; II. 43,3, where Tacitus gives the following description – *ingenio violentum et obsequii ignarum, insita ferocia....*). Because of his independence of spirit, Tiberius chose him to be legate (governor) of Syria to "keep a watchful eye" on Germanicus and Agrippina in the east. Piso's interpretation of his mission was, however, surely a caricature of what was intended, and the relationship between all concerned became a fiasco which risked the whole purpose of Germanicus' mission, with his and Piso's staff bickering in public and finally physically fighting each other (see Shotter, 1974b).

The description of Piso as Germanicus' "enemy" (*inimicum*) probably refers to Germanicus' act of formally renouncing their friendship when he became convinced that Piso was trying to poison him (*Ann.* II. 70,3).

murderer: there was little other than very circumstantial evidence of Piso's guilt on this charge (*Ann.* III. 14,2); essentially, he was convicted because public opinion was obsessed with the "heroic" qualities of Germanicus and needed a scapegoat (*Tib.* 52; *Cal.* 2ff), refusing to accept that the young man could have succumbed to a natural death.

He reached the praetorship: unless Suetonius is in error, it is natural to understand this post as coming in the interval between the death of Germanicus in A.D. 19 and the fall of Sejanus in A.D. 31.

amongst the accomplices of Sejanus: that is, in A.D. 31. The indictment pressed against Vitellius is recorded by Tacitus (*Ann.* V. 8) as using his office as prefect of the *aerarium militare* ("military treasury") to provide funds for Sejanus' "revolution". No doubt, many people were *wrongly* accused in the aftermath of Sejanus' fall, as scores were settled and real accomplices tried to save themselves by implicating others. It is likely – though never said – that, after the death of Germanicus, Vitellius had remained close to his widow, Agrippina; there is some evidence to suggest that Tiberius himself came to suspect a connection between Sejanus and Agrippina (Shotter, 1989, 21ff), and in any case some of Agrippina's friends seem to have seen in Sejanus a possible source of protection against Tiberius.

Lucius Aelius Sejanus was sole prefect of the praetorian guard from A.D. 15 until his fall in A.D. 31 (*Ann.* IV. 1, 2–4), and is generally seen as the most pernicious influence at work during Tiberius' reign. By murder and intrigue he sought to play the two parts of the imperial house (*Julii* and *Claudii*) off against each other, and emerge as the only person upon whom Tiberius could place his hopes for the future.

Because of the loss of the text of Tacitus' *Annals* at the relevant point, we cannot be certain why precisely Sejanus fell from grace, though Tiberius subsequently wrote that it was because of his intrigues against the children of Germanicus, whom Tiberius had probably intended as his heirs (*Tib.* 61). For a discussion of Sejanus and his role, see Shotter, 1992, 41ff.

put under his brother's supervision: it was not uncommon for accused or convicted persons to be put under the supervisory custody of a magistrate or a relative. In this case, the brother involved was probably Aulus, who was to become consul in A.D. 32. However, since it is clear from Tacitus (*Ann.* V. 8,3) that some passage of time was involved, and since Aulus died whilst in office, it is possible that the brother to whom Publius Vitellius was entrusted was Lucius, who was to be consul in A.D. 34.

with a scribe's knife: according to Tacitus, he acquired this on the pretext of writing; he is said to have written up the speech which he delivered at the trial of Piso (Pliny *Nat. Hist.* XI. 187). Tacitus does not mention Vitellius' "change of heart" on the question of suicide.

4 Lucius Vitellius: he was consul in A.D. 34, and in the following year was made legate of Syria with an overriding *imperium* to handle the renewed threat posed by Parthia to stability in the area (Tac. *Ann.* VI. 32,5; Dio LIX. 27). There is no doubt that his conduct of this episode in his career was exemplary (*prisca virtute*), and that it was his skilful combination of diplomatic and military initiatives that secured a favourable outcome. It is worth making the point that at this stage of Tiberius' life, when the emperor had "retired" and was supposed by many to be out of touch with events, he made one of the most imaginative provincial appointments of his whole reign.

Artabanus, the Parthian king: in Germanicus' arrangements in the east of A.D. 17–19, Artabanus was put on the Parthian throne, and Zeno (Artaxias) on that of Armenia. This arrangement remained stable until the latter's death in A.D. 34; misled perhaps by Tiberius' withdrawal from Rome into thinking that the emperor would pay little attention to events in the east, Artabanus put his own son on the vacant Armenian throne, and wrote insolently to Tiberius. The emperor replied by replacing both Artabanus and his son and by sending Lucius Vitellius with special powers to enforce a new settlement; after a short period of largely diplomatic confrontation, Artabanus agreed to accept the Roman nominee for the Armenian throne (Mithridates), in return for a guarantee of his own position in Parthia. He "submitted" in the manner described by Suetonius, and sent his son, Darius, to Rome as a guarantee of his good faith (*Ann.* VI. 31–7 and 41–4; Dio LVIII. 26; Josephus *Ant. J.* XVIII. 4,5). The time-scale for the completion of these events is unclear, since both Suetonius (*Cal.* 14) and Dio (LIX. 27,3) ascribe the successful outcome to Caligula's reign; only Josephus places the conclusion in Tiberius' reign.

to the legionary standards: the standards (see note above on *Galba* 12,2), images and altars were kept in the "regimental chapel" at the rear of the headquarters building (*principia*); the standards were viewed as having a religious significance (*Ann.* I. 39,7). Dio adds that Artabanus paid homage also to the images of Augustus and Caligula.

two more consulships: that is, in A.D. 43 and 47; both marked out the esteem in which Vitellius was held, for not only did he hold these consulships with the emperor as his colleague, but on the first occasion the office enabled him effectively to govern Rome whilst Claudius joined his military expedition to Britain, and the second occasion saw Vitellius and the emperor as colleagues in the censorship also.
and the censorship: Vitellius held the censorship along with Claudius in A.D. 47–8 (*Div. Claud.* 16,1; *Ann.* XI. 13,1); Tacitus (*Ann.* XII. 4) specifically mentions the ejection of Silanus from the senate *per edictum Vitellii*, and adds that Vitellius used the censorship to ingratiate himself with Agrippina (*nomine censoris servilis fallacias obtegens ingruentiumque dominationum provisor*). The censorship had been one of the most respected and influential of republican offices, being held for a period of eighteen months in every period of five years by two senior ex-consuls. The chief tasks were the assessment of the Roman people for taxation-purposes, the overseeing of the state's "moral fibre", regulation of the membership of the senate, and the negotiation of state-contracts. Sulla abolished the office during his dictatorship, but it was restored by Pompey and Crassus in 70 B.C. It lapsed again during the civil wars until Augustus attempted to revive the office in 22 B.C. However, on that occasion, the two censors (Paulus and Plancus), resigned within days apparently feeling unable to exercise the office in the face of the *imperium* of the *princeps*. Thereafter, emperors from time to time exercised a *censoria potestas*, apparently based on their *imperium*, until Claudius again revived the office in A.D. 47–8, occupying it himself with Lucius Vitellius as his colleague. They conducted a full period of censorial activities, of which perhaps the most notable were the admission of some Gallic nobles to membership of the senate (*Ann.* XI. 23–5) and the enlargement of the patriciate (*Ann.* XI. 25). The office lapsed again until occupied by Vespasian and Titus in A.D. 73–4; Domitian in A.D. 84 had himself entitled *censor perpetuus* (*Dom.* 8,3). Thereafter, emperors appear to have exercised censorial functions as and when they saw fit. For Claudius' censorship, see Levick, 1990, 98–101.
deputised for Claudius: there was no "official" position of deputy to the *princeps*, though informally such occasions as this were covered by leaving a trusted adviser in charge when the *princeps* had to be absent from Rome – as Maecenas for Augustus, and Seneca for Nero.
on his expedition to Britain: for the details, see Frere, 1987, 48ff. Claudius joined the expedition in the latter part of the campaigning-season of A.D. 43 for the formal capture of Colchester (Camulodunum), the chief centre of the British leaders, Caratacus and Togodumnus. Although there were many arguments favouring the annexation of Britain, Claudius' *personal* involvement indicates that he was probably trying to identify his interests with those of his legions in order to "neutralise" the impression given at the time of his accession by his association with the praetorian guard – a familiar theme in the events of A.D. 68–9. It was also important to Claudius to recapture the sense of dynamism that characterised Caesar's campaigns to Britain in 55 and 54 B.C. For the "publicity", see *RIC I²* (Claudius), 30.

his reputation suffered: Tacitus (*Ann*. VI. 32, 6–7) draws a sharp contrast between his conduct at Rome (*sinistra....fama*) and his probity in the provinces (*prisca virtus*).

Perinfamis is one of a number of intensifying *per-* compounds found in Suetonius; this one is a rare usage.

windpipe: the plural, *arterias*, is used because of the division of the windpipe into the two bronchial tubes.

as a medicine: *fovere* is frequently used of the relief provided by medicines.

constantly and in public: it has been suggested that Asiaticus' reference to the *os impudicum* of his accuser, Vitellius, may have been an allusion to this practice (*Ann*. XI. 3,2).

5 **inventive in flattery:** see *Ann*. VI. 32,7, where Tacitus contrasts his behaviour at the court of Caligula and Claudius with his conduct as legate of Syria under Tiberius (also Dio LIX. 27).

the cult of Gaius Caesar as a god: the question of Caligula's divinity is difficult to resolve, since despite the assertions in classical writers, no coin or cult-site survives to offer positive support for the claim; nor do provincial inscriptions exceed the "norm" for most emperors. The account provided by Dio (LIX. 27) of Vitellius' involvement with a cult of Caligula is that the emperor, fearing Vitellius as a potential rival, had planned to put him to death on his return from Syria in A.D. 40, but that by obsequious behaviour, including the establishment of the cult, Vitellius not only won a reprieve, but admission into Caligula's most intimate circle. It is possible that the connection between Vitellius' brother and the family of Germanicus may have helped. For a discussion of the emperor's divinity, see Taylor, 1931 and Ferguson, 1970, 88ff; a review of the evidence relating to the divinity of Caligula may be found in Barrett, 1989, 140ff. The practices mentioned in the present passage are discussed in Ogilvie, 1969.

with his head covered: this practice is traced back as far as Aeneas (Virgil *Aen*. III. 405–7). Plutarch (*Roman Questions* 10) explains it as a sign of humility, as a way of avoiding hearing ill-omened sounds, and as a symbolic representation of the soul's concealment within the body.

turning himself: Romans approached a god on the left side, and after prayer turned to the right before falling to the ground in adoration (Lucretius V. 1198–1200). Dio records an occasion (LIX. 27,6) when Caligula, during converse with the goddess, Luna, asked Vitellius if he, too, could see the goddess; Vitellius' adroit reply was that the gods revealed themselves only to each other.

Claudius was obsessed: a feature of the Claudian tradition to which frequent allusion is made (e.g. *Div. Claud*. 25 and 29; *Ann*. XII. 7, 5–7; XI. 35,1).

Addictus properly means one who was enslaved for debt.

wives: Claudius was married four times; the first two, Plautia Urgulanilla and Aelia Paetina, were divorced before he became *princeps* in A.D. 41. His third wife was Valeria Messalina who was executed in A.D. 48 following her bigamous marriage to a young noble, named Gaius Silius (*Ann*. XI. 26–38); her place was taken, after considerable disuccsion (*Ann*. XII. 1) in which the names of several candidates were put forward, by Agrippina, the mother of Nero, who poisoned Claudius in A.D. 54 (*Ann*. XII. 7, 5–7).

freedmen: Suetonius lists them in *Div. Claud.* 28; the most powerful were Narcissus (his secretary) and Pallas (his financial adviser).

He asked Messalina: her influence with him was strong (see *Ann.* XI. 1–3, where he is recorded as having secured for her the condemnation of Valerius Asiaticus).

to take off her shoes: according to Ovid (*Ars Am.* II. 211–2), this was a common practice signifying the lover's enslavement to his mistress. The *socculus* was a woman's shoe which was often decorated with gold and pearls (Pliny *Nat. Hist.* IX. 114). Of Greek origin, the shoe was popular with comic actors, but considered effeminate if worn by men.

and his tunics: most Roman men wore two tunics under the toga, though Augustus is said (*Div. Aug.* 82) to have worn as many as four in winter.

Osculabundus is a verbal adjective not found prior to its use in the present passage.

Narcissus and Pallas: the two most powerful of Claudius' freedmen. Narcissus was the emperor's secretary (*ab epistulis*; see Introduction 1), who disposed of much patronage in Claudius' reign (e.g. *Div. Vesp.* 4,1). Dio (LX. 19, 2–3) records how Claudius sent him to the Gallic coast in A.D. 43 to encourage the legions to embark for Britain. He was later instrumental in the execution of Messalina, but supported the claim of Aelia Paetina (Claudius' divorced second wife) to re-marry the emperor. Losing out to Agrippina and Pallas who supported her, Narcissus undertook to forward the claims of Britannicus to succeed his father; following Nero's accession in A.D. 54, Narcissus committed suicide (*Ann.* XIII. 1,4). Pallas was the financial adviser to Claudius (*a rationibus*), and gained enormous power as a result of the emperor's marriage to Agrippina. Nero dismissed him in A.D. 55, and he died seven years later as a result of poison administered on Nero's instructions (*Ann.* XIII. 14,1 and XIV. 65,1). He was hated for his arrogance (*Ann.* XIII. 23, 1–3), and envied for his wealth (Juv. *Sat.* XIV. 329).

altar to the Household gods: such altars might stand in the main entrance-hall (*atrium*) of a house or in a bedroom; many examples survive in Pompeii.

Secular games: the *ludi saeculares* took the place of the *ludi Tarentini* of the republic; the games lasted for three days and three nights, and took place on the *Campus Martius*, near a volcanic fissure (*Tarentos*), where an altar to Dis and Proserpina stood. The site has been identified (Platner and Ashby, 1929, 508–9), and inscriptions relating to celebrations by Augustus and Septimius Severus have been found. The games were scheduled for celebration every 100 (or 110) years; Augustus celebrated them in 17 B.C., (the occasion for Horace's *carmen saeculare*), Claudius in A.D. 47, and Domitian in A.D. 88; on the latter occasion, Tacitus (as a *quindecemvir sacris faciundis*) officiated, and apparently described them at some length in a lost portion of the *Histories* (*Ann.* XI. 11, 1–2). Claudius' celebration was intended to mark Rome's eight hundredth anniversary.

Section 3

1   **of a stroke:** this appears to be what is meant by *paralysis*. The date of his death is not recorded, though he had, through Agrippina's influence, escaped a prosecution in A.D. 51, when he is described by Tacitus as being a man *validissima gratia, aetate extrema* (*Ann.* XII. 42,4).

two sons: that is, the future emperor (Aulus) and his brother, Lucius (see below on 15,2).

Sextilia: her goodness is generally attested (see also Tac. *Hist.* II. 64,2). Despite Vitellius' rebellion against Otho, that emperor looked after her (Plut. *Otho* 5,2 and 16,2). Following his victory in April of A.D. 69, Vitellius honoured his mother with the title, Augusta (*Hist.* II. 89,2); she died shortly before his own fall, worn out and sorrowful, with her reputation intact (*Hist.* III. 67,1). Suetonius records a rumour (below in 14,5) that Vitellius poisoned her.

consuls in the same year: that is, in A.D. 48, when their father was censor with Claudius. Aulus opened the year as *ordinarius*; his brother was *suffectus* later in the year. Lucius also in A.D. 60 or 61 succeeded his brother in the proconsulate of Africa (see below in 5).

a public funeral: a funeral at the state's expense was first accorded to the dictator, Sulla, in 79 B.C. It had to be authorised by a decree of the senate, and a magistrate would be instructed to deliver the funeral-panegyric, as Tacitus did (as consul in A.D. 97) for Verginius Rufus (Pliny *Epp.* II. 1,6).

with a statue: this too required the senate's authorisation (see above on *Galba* 23). Vitellius celebrated his father's achievements on his own coinage (*RIC I²* (Vitellius), 7).

loyalty: the latin word, *pietas*, (best-known perhaps for Virgil's frequent attribution of it to Aeneas), represented a combination of a sense of duty, loyal devotion to the gods, and to ones family. Octavian was able to make a virtue out of it through his cultivation of the memory of Julius Caesar, and his refusal (albeit, eventual) to co-operate with his father's assassins. Although it might be argued that *pietas* was due to those emperors who had been deified, it was due principally to the living emperor as "father of the national family" (*pater patriae*). Because of this, treason (*maiestas*) might be regarded as *impietas* (*Ann.* VI. 47,2; Bauman, 1972).

2   **Aulus Vitellius....was born:** this date-of-birth is irreconcileable with calculations given (below in 18) for the length of his life. Both Tacitus (*Hist.* III. 86,1) and Suetonius give his age at death as being in his fifty-seventh year. Only Dio (LXV. 22,1) has the correct figure; Drusus Caesar and Norbanus Flaccus were consuls in A.D. 15 (*Ann.* I. 55,1); Drusus, the son of Tiberius, is characterised as hard and cruel (*Ann.* I. 29,4; I. 76,5; Wiedemann, 1992, 172f); he was poisoned in A.D. 23 by his wife, Livilla, at the instigation of Sejanus, the prefect of the praetorian guard (see above on 2,3; *Ann.* IV. 8–10). Gaius Norbanus Flaccus had been praetor in A.D. 11; either he or his brother (consul in A.D. 19) was murdered at the time of Caligula's assassination in A.D. 41. For their ancestry, see Syme, 1939, 325.

so long as he was alive: the only record of a provincial post prior to Galba's appointment of him to Lower Germany is the proconsulate of Africa, held in A.D. 60 or 61, evidently after his father's death.

Genitura was a horoscope predicted at birth.

sent out to the legions: that is, to the legions of Lower Germany – an appointment made by Galba in the summer or autumn of A.D. 68 to fill the vacuum left by the murdered Fonteius Capito. Tacitus (*Hist.* I. 9,1) says of the appointment that it seemed justified – to Galba, that is – by Vitellius' paternal credentials.

mourned her son: Tacitus (*Hist.* II. 64,2) summarises the reply of Sextilia to her son's first letter after his proclamation in Germany.

on Capreae: the island was acquired by Augustus, and a group of twelve villas was built there. In A.D. 27, Tiberius retired to the *villa Iovis*, and spent there much of the last ten years of his life (*Ann.* IV. 67; Shotter, 1989, 17f and 1992, 59ff). The aged emperor is said to have devoted himself whilst there to a life of debauchery and bestiality (*Tib.* 40–3; Marañon, 1956, 204ff). Dio (LXIV. 4,2) refers to Vitellius as a favourite of Tiberius; the debate on the nature of life on Capreae with Tiberius has been lengthy (e.g. Levick, 1976, 201ff); for the villa itself, see Boethius and Ward-Perkins, 1970, 324–6.

spintria: see Suetonius (*Tib.* 43,1) and Tacitus (*Ann.* VI. 1,4). Vitellius, according to the date-of-birth given by Suetonius, would have been in his nineteenth year when his father became consul. The allegation made here is not found in any other writer, and it is typical of Suetonius to introduce such a serious charge with a vague *existimatusque*.

Section 4

every kind of vice: at various points, Tacitus refers to Vitellius' *lucus*, *torpor*, *ignavia* and *socordia* (see also below in 17,2).

his passion for chariot-racing: he received an injury which left him lame (see on 17,2), whilst driving with Caligula; that emperor's enthusiasm for the races is recorded in *Cal.* 54–5.

his love of dice: Claudius' avid gambling is well-recorded (*Div. Claud.* 33,2 and Seneca *Apocol.* 14).

greater favour with Nero: see Tacitus (*Hist.* II. 71,1). Nero's chariot-driving and dice-playing are well-documented (*Nero* 22,1; 24,2; 30,3; 53). Dio (LXV. 2–5) records Vitellius' debauched habits, but also mentions a better side to his character (LXV. 6).

a particular service: the use of *peculiaris* for "particular" is almost unique.

at the Neronian games: Nero established this quinquennial celebration in A.D. 60 (*Nero* 12,3; *Ann.* XIV. 20,1); the *Neronia* were set up after the Greek fashion, and furnish strong evidence of Nero's growing phil-hellenism. He instructed that the presidency of the games should be exercised not (as was normal) by an ex-praetor, but by ex-consuls chosen by lot – hence, the presence of Vitellius. Tacitus mentions a single celebration in A.D. 65 (*Ann.* XVI. 4,1), though the games were discontinued at Nero's death. Domitian instituted an alternative (*Dom.* 4,4), but we find a mention of a celebration of *Neronia* as late as A.D. 242 (Victor *Caes.* 27).

lyre-players: precisely, a *citharoedus* was an artist who played the lyre, *and* sang to its accompaniment. Although Nero had earlier performed at Naples, his first performance *in Rome* was in A.D. 65, when people clamoured to hear the "divine voice" (*Nero* 21,1). The climax of the emperor's artistic career was his visit to Greece in A.D. 67, when he competed in all the festivals and carried off 1,808 first-prizes (Griffin, 1984, 143ff).

though everyone was calling: *quamvis* followed by a participle is a post-Augustan construction.

So he left the theatre: this detail does not appear in Tacitus' account (*Ann.* XVI. 4).

Section 5

favour of three emperors: that is, Caligula, Claudius and Nero.

political honours: that is, the posts of the senatorial *cursus honorum*, culminating with his consulship in A.D. 48 and the proconsulate of Africa in 60 or 61 (see below). Tacitus (*Hist.* III. 86,1) ascribes Vitellius' success entirely to his father's reputation.

highest priesthoods: two are known: he was one of the Arval Brethren in Nero's reign, and a *quindecemvir sacris faciundis* (see *RIC* I² (Vitellius), 70).

proconsulship of Africa: in A.D. 60 or 61 (*Hist.* I. 70,1).

in charge of public works: the various curatorial posts (of public works, roads, aqueducts, of the Tiber) were established at Rome by Augustus (*Div. Aug.* 37); they were often held by ex-consuls, though the "minimum qualification" was to have held the praetorship. It is not clear when Vitellius held this post, though it may have been between the praetorship and consulship, as an alternative to commanding a legion (*legatio legionis*).

his enthusiasm for these: Tacitus (*Hist.* II. 97,2) praises Vitellius' tenure in Africa.

for two years without a break: *biennio continuato* is an ablative expressing duration of time.

when his brother succeeded him: Lucius Vitellius had also succeeded his brother directly in the holding of the consulship in A.D. 48.

as his deputy: it was normal for provincial governors to enjoy the services of deputies (*legati*), to whom they could give certain functions. Usually, a consular proconsul had three who were chosen by himself, but approved by the emperor; they were of equal or inferior rank to the proconsul himself.

in his post in Rome: that is, as *curator* (see above).

to have stolen: the verb, *surripere*, is used elsewhere of thefts of religious objects.

to have replaced: a similar allegation was made against Julius Caesar (*Div. Iul.* 54); the form, *aurichalcum*, arises due to an erroneous derivation from *aurum*; it in fact derives from the Greek word for "mountain", the source of part of the alloy. Orichalcum was used for minting *sestertii* and *dupondii* in the coinage-system. An indication of the degree of the fraud here described is that one hundred *sestertii* (or two hundred *dupondii*) were equivalent to a single gold *aureus*; thus, in weight, approximately three thousand grammes of orichalcum were taken as equivalent to 7.25 grammes of gold.

Section 6

Petronia: after her divorce from Vitellius, she married Gnaeus Cornelius Dolabella (see above on *Galba* 12,2); this marriage so enraged Vitellius that he had Dolabella murdered early in his reign, doing his reputation great harm (*Hist.* II. 63–4); Dolabella had by some been considered as a possible succesor to Galba.

whose father: Publius Petronius was *consul suffectus* in A.D. 19, and proconsul of Asia for six years (A.D. 29–35); he became governor of Syria under Caligula, and was given the task (later rescinded at Petronius' persuasion) of supervising the erection of the emperor's statue in the Temple at Jerusalem (Philo *Leg.* 31; Barrett, 1989, 182ff). Seneca notes that Petronius was a close friend of Claudius (*Apocol.* 14). Petronius himself married a Vitellia (*Ann.* III. 49,2), though it is not clear what

her relationship was with the emperor; their son was the distinguished Petronius Turpilianus, who had been given by Nero the task of defending Italy against Vindex and Galba in the spring of A.D. 68 (Shotter, 1975, 67f), and who was subsequently murdered on Galba's orders (*Hist.* I. 6,1).

blind in one eye: *altero oculo* is an ablative of respect.

on condition that: Suetonius follows *sub condicione* with a number of constructions (*si, ut, ne*).

freed from his father's control: an extremely cumbersome process whereby a son who was freed from paternal control (*patria potestas*), so that he could inherit property in his own right. The son was sold three times to a fictitious purchaser, and was freed from his father's control after the third sale. Two cases are mentioned in Pliny's *Letters* (IV. 2; VIII. 18).

charging him: *insimulare*, although not used elsewhere by Suetonius, is used here, as by other authors, to indicate the making of a *false* accusation. Occasionally, however, it can be used simply as a synonym of *accusare*.

parricide: in this case, of course, only *intended*.

Galeria Fundana: Tacitus (*Hist.* II. 64,2) praises her for not associating herself with the horrors of civil war, though Dio (LXV. 4) talks of her extravagance in sharing her husband's belief that Nero's *domus aurea* was poorly-appointed and inadequate for their requirements. Tacitus also (*Hist.* II. 60,2) reveals that she protected the Othonian, Galerius Trachalus, a relative of hers.

a boy and a girl: Vitellius, at Lyons on his way to become emperor, presented his son to his army wrapped in a military cloak, and named him *Germanicus* (*Hist.* II. 59,3). The boy was with his father when he surrendered power (*Hist.* III. 67), and was later put to death by the Flavian leader, Mucianus (below in 18). For the daughter, see above on *Otho* 8,1, where Suetonius mentions the story that Otho had proposed a marriage between his son and Vitellius' daughter. Both children were featured on Vitellius' coinage (*RIC* I² (Vitellius), 57).

stammered: the form, *titubantia* (used here and in *Div. Claud.* 30), occurs only in Suetonius.

Section 7

1 **Galba appointed him:** for the reason for this vacancy, see above on *Galba* 11. Galba's appointment of Vitellius is seen by Tacitus as totally inadequate, and based upon his father's reputation (*Hist.* I. 9,1 and III. 86,1). For the legions in Lower Germany, see below in Appendix I.

in Lower Germany: The Germanies (*Superior* and *Inferor*) were military districts rather than provinces, and any civilian jurisdiction (for example, in financial matters) was exercised from neighbouring Belgica. It appears that, after the revolt of Antonius Saturninus in A.D. 88–9, their government was altered in a way that made them more like regular provinces.

of Titus Vinius: for his influence over Galba, see above on *Galba* 14,2.

for "the Blues": there were four factions in circus-racing, which excited enormous and obsessive enthusiasm; Pliny (*Nat. Hist.* VII. 186) observes that one enthusiast even threw himself on to the funeral-pyre of a dead driver. The factions were "Red" (*russatus* or *russeus*), "White" (*albus*), which were the original two, together with

"Green" (*prasinus* or *viridis*) and "Blue" (*venetus*). Many emperors were involved with the factions: Caligula, Nero, Domitian, Lucius Verus, Commodus and Elagabalus all favoured "the Green", whilst Vitellius and Caracalla followed "the Blue"; Vitellius (see above on 4) personally took part as a "Blue" driver (Dio LXV. 5,1). In general, see Veyne, 1992, 392ff.

obsessed with the thought of food: see also Dio (LXV. 2), who provides a catalogue of Vitellius' self-indulgent habits.

huge appetite: as in English, the latin word (*gula* or "gullet") is used for the habit for which it was employed.

than a sign of favour: thus Suetonius uses the anecdote of Galba's view of Vitellius effectively to contradict the views expressed by Tacitus and others (*Hist.* I. 9,1).

2   **in such stretched circumstances:** so Tacitus (*Hist.* II. 59,2) describes Vitellius in the early stage of his "campaign" as *vetere egestate conspicuus* (also Plut. *Galba* 22,5).

his wife and children: Tacitus (*Hist.* I. 75,2) says that Vitellius wrote to Otho's brother, making him responsible with his life for the safety of his mother and children; no mention is made in that context of Galeria Fundana.   The issue of whether a governor of a province could be accompanied by his wife had been the subject of a debate in Tiberius' reign, as a result of some "notorious" cases – Agrippina (the wife of Germanicus), Plancina (the wife of Gnaeus Piso), and Sosia Galla (the wife of Gaius Silius); see *Ann.* III. 33,1 and IV. 20,6, in which Tacitus reports a decision of A.D. 24 that, whilst governors would not be prevented from taking their wives with them to the provinces, they would be held personally responsible for any misconduct on their wives' parts.

in an attic: the neuter-plural of *meritorius* is used as a noun, meaning "lodgings". Petronius (*Satyricon* 38) describes a vulgar-rich type who let his attic (*cenaculum*) to make money.

Suetonius here uses *abdere* with an ablative of place (as in *Otho* 6,3), though this construction was mostly poetical in post-Augustan latin. In *Galba* 20,2, he uses *in* with an accusative case.

let his own house: Suetonius alone uses *ablocare* for *locare* in this sense.

from his mother's ear: that is, Sextilia.   The *uniones* were the most highly-prized of all pearls, and came from the Red Sea.   Pliny (*Nat. Hist.* XII. 2) derives the name from the fact that each pearl was unique.   The self-indulgence of Roman women in the use of pearls was a subject of criticism at the time (Seneca *De Ben.* VII. 9,4).

pawned: *pignare* was used for *pignori dare*.

a crowd of his creditors: Dio (LXV. 2–5) gives considerable detail on Vitellius' extravagance, recording that he was often lost in the forum amidst the crowd of his creditors.   Dio also has the story of his creditors' efforts to delay his departure for Germany (LXV. 5,3).

Sinuessa and Formiae: both towns lay on the *via Appia* near the borders of Latium and Campania.   The site of Formiae is now the town of Mola di Gaeta, whilst the ruins of Sinuessa lie some eighteen miles away at the foot of Monte Dragone.

whose public taxes: we have no information as to how this situation had arisen, though Vitellius had presumably purchased the right to collect the indirect taxes of these communities (Stevenson, 1939, 148ff).

false accusations: *calumniae* could be either false accusations against a person, or convictions for having made false accusations.

instituted proceedings: *iniuriae* could cover offences involving violence, nuisance or defamation; the *formulae* were the forms in which the praetor related the law to the case in hand.

3   **he found the army hostile:** this hostility was of course directed towards Galba (see above on *Galba* 9–11; Tac. *Hist.* I. 8). The chief reasons for the hostility were Galba's murder of Fonteius Capito and "dismissal" of Verginius Rufus, and the pressure to which the troops had been subjected after Nero's suicide to swear allegiance to Galba.

with hands outstretched: the hands were stretched out and turned upwards to heaven in the attitude of thanks to the gods – on this occasion, for the arrival of Vitellius.

whose father: see above on 2,4 (Tac. *Hist.* I. 9,1 and I. 52,4); the feeling was evidently that a man of Vitellius' standing would be better able to "represent" them, even to the point of challenging Galba for power.

in the prime of life: Vitellius' age (53 years) would appear to be a little outside the normal interpretation of *aetate integer*, which would naturally refer to a younger person with much life ahead of him.

In such expressions, Suetonius applies *integer* sometimes to the person concerned (qualifying it with the ablative, *aetate*), or makes it agree with *aetas*.

common soldiers: *miles caligatus* is an alternative expression for the more usual *gregarius miles*; it refers to the military boot (*caliga*), made of leather and with soles studded with nails. The word, of course, provided the nickname of the emperor, Gaius *Caligula*.

Quoque ("even") serves to emphasise the unusual nature of Vitellius' behaviour (Mooney, 1930, 634).

in wayside inns: Suetonius typically distinguishes between the stop-over points for beasts of burden (*stabula*) and the inns for travellers (*deversoria*); his instinct and training would encourage him to choose the correct word in such a context.

affable: Vitellius' "affability" (*comitas*) is said by Tacitus (*Hist.* I. 52,2) to have been his supporters' interpretation of characteristics in the emperor which others thought of as indicating lack of taste and judgement.

he had had breakfast: breakfast (*iantaculum*) was a meal taken at the third or fourth hour (that is, of the daylight-day), and consisted usually of bread dipped in wine or honey.

Section 8

1   **he entered the camp:** Tacitus (*Hist.* I. 52,1) describes Vitellius' careful inspection of the camp on his arrival on December 1st, A.D. 68. There were three legionary fortresses in Lower Germany; the most important was the double fortress (for legions V and XV) at Xanten (Vetera), which was the headquarters of the army of

Lower Germany and presumably Vitellius' destination. The other fortresses were located at Neuss (Novaesium: for legion XVI) and at Bonn (Bonna: for legion I).

to remove the punishments: also described by Tacitus (*Hist.* I. 52, 1). Some of these were men who had been "too loyal" to Nero or Verginius Rufus in the spring of A.D. 68. Some of such punishments are described elsewhere by Suetonius (*Div. Aug.* 24,2).

defendants' anxieties: *sordes* were clothes of mourning, and often worn by those on trial in order to elicit sympathy. The figurative description of its removal by Vitellius refers, of course, to the dropping of the charges concerned.

after hardly a month: Vitellius had arrived on December 1st; on January 1st, A.D. 69, whilst at Cologne, he heard of the decision of two legions of Upper Germany not to renew their oath to Galba. He passed on this news to the Lower army, and on January 2nd, the soldiers of legion I (under Fabius Valens) hailed him as emperor (*Hist.* I. 56–7).

to what day it was: the day after the *Kalends* (that is, January 2nd) was regarded as unlucky for embarking upon any undertaking; the same was thought to be true of the days following the *Nones* and the *Ides*.

in his indoor clothes: cf. *Otho* 12,1. Suetonius uses *in* or a simple ablative to describe the clothes in which a person was dressed; earlier writers generally preferred *cum*.

he was hailed as emperor: see Tac. *Hist.* I. 57,1.

through the crowded streets: that is, of Cologne (Colonia Agrippinensis – see below on 10,1); this interpretation of *vici* as "streets" or "districts" is much to be preferred to "villages", which would imply a much longer journey.

from the temple of Mars: that is, of course, in Cologne. Suetonius later (in 10,3) describes Vitellius' dedication in the same temple of the sword used by Otho to commit suicide.

2 **to his quarters:** the *praetorium* was the house of the commander.

the chimney had caught fire: the most likely meaning of a difficult expression (*ex conceptu camini*); *conceptus* appears to be connected with fire in only one other passage (Pliny *Nat. Hist.* XVI. 208). The *caminus* was a fire-place, fitted with a chimney, and burning logs; it was commonly used for providing heat in winter in military buildings.

Vitellius said: it was not uncommon for commanders to offer favourable interpretations to what appeared to be unfavourable signs (Frontinus *Strateg.* I. 12). *Quidem*, as often, is used to draw attention to a *bon mot*.

a light is lighting: it seems possible that the whole saying was a quotation from a tragedy, since the addition of *deus* at the end would produce a line in the *iambic senarius* metre used in tragedy.

As the line stands, *adluxit* is used impersonally, for which there is no known parallel.

The army of Upper Germany: see Tac. *Hist.* I. 57,1. On January 1st, the two legions at Mainz (Moguntiacum), the military headquarters of Upper Germany (legions IV and XXII), had destroyed Galba's images, and bound themselves instead to the senate and people (above in *Galba* 16,2; Plut. *Galba* 22,3).

he readily took the title, Germanicus: so also Tacitus (*Hist*. I. 62,2). Plutarch, on the other hand (*Galba* 22,7), says that Vitellius had been hesitant over acceptance, and implies that it was the effects of over-indulgence in food and drink that made him accept. Vitellius' mother refused to recognise her son as *Germanicus* (see above on 3,2).

that of Augustus: *cognomen* has to be understood with *Augusti*. Tacitus (*Hist*. II. 62,2) says that Vitellius delayed acceptance of the title, *Augustus*, even though the senate had voted it to him along with other honours, when it had heard of Otho's defeat and death (*Hist*. II. 55,2). Vitellius dated his reign from the day of the senate's vote (April 19th), but he does not appear to have accepted the title, *Augustus*, until pressurised by the people in August (Tac. *Hist*. II. 90,2).

refused the title of Caesar for all time: Tacitus twice mentions this refusal (*Hist*. I. 62,2 and II. 62,2), as does Plutarch (*Galba* 22,7). However, Tacitus says that later, as the Flavian forces advanced, Vitellius did express the desire to be acclaimed as *Caesar* (*Hist*. III. 58,3). Vitellius' coins from Rome begin simply with the inscription, A VITELLIVS IMPERATOR GERMANICVS, to which AVGVSTVS was later added; CAESAR never appears, although it is found on some coins minted in Alexandria, where officials were presumably unaware of the emperor's wishes (see *RIC* I² (Vitellius), pp. 268ff and Milne, 1971, p. 11).

Section 9

As soon as news reached Germany: Tacitus (*Hist*. I. 64,1) says that one column of Vitellius' troops, under Fabius Valens, had already set off and had reached the river Moselle; the news made no difference to them.

he divided the army into two: Suetonius here oversimplifies the arrangements; Tacitus shows (*Hist*. I. 61) that the forward-group of Vitellius' troops was divided between Valens and Caecina; Valens marched with approximately forty thousand men (from legions I, V, XV, and XVI, with auxiliary units) through Gaul to enlist volunteers and gather money, aiming at an entry into Italy via the Cottian Alps. Caecina took approximately thirty thousand men, spearheaded by legion XXI, by the direct route into northern Italy. Vitellius was to lead the rest – perhaps sixty thousand men – afterwards; his group included eight thousand men from Britain.

a lucky omen: Tacitus tells the same story (*Hist*. I. 62,3); the same omen appears to have presaged Germanicus' victory over Arminius in A.D. 16 (*Ann*. II. 17,2, where it is described as *pulcherrimum augurium*.).

circled the standards: *lustrare*, of course, carries the connotation of religious purification. Because this was often achieved by a procession of priests encircling a sacred object, the verb itself came to mean "circle".

was moving off: normally *movere* requires *se*, when used in this sense.

in many places: Suetonius frequently uses *plurifariam*, though it is not found in any earlier writer. The form of the word is the feminine accusative singular of the adjective.

suddenly collapsed: it is recorded that the deaths of both Caesar (Dio XLIV. 18) and Nero (*Nero* 46,2) were preceded by such omens.

the laurel wreath: Galba had a similar experience (*Galba* 18,3).

Aquam has to be understood with *profluentem*.

at Vienne: the town of Vienne (Vienna) was situated in Gallia Narbonensis on the bank of the Rhone, opposite to Lyons. There was a fierce rivalry between the two (*Hist.* I. 65), based partly on historical events and differing loyalties – for example, with regard to Vindex's rebellion in A.D. 68. The rivalry probably originated in the fact that, whilst Lyons (Lugdunum) was a planted *colonia* of Roman citizens, Vienne developed out of the chief centre of the tribe of the Allobroges. The Roman remains in the town are distinguished for the temple of Augustus and Livia (Boethius and Ward-Perkins, 1970, 348), which was apparently modelled on Augustus' temple of Mars the Avenger, dedicated in the Forum of Augustus in Rome in 2 B.C.

a cock perched: Suetonius offers no explanation of this until c. 18, where he relates it to Vitellius' ultimate defeat at the hands of the Flavian general, Antonius Primus, who came from Toulouse (Tolosa), and who as a boy had enjoyed the nickname of *Beccus*, or "cock's beak". It is worth noting that had the bird in question been an eagle, it would have been interpreted as a sign of coming power (cf. *Div. Claud.* 7).

his deputies: that is, Fabius Valens and Aulus Caecina Alienus, who were responsible for Otho's defeat at Bedriacum (*Otho* 9,2). Valens had been given the command of legion I by Nero, and executed Fonteius Capito (his commander) on Galba's behalf (*Galba* 11), also persuading the legions of Germany to swear (albeit unwillingly) their allegiance to Galba. Valens' view that Galba had not rewarded him sufficiently for these services prompted him to persuade Vitellius to make a bid for power. After the victory, he and Caecina were made consuls, and given the command of Vitellius' defence of Italy against the Flavians. Valens, however, was too ill to take a full part in the campaign; when trying to bring the Gallic provinces in on Vitellius' side, he was captured and put to death. Tacitus entertained a low view of his character (*Hist.* I. 66,2; II. 56,2; III. 62). Caecina was quaestor in Baetica in A.D. 68, and early on came in on Galba's side, for which he was given a legionary command (probably of legion IV) in Upper Germany. However, when Galba ordered his prosecution for corruption, Caecina brought the legions of his province over to Vitellius. Like Valens, he was given a command by Vitellius and, with Valens, was chosen to lead Vitellius' troops against the Flavians, but betrayed his cause (*Hist.* II. 99–101). He was eventually put to death in A.D. 79, on the orders of Titus, for conspiring against Vespasian (Dio LXVI. 16). Tacitus (*Hist.* II. 101) goes out of his way to counter the view, put forward by early Flavian writers (who were reflecting the early Flavian propaganda), that Caecina's betrayal of Vitellius was an act of patriotism; Tacitus' more down-to-earth opinion was that Caecina was a man to whom treachery was second nature.

Section 10

1   **the outcome of the battle of Bedriacum:** see in *Otho* 9,2 (also Tac. *Hist.* II 57,1 and Dio LXV. 1,2a).

     and Otho's death: see *Otho* 11.

     praetorian cohorts: Augustus maintained nine cohorts (of one thousand men each) and ten squadrons of cavalry. The guard did not, however, become a major force in politics until brought together into a single fortress by Tiberius, at the instigation of

Sejanus. Caligula and Claudius appear to have kept eleven or twelve cohorts, and Vitellius (*Hist*. II. 93,2) later raised the number to sixteen. In the Flavian period, Vespasian reduced the number once more to nine, but it was increased again to ten. (For the prefects, see above on *Galba* 14,2). The disbanding of the cohorts, mentioned in the present passage, had two chief motives: in the first place, in the recent struggle the guard had been devotedly loyal to Otho, and secondly, the legions – and those from Germany in particular – were strongly envious of the guard's superior service-conditions and rates of pay. Tacitus (*Hist*. II. 67,1) says that the praetorians dismissed by Vitellius resumed service under Vespasian.

terrible conduct: that is, their desertion of Galba and support of Otho earlier in the year.

Pessimi exempli is a genitive of quality.

ordered them to hand over: the sense of this passage – indeed the normal use of *exauctorare* – would suggest that the payments associated with honourable discharge were not made. Tacitus, however (*Hist*. II. 67,1), contradicts this impression; in this case, each man will have received twenty thousand *sestertii*. The handing-over of arms would have included also the standards; when these men resumed service in Vespasian's cause, Antonius Primus, the Flavian general, spurred them on by pointing out to them *their* standards, now raised by their Vitellian replacements (*Hist*. III. 24,3).

petitions: thus, one of the imperial "secretaries", who specifically handled such petitions, was entitled *a libellis* (see Introduction 1). Plutarch (*Galba* 27,5) also put the number at one hundred and twenty, whilst Tacitus says that the number exceeded this, and in very similar language describes the action of Vitellius (*Hist*. I. 44,2).

This would have seemed: elsewhere, referring to Otho, Tacitus says that the first act of a new emperor should have been to punish those responsible for such an act (Shotter, 1991a, 3299ff).

2 **as if he were triumphing over them:** Tacitus records that Vitellius was encouraged in this attitude by Junius Blaesus, the governor of Lugdunensis (*Hist*. II. 59,2).

sailed along rivers: presumably, the Saone (Arar) and the Rhone (Rhodanus) are meant.

exquisitely decorated: *delicatissimum* is used of something that is luxurious beyond normal acceptability.

most lavish banquets: Tacitus (*Hist*. II. 62,1) provides a vivid description of Vitellius' tasteless and unbearable behaviour.

exercised no discipline: this and the outrages committed by Vitellius' troops are recurring themes in Tacitus' account (*Hist*. II. 56; 68; 71; 87), though the behaviour later in the year of the Flavian troops under Antonius Primus cannot be described as any more salutory (*Hist*. III. 33).

they freed slaves: the proper latin form, as here, was "to claim (*asserere*) someone for freedom (*in libertatem*)".

3 **He eventually reached the battlefield:** that is, at Bedriacum; both Tacitus (*Hist*. II. 70) and Dio (LXV. 1,3) provide vivid descriptions of Vitellius' conduct on this occasion.

disgusted some of those: Tacitus describes the scene (*Hist.* II. 70,1) and this reaction on the part of some of his party (*Hist.* II. 70,3). According to Dio (LXIV. 10,3), forty thousand men were killed in the battle.

Abhorrere unusually here takes an accusative (*tabem*).

preposterous utterance: Tacitus does not report this, but gives a similar example in the case of the death of Junius Blaesus (*Hist.* III. 39,1; see also below in 14,2). On this occasion, Tacitus indicates that he was sufficiently horrified to quote Vitellius' actual words.

and better still: it should be noted that the comparative (*melius*) expresses an advance on a state of affairs already described with a superlative (*optime*).

Still, to palliate: *setius* is equivalent to *minus*.

stone erected in Otho's memory: Otho's grave was simple (*Hist.* II. 49,4; Plut. *Otho* 18,1); thus, the use of the word, *mausoleum*, represents a tasteless insult on Vitellius' part.

he further sent the dagger: it was common to dedicate an enemy's weapon to a god (e.g. *Cal.* 24,3; Tac. *Ann.* XV. 74,2).

to Cologne: the significance rests in the fact that Vitellius was first saluted there (see above on 8,1). The original name was *Oppidum Ubiorum* ("The Settlement of the Ubii"); Germanicus' daughter, Agrippina, was born there, and she persuaded her husband, the emperor Claudius, to plant a *colonia* of veterans there in A.D. 51; hence, the new name, *Colonia Agrippinensis* (Tac. *Ann.* XII. 27,1).

to Mars: Vitellius had been given the sword of Julius Caesar from this same temple when he set out on his campaign (see above on 8,1).

in the Apennines: Vitellius went from Cremona to Bononia (Bologna; Tac. *Hist.* II. 71,1) at the foot of the Apennines. He *may* have then crossed to Florentia (Florence), and thence to Rome along the *via Cassia*.

all-night celebration: the *pervigilium* was nominally a religious celebration – in this case, for victory over Otho –, but this one took the form of all-night orgies (Tac. *Hist.* II. 68,1). There was a shrine of Jupiter Appenninus at the highest point of the *via Flaminia*; the *pervigilium* may have taken place there.

Section 11

1   **sound of a bugle:** see Vegetius *De Re Mil.* II. 22; the *classicum* seems generally to have been a signal for battle, given in the presence of and by the order of the *imperator* (general).

wearing his military cloak: Tacitus (*Hist.* II. 89,1) says that Vitellius exchanged the *paludamentum* ("military cloak") for the *toga praetexta* at the Milvian Bridge; his coinage shows him in both modes of dress (*RIC* I² (Vitellius), pp. 275–7).

insignia of the various units: the *signum* was properly the emblem of the maniple (two centuries), whilst the *vexillum* usually refers to cavalry-standards.

with their officers' cloaks: that is, wearing the *sagum* (or *sagulum*); the form, *sagulatus*, appears to be used only here – *sagatus* being more common.

ordinary soldiers: although early emperors – Augustus, in particular – were careful about identifying themselves too closely with their soldiers, it was clearly appropriate in the context of the events of A.D. 68–9, and normal by Suetonius' time, for emperors so to identify their interests.

2   **to every human and divine scruple:** see also Tac. *Hist.* II. 91,1 and Dio LXV. 2,1.
Battle of the Allia: July 18th, a day marked on the religious calendar. This was the day, in 390 B.C., when the Romans were badly defeated by Gauls at the river Allia, a tributary of the Tiber. Tacitus (*Hist.* II. 91,1) also notices the anniversary, and the fact that on the same day (in 477 B.C.), the three hundred Fabii were killed at the river Cremera by the army of neighbouring Veii; it is possible that the defeat at the Cremera arose as a "doublet" of the loss of the three hundred Spartans at Thermopylae.
post of chief priest: the post of *pontifex maximus* was elective in the republic, and subject to the same level of corruption as other elective offices. Augustus assumed the post himself in 12 B.C., after the death of the then-occupant, his former triumviral colleague, Marcus Lepidus. Thereafter, it was part of the imperial titulary until renounced as pagan by Gratian in the early 380s. The chief priest was "chairman" of all the priestly colleges, and exercised particular tutelage over the Vestal Virgins; the post carried with it an official residence – the *regia* – in the forum-area (Boethius and Ward-Perkins, 1970, 88).
settled the magisterial elections: Tacitus (*Hist.* III. 55,2) says that these were fixed for "*many* years ahead". The emperor's part in the election-process is discussed in some detail in Shotter, 1966. Caesar had fixed elections in advance, though Tiberius (*Ann.* II. 36) had resisted it, presumably because it would have impaired his ability to exercise an on-going "quality-assessment" of candidates. Tacitus (*Hist.* II. 71,1 and 91,2) says that Vitellius did himself go through the formalities of an election-process.
consul for life: Vitellius is certainly described on one inscription (*ILS* 242) as COS PERP. Caligula declined a similar offer (Dio LIX. 6,5), and Nero was offered continuous consulships (Tac. *Ann.* XIII. 41,5). Domitian was made consul for a ten-year period (Dio LXVII. 4,3).
funeral-offerings to Nero: for Vitellius' attitude to Nero, see above in 4. Tacitus (*Hist.* II. 95,1) and Dio (LXV. 7,3) have the same story. The significance of the use of the *Campus Martius* was that it was possible from it to see the point on the Pincian hill, where the family-tomb of the Domitii stood, in which Nero's remains were placed (*Nero* 50).
the master's repertoire: it is possible that a *liber dominicus* existed, which contained Nero's compositions and favourite pieces. The term, *dominus*, was not normally used of any emperor prior to Domitian (*Dom.* 13,1). In this case, the *mastery* probably refers to Nero as a skilful practitioner on the lyre.
Diceret is occasionally used in such a context for *caneret* (cf. Virgil *Aen.* I. 1).
Nero's songs: see *Nero* 21 and 38,2; Dio LXI. 20 and LXII. 18,1; Tac. *Ann.* XV. 33. Although some of Nero's subjects admired this aspect of his accomplishments, others picked it out as a reason for his removal – as did Vindex (Dio LXIII. 22,5).
leap to his feet: a regular way of showing enthusiasm (*Div. Aug.* 53,1).

Section 12

actors and charioteers: see above in 4 and 7,1. Tacitus also mentions Vitellius' proximity to these groups (*Hist.* II. 71,1 and 87,2).

ex-slave, Asiaticus: Asiaticus was an infamous freedman of Vitellius, who is ranked with the worst of his class (Tac. *Hist.* II. 95, 2–3; IV. 11,3). He was crucified – that is, as a *slave* – by the victorious Flavians, even though Vitellius had conferred equestrian status upon him. Plutarch (*Galba* 20,3) wrongly associates him with Galba.

vinegar-drink: *posca* was a mixture of vinegar and water which made up a drink favoured by lower-class Romans, soldiers and slaves (SHA. *Life of Hadrian* 10).

at Puteoli: the modern town of Pozzuoli, situated on the northern end of the fashionable Bay of Naples; it was one of Italy's chief ports – hence its choice by Asiaticus.

but almost immediately: the *-que* of *statimque* seems here to carry the force of "but" (cf. Sallust *Cat.* 3,3).

became very annoyed: *gravatus* is used as a deponent by Suetonius, though followed by *ob* only here; normally it takes an accusative and infinitive.

travelling trainer of gladiators: the word, *circumforaneus* (or *circumforanus*), means "travelling around to markets and fairs". The *lanista* was properly the "trainer" in a gladiatorial school, but clearly he also put on shows as well as selling and letting-out gladiators (Wiedemann, 1992, 106).

of a show: with *muneris, gladiatorii* has to be understood. The word, *munus*, indicates that the putting-on of such shows was a *duty* incumbent upon national and local leaders (Wiedemann, 1992).

provincial appointment: that is, as proconsul of Africa in A.D. 60 or 61 (see above on 5).

on the first day of his reign: that is, April 19th, A.D. 69 (see on *Otho* 11,2). The "timing" differs a little in Tacitus (*Hist.* II. 57,2), who places it at the point where Vitellius, still on his march from Germany, heard the news of Bedriacum and of Otho's suicide.

the golden rings: that is, the symbol of membership of the equestrian order (see on *Galba* 10,3).

Super cenam means "during dinner"; the use of *super* in such a temporal sense is comparatively rare, and restricted to a few phrases (Mooney, 1930, 632), though this particular expression is frequent in Suetonius (e.g. *Div. Tit.* 8,1).

everyone had been begging: Tacitus (*Hist.* II. 57,2) has the same story, and puts the change down to the emperor's *mobilitas ingenii*.

Section 13

1   **especially addicted:** Suetonius commonly intensifies *praecipue* with *vel* to give a superlative sense.

high-living and cruelty: all sources provide examples of this (Tac. *Hist.* II. 62,1 and 95; Dio LXV. 2). Interestingly, Eutropius (VII. 18) increases Suetonius' "three meals a day, and sometimes even four" to "four or five"! The present section deals with "high-living" (*luxuria*); examples of "cruelty" (*saevitia*) are given below in 14.

and sometimes even four: they are detailed by Dio (LXV. 4, 2–3). On the formation of adverbs ending in *-fariam* (*trifariam...quadrifariam*), see above on 9.

breakfast: on the *iantaculum*, see above on 7,3; it was not normally a substantial meal, though Vitellius made it so.

lunch: this was followed by a rest, exercises, bathing, and then dinner.

drinking-session: it was very unusual to eat anything at the *comissatio*.

He coped with this easily: his fellow-diners were evidently less resilient and fortunate (Dio LXV. 2, 2–3); Dio adds an anecdote about Vibius Crispus, who remarked that being ill saved him from a worse fate.

self-induced vomiting: a common practice in Rome (*Div. Claud.* 33), though it was deplored by some (Seneca *Ad Helv.* 10,3).

The huge expense imposed both on the state and on the emperor's hosts is alluded to by Dio (LXV. 3–4), who claims that Vitellius spent nine hundred million *sestertii*, including one million on one dish alone. Although the text of Dio is uncertain at this point, the historian seems to say that Vitellius' friends spent four million *sestertii* in just a few days on entertaining him. Interestingly, "multiplication" has evidently extended Suetonius' four hundred thousand *sestertii*. Nero, too, was in the habit of inviting himself to friends' houses for dinner (*Nero* 27,3).

2 **The most notorious:** Suetonius almost always uses *famosus* in a pejorative sense; the unnecessary *super ceteras* emphasises the notoriety still further.

to mark his arrival: it was normal to entertain a friend or relative who had just completed a journey.

the best fish: the fish most popular at gourmet dinner-parties were sturgeon, bream, pike, mullet, lampreys and turbot; Juvenal (*Sat.* IV) tells the story of a fisherman who presented a "prize-fish" to Domitian.

seven thousand birds: there was a variety of favoured species, including grouse, snipe, partridge, quail, peacock, pheasant, guinea-fowl, crane, stork and flamingo.

that dish: a *patina* was a deep earthernware-dish which could be used for cooking and serving. Pliny (*Nat. Hist.* XXXV. 163) says that Vitellius' *patina* cost one million *sestertii*, and required a specially-constructed kiln for firing it. Dio (LXV. 3,3) says that it was impossible to make an earthernware-dish of sufficient size for Vitellius' requirements, and one of silver was manufactured instead. This survived until Hadrian had it melted down. Vitellius was not alone in such extravagance; Pliny (*Nat. Hist.* XXXV. 163) mentions the Flavian general, Licinius Mucianus, as having dishes which were as broad as the Pomptine Marsh.

shield of Minerva: the two chief suggestions for the identification of the statue involved are the bronze of Athena Promachos, a work of Pheidias on the Acropolis at Athens, which stood 50–60 feet in height. An alternative is the statue, again by Pheidias, of Athena in the Parthenon, whose shield was famous for the scenes embossed on either side. It is possible that, by using the Greek word here, Suetonius is retaining Vitellius' play-on-words – πολιοῦχος meaning "Defender of the city", and πολυχόος, meaning "of large capacity" or "pouring much".

livers of scar-fish: it is not certain what type of fish *scarus* was, though Pliny (*Nat. Hist.* IX. 62) describes it as the most highly-prized of fish, which had been brought from the eastern Mediterranean by Optatus, who was prefect of the fleet (*praefectus classis*) under Tiberius, and introduced into the sea off Latium.

Such a recital of dishes and their origins may be preserved from an original account of the proceedings. It was a typical affectation of the nouveaux-riches of the principate to provide such a catalogue for their guests (see Horace *Sat.* II. 8).

of pheasants: Suetonius and Pliny (in *Nat. Hist.*) employ the feminine form of the word *(phasianae)*. Tradition said that the bird was introduced from Phasis (in Colchis) by the Argonauts (Seneca *Ad Helv.* 10).

and peacocks: this delicacy was introduced from Asia, and first served in the first century B.C. by Hortensius, the orator (Pliny *Nat. Hist.* X. 45). The serving of the brains of animals is mentioned also by Dio (LXV. 3,3).

tongues of flamingoes: this dish was introduced from the Nile by Apicius, the gourmet of the Augusant period (Pliny *Nat. Hist.* X. 133). The bird itself is said to have been offered as a sacrifice in Caligula's supposed dedication of a temple to himself *(Cal.* 22).

guts of lampreys: lampreys were brought from Sicilian waters, and cultivated in fish-ponds in Rome in the gardens of the rich (Juv. *Sat.* V. 99). Augustus' friend, Vedius Pollio, was notorious for throwing offending slaves into his lamprey-pool (Dio LIV. 23,1; Pliny *Nat. Hist.* IX. 77).

had been fetched: the widely-flung provenances of Vitellius' dishes is mentioned also by Dio (LXV. 3,1).

triremes commanded by senior captains: the importance of the mission was indicated by the fact that the triremes were commanded not by the usual trierarchs, but by navarchs who normally commanded larger vessels. Vitellius was not alone in using the fleet for such a personal purpose (see note above on *livers of scar-fish*).

3 **bits of flesh:** the singular, *viscus*, is used instead of the more usual plural, *viscera*.

and spelt-cake: the manuscripts are corrupt here, and *farris frusta* ("bits of spelt-cake") seems to provide the most reasonable restoration; some, however, regard the following *paene* as a corruption of *panem*. The *general* sense is, however, clear. For such outlandish greed, cf. Terence *Eunuchus* 491 and Suet. *Div. Claud.* 33.

The cakes *(liba)* were either placed on the altar or burned in the fire.

of previous days' meals: cf. *Tib.* 34,1 and *Cal.* 58.1.

Section 14

1 **punish, even execute:** it is not clear how great a difference is intended between *necem* and *supplicium*; although the latter can mean any kind of punishment, more often than not in both Suetonius and Tacitus it means specifically *capital* punishment.

share in his power: cf. *Tib.* 25,3. *Adlicefacere* is a post-Augustan compound sometimes used (pleonastically) for *adlicere*.

into a drink of cold water: the same method that was employed to administer poison to Claudius' son, Britannicus (Tac. *Ann* XIII. 16,3).

2 **money-lenders:** a voracious breed with whom Vitellius had had many dealings (above on 7,2), and whose activities were restricted by Vespasian *(Div. Vesp.* 11).

debt-collectors: the *stipulatores* lent money by a verbal agreement, though cases of default were dealt with by a court-procedure.

tax-collectors: the word, *publicani*, could be used to apply either to those who bought the collection-right from the state, or to the men who performed the actual task of collection (Lintott, 1993, 75ff).

tolls: *portoria* were levies on goods carried through a country or over a chargeable "obstacle" (e.g. a bridge); the levy might also be made on vehicles or people. The

better-known use of the term relates to the "harbour-dues" paid on imported merchandise (*Div. Iul.* 43,1).

one of these: although it is widely assumed that the person to whom allusion is made was Junius Blaesus, governor of Lugdunensis (see above on 10,2), whose poisoning at Vitellius' hands is described by Tacitus (*Hist.* III. 39,1), there is no pressing reason to make the identification in the present case.

in his presence: Suetonius makes frequent use of *coram* as an adverb.

when another man: it is, of course, difficult to know the circumstances in anecdotes that are left half-told: there could well have been more to some of these than at first sight appears, particularly in view of Otho's popularity. Compare, for example, Balsdon's "explanation" of the case in Caligula's reign involving the selling of hot water (Dio LIX. 11,6; Balsdon, 1934, 43f).

3 **"You are my heir":** it was common practice for members of the nobility to name the emperor in their wills; the reason for this might vary from genuine friendship or political pragmatism to a realisation that, if the emperor was named as part-heir, he might then leave the remainder of the will in tact. Generally, the more reasonable emperors, though politically flattered by the implied compliment, refused such legacies if the *testator* had children of his own, or unless a genuine personal friendship was involved. However, Caligula (*Cal.* 38,2), Nero (*Nero* 32,2) and Domitian (*Dom.* 12,2) are on record as having been more grasping and mercenary, though it is possible that their attitudes represented a response to what they saw to be empty flattery; nonetheless, such legacies might form a lifeline for extravagant emperors.

He even put: for similarly tyrannical behaviour on Domitian's part, see *Dom.* 10,1 and Pliny *Panegyric of Trajan* 33.

hopes of overthrowing him: *nova spe* is really an abbreviated version of *spe rerum novarum* (that is, "revolution").

4 **jesters:** the word, *vernaculi*, derives from *vernae* (or "slaves born in the home"); these were traditionally encouraged by their masters in a kind of urbane impertinence (Tac. *Hist.* II. 88,2) and wittiness, which may have been the origin of the "counter-proclamation" put up following the banning of astrologers.

fortune-tellers: see above on *Otho* 4,1.

as each was charged: *deferre* meant "to lay information", and the criminal-justice system in Rome depended on those private individuals (*delatores*), who laid information for profit, receiving a proportion (25% or 50%) of a convicted person's property. Inevitably, this was a corrupt system as there was clearly an incentive to ruin rich and influential people. The informers were by many (including Tacitus) regarded as the real cancer in the political system of the early principate (*Ann.* I. 73, 1–2; 74, 1–2; II. 27,1), though Tiberius blindly referred to them as the "guardians of the law" (*Ann.* IV. 30, 3–5). Their activities were from time to time discouraged (*Cal.* 15,4; *Nero* 10, 1; *Dom.* 9,3 and 10,1; Pliny *Panegyric of Trajan* 34 and 44), but most emperors who began by discouraging them, sooner or later reversed this. It was almost inevitable that the state would have to rely on such people, in the absence of a proper public prosecution service.

his case unheard: the use of *inauditus* in this technical legal sense is post-Augustan (cf. *Galba* 14,3).

because...a notice was put up: this is the only instance in Suetonius' writings in which an indicative is used after *quod* when it introduces a reason for accusing, blaming, or being angry with someone.

his edict: the edict is mentioned by Tacitus (*Hist.* II. 62,2), though in his account Vitellius seems not to have reached Rome when it was issued. Dio, on the other hand (LXV. 1,4), says specifically that Vitellius was in Rome at the time.

The Chaldaeans: an alternative name for *mathematici*; its origin lay in the fact that the Babylonian priest, Berosus (c. 340–270 B.C.), was the first Chaldaean to practise astrology in Greece.

was put up saying: it is possible that the latin should have *edicere* (from *edictum*) rather than the *dicere* of the manuscripts.

a great good: it was common for religious reasons to prefix an edict with the formula *bonum factum*, or B F.

by the same date: Dio (LXV. 1,4) has the same story, though he gives it a different slant. He fails to mention the deadline of October 1st, but says that the astrologers' deadline was December 18th, the day on which the emperor actually died, and comments upon the accuracy of the prediction.

be no more: a witty variant on the reference in Vitellius' edict to Rome and Italy; the astrologers' "edict" lays down that Vitellius should be "nowhere on earth" (*ne....usquam esset*).

5   **suspected of:** Suetonius' construction is *suspectus in* (cf. *Hist.* I. 13,3); Suetonius follows it with *quasi*, whereas Tacitus normally uses *tamquam* (*Hist.* III. 35,2).

his mother's death: Sextilia (see above on 3,1); there is no mention in Tacitus' account of this allegation.

a woman of the tribe of the Chatti: Tacitus (*Germ.* 8) describes the high regard in which the German tribes held prophetesses (cf. Strabo VII. 293 of the Cimbri in particular). A prophetess of the Bructeri, named Velaeda, was active in encouraging the revolt on the Rhine in A.D. 69 of Julius Civilis (*Hist.* IV. 61,2); she was brought to Rome in Vespasian's reign, and succeeded by another, named Ganna, during the reign of Domitian (Dio LXVII. 5,3). The Chatti lived on the east bank of the Rhine, and were the subject of major military activity in Domitian's reign (Tac. *Germ.* 30–1 and 37,6).

Section 15

1   **in the eighth month:** that is, in August of A.D. 69, counting *not* from his *dies imperii* in April, but from his proclamation on the Rhine in January. The order of events is not clear, and Suetonius may be in error over details. Tacitus does not specify the time at which the legions of the Danube joined Vespasian (*Hist.* II. 85ff), but it is certain that others had preceded them in this act – the Egyptian legions on July 1st, the legions of Judaea at some stage in the first two weeks of July (*Hist.* II. 79; *Div. Vesp.* 6,3), whilst the Syrian legions also joined Vespasian before mid-July (*Hist.* II. 81,1). The confusion may have arisen from a misunderstanding based upon the actions of a detachment of the Moesian legions, which in April had come to Italy to support Otho; on hearing of his suicide, they temporarily occupied Aquileia and declared for Vespasian. On that occasion, however, they were persuaded eventually to accept Vitellius as emperor.

the armies stationed in Pannonia...: for details, see below in Appendix I. It is clear that these armies had no suitable candidate of their own, and that the initiative was seized by Antonius Primus (*legatus* of legion VII Galbiana in Pannonia), who, being too "junior" to make a credible claim on his own behalf, nailed his colours to the Flavian mast (see *Hist.* II. 86; Shotter, 1977).

armies in Judaea and Syria: Vespasian was himself *legatus* in Judaea; Mucianus, *legatus* in Syria, was not naturally well-disposed towards Vespasian, but was persuaded by Vespasian's son, Titus, that he and Vespasian should co-operate (*Hist.* II. 5–6; 74,1).

The adjective, *Syriaticus*, seems sound in the manuscripts, though Suetonius normally uses *Syriacus*.

He conducted a levy in Rome: see Tac. *Hist.* III. 58,2.

after regular service: that is, they would achieve the benefits normally available only after many years of service – praetorian soldiers sixteen years, legionaries and soldiers of the urban cohorts twenty years, and auxiliaries twenty-five years.

Iusta militia is regular service in the army for a stated term.

benefits: these came in the form of land or money, though the values established were –

praetorians	:	5000 *denarii*
legions	:	3000 *denarii* (under Augustus, but halved by Caligula – *Cal.* 44)

2 **when the enemy was pressing:** by land there were two prongs to the Flavian attack; Antonius Primus with troops from the Danubian provinces had occupied north-east Italy, defeated the Vitellians at the second battle of Bedriacum, and subjected Cremona to a savage assault. Mucianus was following behind through the Danube provinces with legion VI and thirteen thousand troops detached from legions, making up what Tacitus calls *ingens agmen* (*Hist.* II. 83,1). Vespasian himself travelled westwards more slowly through Egypt in order to gather funds and presumably to put himself into a position from which he could threaten Italy's grain-supplies. By sea, Mucianus organised the Pontic fleet to blockade eastern Italy (*Hist.* II. 83,2); the Ravenna-fleet deserted to Vespasian under Lucilius Bassus (*Hist.* II. 100,3), as did the Misenum-fleet a little later (*Hist.* III. 56–7).

commanded by his brother: on Lucius Vitellius, see above on 3,1 and 5. The accounts of Suetonius and Tacitus differ somewhat: Lucius Vitellius was, according to Tacitus (*Hist.* III. 55,2), put in command of the city of Rome, and subsequently sent to put down a revolt in Campania (*Hist.* III. 58,1). The task of winning back the Misenum-fleet was entrusted to Claudius Julianus, its ex-commander, with an urban cohort and a band of gladiators (*Hist.* III. 57,2); he, however, went over to Vespasian, occupying the Campanian town of Tarracina, though it was soon won back by Lucius Vitellius (*Hist.* III. 76).

the same armies and generals: see above on 9,1. Caecina and Valens had defeated Otho at the first battle of Bedriacum (*Otho* 9,2). On this occasion, however, Valens, the more trustworthy and efficient of the two, was incapacitated through illness; thus the effective command was in the hands of Caecina (*Hist.* II. 99; Dio LXV. 10, 1–2). The advance Vitellian force consisted of legions V and XXII, with detachments of I (Germanica), XIV, XV and XVI; to the rear came

legions I (Italica) and XXI, with detachments from the three British legions (II, IX and XX) and some auxiliaries. A troop of cavalry was sent ahead to seize Cremona (*Hist.* II. 100,1).

defeated....either by superior strength: the decisive second battle of Bedriacum was fought in October of A.D. 69 by the Vitellians against a Flavian army led by Antonius Primus. Mucianus had not yet reached Italy, and there was a developing rivalry between himself and Primus over who should win the glory of taking Rome. Primus should have waited for Mucianus in the north, though the advancing season and deteriorating weather represented strong arguments in favour of speed. Tacitus provides a vivid description of the battle of Bedriacum (*Hist.* III. 21–5). Antonius' army went on to sack Cremona as an act of revenge for the humiliation handed out by Vitellius to legion XIII earlier in the year (*Hist.* III. 26ff; *Otho* 10,1).

....or by treachery: of Vitellian leaders who betrayed their cause the most significant were Lucilius Bassus, prefect of the Ravenna-fleet (Tac. *Hist.* III. 12), though he was so timorous about it that the fleet chose as its new leader the vigorous Cornelius Fuscus. Another major defection was that of Caecina who was negotiating with the Flavians before Bedriacum and tried to persuade his troops to join the Ravenna-fleet; most were hostile to this and put Caecina under arrest, entrusting themselves instead to two "loyalists", Fabius Fabullus (*legatus* of legion V) and Cassius Longus (*Hist.* II. 99–100 and III. 13–4). The consequent disarray on the Vitellian side provided Antonius Primus with an unmissable opportunity. After Bedriacum, prominent defectors were Claudius Julianus (see above), Claudius Apollinaris (prefect of the Misenum-fleet), together with the praetorian prefects, Julius Priscus and Alfenus Varus (Tac. *Hist.* III. 61).

made a deal: Tacitus (*Hist.* III. 63) says that following the surrender of Vitellian troops at Narnia, Antonius Primus and his colleague, Arrius Varus, offered Vitellius safety for himself and his family, together with a sum of money, if he abdicated. This offer received "official" Flavian backing from Mucianus.

Flavius Sabinus: Vespasian's elder brother had enjoyed a distinguished career (*Hist.* III. 75,1), participating in Claudius' British expedition of A.D. 43, and governing Moesia for seven years before being appointed by Nero (c. A.D. 56) as prefect of Rome (*praefectus urbi*). His tenure of this post is not entirely clear, as he evidently was *not* holding it in A.D. 61 (*Ann.* XIV. 42,1), but was in Nero's later years since he was deposed by Galba and subsequently reinstated by Otho. Tacitus indicates (*Hist.* III. 75,1) that prior to A.D. 69 Sabinus was regarded as the most significant member of the Flavian family, which probably helps to explain Mucianus' intense jealousy of him. Vitellius tried to surrender to Sabinus, and many thought that Sabinus should have used the opportunity to take power for himself. However, during the negotiations, Vitellius' supporters beseiged Sabinus on the Capitolium, set the temple of Jupiter on fire, and captured and killed Sabinus (see below in 15,3 and Tac. *Hist.* III. 64–75).

a hundred million sestertii: Tacitus does not specify a figure.

on the steps of the Palace: Tacitus (*Hist.* III. 74,2) has the same expression in his description; the force of *pro* seems to couple the ideas of "standing *on*" and "speaking *from*".

that he was retiring: *Hist.* III. 68,2.

the crowd, however: there are again verbal similarities with Tacitus' account (*Hist.* III. 68,3).

at dawn: the expression, *primo diluculo*, seems to indicate that period when it is light, but the sun is not yet up.

mourning-clothes: see *Hist.* III. 67; Tacitus says that Vitellius' main theme was his desire to secure peace, and that he choked with emotion as he spoke. The detailed order of events as given by Suetonius differs a little from that in Tacitus. Tacitus says nothing of Vitellius' use of a text (*libellum*) for his speech.

3   the crowd....interrupted him: in Tacitus' account, whilst Vitellius had been making his way to the *rostra*, the crowd heaped on him inappropriate flattery, whilst the soldiers were "menacingly silent". There was a loud protest when he said that he would deposit his *imperator's* dagger in the temple of Concord (that is, as a symbol of resignation).

he plucked up his courage: Tacitus' account suggests no positive action on Vitellius' part; rather, he was *consilii inops* (*Hist.* III. 68,3). Dio, following Suetonius, refers to Vitellius' vacillation (LXV. 16, especially 16,3). The force of Tacitus is that the positive action that followed – that is, the attack on Flavius Sabinus – was due to Vitellius' followers rather than to Vitellius himself.

a sudden attack: *Hist.* III. 69. This attack on Sabinus' retinue was made near the Basin of Fundanius on the Quirinal, from where Sabinus tried to find safety by escaping to the Capitolium.

Flavian sympathisers: the first reference in Suetonius to Vespasian's followers as *Flaviani*, after his gentile name of *Flavius*. The scene was evidently very confused (*Hist.* III. 69, 3–4); apparently amongst those with Sabinus were the consuls (Quintius Atticus and Caecilius Simplex), some senators and *equites*, and (prominently) a lady named Verulana Gratilla. Sabinus also managed to bring into his group his own family and his nephew, Domitian.

defeated them by setting fire: *Hist.* III. 71ff; Tacitus says (71,4) that it was not clear whether the fire was caused by the attackers or by the beseiged, and denounces it as the most evil act in Rome's history (72,1).

temple of Jupiter: Tacitus (*Hist.* III. 72, 2–3) uses the occasion to give a brief history of the famous temple. It was founded by the king, Tarquinius Priscus, and brought to completion by his two successors, Servius Tullius and Tarquinius Superbus; its dedication was one of the first acts of the newly-established republic (though on these dates and traditions, see Gjerstad, 1962). More recently it had been destroyed in 83 B.C. in Sulla's march on Rome, and restored by Galba's ancestor, Quintus Catulus (see above on *Galba* 2); for a commemoration of this on a *denarius* of 78 B.C., see Crawford, 1974, p.399. Although over the years its furnishings and decoration had come to reflect Rome's growing status and opulence, its plan had remained very firmly and clearly rooted in the tradition of Etruscan temple-architecture (Boethius and Ward-Perkins, 1970, 92–3). Domitian (*Dom.* 1,2), Sabinus' sons and the consul, Simplex, escaped, but Sabinus and the other consul (Atticus) were taken in chains to Vitellius, who was unable to resist his supporters' demands for Sabinus' death. Atticus saved himself by confessing to personal responsibility for the fire, thus exonerating the Vitellians (Tac. *Hist.* III. 73–5).

house of the emperor, Tiberius: see note on *Otho* 6,2 and Boethius and Ward-Perkins, 1970, 204–5. The house was built on the site which had previously been occupied by the house of his father, Ti. Claudius Nero.

he was sorry: note the personal use of *paenitens* (normally found in impersonal form); it is usually followed by a genitive (*facti*).

shifted the blame: as in *Hist*. III. 70,4, where Vitellius blamed his soldiers for breaking the agreement with Sabinus.

he convened a public meeting: from the description of this, it is tolerably clear that Suetonius has mistakenly transferred these details from the earlier occasion when Vitellius had addressed the people from the *rostra* (above in 15,2; *Hist*. III. 67ff).

and swore an oath: Tacitus nowhere mentions this.

4　**his dagger:** the symbol of the authority of the *imperator*. Tacitus (*Hist*. III. 68,2) names the consul as Caecilius Simplex; since he had sided with the Flavians on the Capitolium, such a re-appearance as Suetonius' order of events requires would be beyond credence. Dio (LXV. 16,6) adds that Vitellius was jeered at for this "offer".

temple of Concord: this was built on the slopes of the Capitoline hill overlooking the forum. According to tradition, it was founded by Camillus in 367 B.C., and restored by Tiberius in A.D. 12 (*Tib*. 20). It ws often used by the senate as a meeting-place (Boethius and Ward-Perkins, 1970, 196).

surname, Concordia: there is no other reference to this, though the goddess, Concordia, appears on Vitellius' coins (*RIC* I² (Vitellius), pp. 274ff), as on those of other emperors.

Section 16

The account of Vitellius' last hours (in 16–17) may be usefully compared with that provided by Tacitus (*Hist*. III. 84–85); the differences in details selected by the two authors is revealing of their approaches (see Loftstedt, 1948, 1ff).

send intermediaries: Tacitus (*Hist*. III. 80,1) shows that these envoys were to be sent to two advancing Flavian columns – one with Antonius Primus on the *via Flaminia*, the other with Vespasian's cousin, Petilius Cerialis, on the *via Salaria*. Those who met with Cerialis' troops were given a rough reception, and one – the stoic, Arulenus Rusticus, who was later executed by Domitian – was injured. The group meeting Antonius Primus was better received, though, as Tacitus shows, one member – the stoic philosopher, Musonius Rufus – nearly caused an incident by his moralising (*intempestiva sapientia* – *Hist*. III. 81,1).

with Vestal Virgins: the Vestals were treated with great respect by Antonius Primus, as accorded with their traditional status (Ogilvie, 1969, 90f); nonetheless, Antonius sent them back with an uncompromising message that the actions of the Vitellians in Rome had destroyed the normal courtesies between enemies (*Hist*. III. 81,2). Dio (LXV. 18,3) says that the Vestals were sent to Cerialis, adding the probably-significant point that by this time the burning Capitolium was in the view of the advancing Flavians.

enemy-troops were closing on Rome: see Tac. *Hist*. III. 82, where it is shown that there were three prongs to the advance – along the *via Flaminia*, along the *via Salaria* (to the Colline gate), and along the Tiber. The Vitellians had tried to arm

everybody in Rome to resist, but they were no match for the Flavians, though the nature of the street-fighting was fierce and led to many fatalities. Probably the most significant victory was that over the praetorian guard which Vitellius had formed from the German legions.

immediately he hid: Tacitus (*Hist.* III. 84,4) says that Vitellius did this *after* the capture of the city, and that he made for his *wife's* house (not his father's). The Aventine hill was an area of traditional significance to the urban plebs of Rome. It is typical of the inquisitive detail favoured by Suetonius that he should mention the presence of the *pistor* and *cocus*, described by Tacitus simply as *infima servitiorum*.

south to Campania: so too Tacitus (*Hist.* III. 84,4); Lucius Vitellius had captured Tarracina (see above on 15,2; also Dio LXV. 20,1).

a vague rumour that....: as often, a clause introduced by *tamquam* replaces an accusative and infinitive.

he allowed himself to be taken: Tacitus attributes this not to a positive decision, but to Vitellius' characteristic *mobilitas ingenii* (*Hist.* III. 84,4).

everything deserted: this coldly "factual" account can be contrasted with the Tacitean version, which seeks to relate in quasi-visual terms the effect of the emptiness upon Vitellius in his terror.

a money-belt: *zona* can mean both the "belt" and the actual "purse".

in the porter's room: again Tacitus omits the detail and describes the hiding-place simply as *pudenda latebra* (cf. Dio LXV. 20,1, who follows Suetonius' details). *Cella* was used of a servant's room; thus the diminutive, *cellula*, here highlights the sordid state which Vitellius had now reached.

tying a dog to the door: the deterring of unwelcome visitors by a dog or the threat of a dog is well-illustrated by the famous mosaic in the entrance-way of a house in Pompeii, bearing the inscription, CAVE CANEM.

Section 17

1   **finding no opposition:** classical latin normally employs *nullo* as the ablative of *nemo*.

searching through: Suetonius does not use *rimari* elsewhere, and may have picked it up from Tacitus' account of the Vitellians' activities in Vienne (*Hist.* II. 29,1).

dragged out by them: Tacitus names the person responsible for this as Julius Placidus (*tribunus cohortis* – *Hist.* III. 84,4).

the whereabouts of Vitellius: the severe contraction of the latin – *ubi esse Vitellium sciret* – is regarded by many as corrupt; an acceptable emendation might be *ubi esset Vitellius si* (or *num*) *sciret*.

even in custody: that is, in the prison (sometimes known as *Mamertinus*), which stood at the foot of the Capitolium. The force of *even* is that most Romans of his standing would have expected custody to mean being committed into the charge of named individuals – much as the emperor's uncle, Publius Vitellius, had been handed over to his brother (see above on 2,3).

his hands were tied: Tac. *Hist.* III. 84,5; Dio LXV. 20,2.

forum: Dio (LXV. 20,3) tries to inject a note of pathos by adding that it was the venue of many of Vitellius' addresses as emperor.

Sacred Way: the road leading from the Palatine to the forum (cf. Dio LXV. 20,3).

subjected to actions: see also Dio (LXV. 20,3) and Josephus (*Bell. Iud.* IV. 11,4); Tacitus adds the pertinent point that Vitellius looked so sordid that people could not feel any pity (*Hist.* III. 84,5).

pulled by the hair: criminals were not allowed to avert their gaze in such situations (cf. Pliny *Panegyric of Trajan* 34).

as happens to criminals: *ceu*, originally a poetical word, is used in post-Augustan latin for *velut*. *trahi* has to be understood with *ceu noxii solent*.

the point of a sword: Tac. *Hist.* III. 85; Dio LXV. 21,1.

2 **others called him "Firebug":** that is, because of the burning of the Capitolium; the same insult was thrown at Nero (Tac. *Ann.* XV. 67,3).

"Fatty": Suetonius uses the word *patinarium*, clearly referring to the enormous *patina* mentioned above (in 13,2).

extremely tall: *enormis* can have this meaning, though its significance is often "shapeless". It should be noted that Suetonius misses some of the detail given by Tacitus (in *Hist.* III. 85), and which was strongly illustrative of Vitellius' attitude and the fickleness of his subjects: particularly relevant was Vitellius' response – "and yet I was your emperor". Instead, the biographer progresses in a natural way from an insult concerning Vitellius' physical appearance to a description of his physical characteristics (cf. Dio LXV. 21, who also captures a degree of pathos).

a protruding stomach: Dio LXV. 20,3.

He was lame: *subdebile* is not found elsewhere.

on an occasion: the adverb, *olim*, is present because of the verbal force of the noun, *impulsu*.

Caligula had been driving: see above on 4.

as an assistant: it is not altogether clear what Vitellius' duties were, though he may have been one of the assistants who refreshed the horses or poured water on the chariot-wheels to prevent overheating. Dio (LXV. 5, 1–2) mentions Vitellius, as emperor, rubbing down chariot-horses.

the Gemonian Steps: Tacitus (*Hist.* III. 85) mentions this as the spot at which Vitellius uttered his *non degenera vox* (see above). The Steps led from the Capitolium to the forum; bodies of criminals were exposed on them, as was that of Sejanus for three days in A.D. 31 (Dio LVIII. 11,5). There is no mention of the *scalae Gemoniae* before the time of Tiberius. Dio (LXV. 21,2) says that Vitellius was beheaded at the Steps; his head was carried around by his murderers, whilst his wife gained custody of the body and gave it a proper burial – hardly possible if Suetonius' version is correct.

tiny dagger-cuts: one of the tortures described as characteristic of Caligula's cruelty (*Cal.* 30,1). There is no mention here of the apparent attempt by a soldier to kill Vitellius, and thus save him from further suffering (Tac. *Hist.* III. 84,5; Dio LXV. 21, 1–2). Tacitus suggests that a possible motive may have been to kill the tribune who had approached Vitellius.

and thrown into the Tiber: common criminals, who had been executed by strangulation in the Mamertine prison were dragged by a hook to the *scalae Gemoniae*, and, after exposure to public gaze, were thrown into the Tiber (see *Tib.* 54,2; 61,4; 75,1; Juv. *Sat.* X. 66; Tac. *Ann.* VI. 19, 3–4).

Section 18

along with his brother: see Dio LXV. 22,1; Lucius Vitellius set out from Tarracina to come to his brother's aid, but encountered troops sent by Antonius Primus and surrendered to them. Although he was promised his life, he was brought to Rome and executed. Tacitus gives two very critical sketches of him (*Hist.* III. 77,4 and IV. 2,3).

and his son: according to Dio (LXV. 22,2), the young Germanicus was killed at the same time as his uncle, but Tacitus (*Hist.* IV. 80,1) says that his execution was ordered by Mucianus a year later.

he was fifty-six years old: Tacitus (*Hist.* III. 86,1) agrees; the difficulties are discussed above in 3,2. If he was born, as Suetonius says there, in A.D. 15 (September 24th) and killed on December 22nd in A.D. 69, then he was, as Dio (LXV. 22,1) says, fifty-four years and eighty-nine days old at the time of his death. There is no satisfactory explanation, except that Suetonius may have used different sources which he omitted to reconcile; in any case, such discrepancies are not unusual in Suetonius (*Galba* 23; *Otho* 11,2).

which I have already mentioned: see above in 9.

a man of Gaul: the adjective, *Gallicanus*, is used exclusively of men deriving from Gallia Cisalpina or Gallia Narbonensis.

Antonius Primus: for a discussion of this man, see Shotter, 1977; he was an asset in the fluid circumstances of civil war, but not one who could be trusted in peacetime (e.g. Tac. *Ann.* XIV. 40,3). Nero banished him, but he was rehabilitated by Galba and given command of legion VII in Pannonia. Otho made no use of him, but Antonius shared the distaste of Vitellius felt by the legions of the Danube; in the absence of credible leaders in the area, Antonius took the initiative in persuading these troops to declare for Vespasian. The Flavian victory in Italy was largely to his credit, and was in his own mind a reason why in Flavian circles he should have been preferred to Mucianus. Mucianus, however, ensured his subordinate status (*Hist.* IV. 11,1) and, despite Antonius' efforts, Vespasian would not reverse this. In later life, Antonius was a patron of the poet, Martial (*Epig.* X. 23), who indicates that Antonius was still alive in A.D. 98 at the age of seventy-five; see *Hist.* II. 86,2 for Tacitus' frank appraisal of him.

of Tolosa: that is, modern Toulouse; the birthplace is celebrated by Martial (*Epig.* X. 99,3).

the nickname, Beccus: the form, *Becco*, also exists; it is dative here by attraction to *cui*.

means: *valet* is used regularly in this sense for *significat*.

cock's beak: Mooney (1930, 372) observes that surprisingly Suetonius fails to notice the coincidence between *gallus* ("cock") and *Gallus* ("a man of Gaul").

Appendix

The distribution of the legions of the Roman army

A: c. A.D. 65 (27 legions)

Spain (Tarraconensis)	VI Victrix
Britain	II Augusta; IX Hispana; XIV Gemina Martia Victrix; XX Valeria Victrix
Germany (Superior)	IV Macedonica; XXI Rapax: XXII Primigenia
Germany (Inferior)	I Germanica; V Alaudae; XV Primigenia; XVI Gallica
Dalmatia	XI Claudia Pia Fidelis
Moesia	VII Claudia Pia Fidelis; VIII Augusta
Pannonia	X Gemina; XIII Gemina
Syria/Armenia	III Gallica; IV Scythica; V Macedonica; VI Ferrata; XII Fulminata; XV Apollinaris
Egypt	III Cyrenaica; XXII Deiotariana
Africa	III Augusta

B: A.D. 68 (December) (30 or 31 legions)

Spain (Tarraconensis)	VI Victrix; X Gemina
Britain	II Augusta; IX Hispana; XX Valeria Victrix
Germany (Superior)	IV Macedonica; XXI Rapax; XXII Primigenia
Germany (Inferior)	I Germanica; V Alaudae; XV Primigenia; XVI Gallica
Gaul (Lugdunensis)	I Italica
Rome	I Adiutrix
Dalmatia	XI Claudia Pia Fidelis; XIV Gemina Martia Victrix
Pannonia	VII Galbiana; XIII Gemina
Moesia	III Gallica; VII Claudia Pia Fidelis; VIII Augusta
Syria	IV Scythica; VI Ferrata; XII Fulminata
Judaea	V Macedonica; X Fretensis; XV Apollinaris
Egypt	III Cyrenaica; XXII Deiotariana
Africa	III Augusta; (I Macriana)

C: A.D. 71 (29 legions)

Spain (Tarraconensis)	VII Gemina (renamed from VII Galbiana)
Britain	II Augusta; IX Hispana; XX Valeria Victrix
Germany (Superior)	I Adiutrix; VIII Augusta; XI Claudia Pia Fidelis; XIV Gemina Martia Victrix
Germany (Inferior)	II Adiutrix; VI Victrix; X Gemina; XXI Rapax
Pannonia	XIII Gemina; XV Apollinaris; XXII Primigenia

Moesia	I Italica; IV Flavia; V Alaudae; V Macedonica
	VII Claudia Pia Fidelis
Syria	III Gallica; IV Scythica; VI Ferrata
Cappadocia	XII Fulminata; XVI Flavia
Judaea	X Fretensis
Egypt	III Cyrenaica; XXII Deiotariana
Africa	III Augusta

(Note: Four legions (I Germanica, IV Macedonica, XV Primigenia and XVI Gallica) were disbanded by Vespasian as a result of their conduct in the events of A.D. 68–70; they were replaced by IV Flavia and XVI Flavia. II Adiutrix was recruited probably by Otho, though some hold it to have been formed from the Ravenna-fleet after its defection to Vespasian during A.D. 69).

Index

Index of Names and Places cited in the Introduction and Text/Translation.

Note: References to Roman personages are listed under gentile names, except in the cases of those emperors and authors who are better-known by either their *praenomina* (e.g. Tiberius) or *cognomina* (e.g. Tacitus).

CLASSICAL TEXTS

Editorial Advisor: Professor M.M. Willcock (London)

Published volumes

AESCHYLUS
THE EUMENIDES, edited by A.J.Podlecki
ARISTOPHANES, edited by Alan H.Sommerstein
ACHARNIANS
BIRDS
CLOUDS
KNIGHTS
LYSISTRATA
PEACE
WASPS
AUGUSTINE
SOLILOQUIES *and* IMMORTALITY OF THE SOUL, edited by G.Watson
CAESAR
CIVIL WAR Books I & II, edited by J.M.Carter
CIVIL WAR Book III, edited by J.M. Carter
CASSIUS DIO
ROMAN HISTORY Books 53.1-55.9, edited by J.W.Rich
CICERO General Editor: Professor A.E.Douglas
TUSCULAN DISPUTATIONS 1, edited by A.E.Douglas
TUSCULAN DISPUTATIONS 2 & 5, edited by A.E.Douglas
ON FATE with **BOETHIUS** CONSOLATION V, edited by R.W.Sharples
PHILIPPICS II, edited by W.K.Lacey
VERRINES II,1, edited by T.N.Mitchell
ON STOIC GOOD AND EVIL: (De Finibus 3 and Paradoxa Stoicorum)
      edited by M.R. Wright
ON FRIENDSHIP and THE DREAM OF SCIPIO: (De Amicitia and
      Somnium Scipionis), edited by J.G.F.Powell
EURIPIDES General Editor; Professor C.Collard
ALCESTIS, edited by D.Conacher
ELECTRA, edited by M.J.Cropp
HECUBA edited by C.Collard
ORESTES, edited by M.L.West
PHOENICIAN WOMEN, edited by E.Craik
TROJAN WOMEN, edited by Shirley Barlow
GREEK ORATORS
I ANTIPHON, LYSIAS, edited by M.Edwards & S.Usher
III ISOCRATES Panegyricus and To Nicocles edited by S.Usher
V DEMOSTHENES On the Crown edited by S. Usher
VI APOLLODORUS c. Neaira, edited by C. Carey
HELLENICA OXYRHYNCHIA
edited by P.R.McKechnie & S.J.Kern
HOMER
ODYSSEY I & II edited by P.V.Jones
HORACE
SATIRES I edited by P.M. Brown
SATIRES II, edited by F. Muecke
JOSEPH OF EXETER